CONTENTS

THE
REFERENCE
SHELF

AMERICAN EDUCATION

edited by ROBERT EMMET LONG

THE REFERENCE SHELF

Volume 56 Number 5

THE H. W. WILSON COMPANY

New York   1984

THE REFERENCE SHELF

The books in this series contain reprints of articles, excerpts from books, and addresses on current issues and social trends in the United States and other countries. There are six separately bound numbers in each volume, all of which are generally published in the same calendar year. One number is a collection of recent speeches; each of the others is devoted to a single subject and gives background information and discussion from various points of view, concluding with a comprehensive bibliography. Books in the series may be purchased individually or on subscription.

Library of Congress Cataloging in Publication Data

Main entry under title:

American education.

   (The Reference shelf ; v. 56, no. 5)
   Bibliography: p.
   1. Education—United States—Addresses, essays, lectures. I. Long, Robert Emmet. II. Series.
LA209.2.A67 1984   370'.973   84–22110
ISBN 0–8242–0699–1

Printed in the United States of America

PREFACE

American education has been the subject of heated debate and general concern at various times in the recent past. In the 1950s, when the Soviet Union took the lead in space exploration through the successful launching of Sputnik, the American educational enterprise was called into question. Some notable books were written on the subject, reports were issued, and educational reforms—particularly in the teaching of science and mathematics—were initiated. During the Vietnam war American education again came to the center of attention. Student riots at Berkeley, Columbia, and other universities ultimately led to curriculum reforms that attempted to make education "relevant" to contemporary social concerns and gave unprecedented attention to ethnic and minority group needs. Not only women's studies and black studies but scores of other special studies flourished during the 1970s. The policy of "open admissions," by which students were admitted to many public universities on the basis of a high school diploma, also had its effect in college classrooms. Remedial courses in the basics of English composition became a normal feature of even the most intellectually respected colleges. These changes were the outcome of neglect of the traditional curriculum in the secondary schools, where college preparatory courses became unfashionable; students took fewer mathematics and science courses, and studied less history, literature, and language. For more than a decade SAT scores of high school seniors have declined steadily, and many graduates of the high schools read today at an eighth grade level or lower. This decline of standards in the secondary schools is the subject of the latest debate on American education.

Criticism of the public schools has increased over the last seven or eight years. In 1981 concern with poor performance levels prompted President Reagan to mandate a special study, undertaken by the National Commission on Excellence in Education; and in 1983 the commission, in its highly publicized report, *A Nation at Risk,* charged that performance in the schools was so derelict that the nation itself was in danger. A number of other reports appeared in the same year, all reaching similar conclusions, but *A Nation at Risk* captured the public imagination with its sense of urgency.

Section I of this volume reprints *A Nation at Risk,* as well as the Twentieth Century Fund's report *Making the Grade,* and the synoptic final section of the Carnegie Foundation study *High School: A Report on Secondary Education in America.* Section II focuses on responses to these reports, commentary that is often critical of the reports themselves—their biases, omissions, and assumptions of the mission of education. Section III deals with the issues that are raised most frequently by the reports.

The editor is indebted to the authors and publishers who have granted permission to reprint the materials in this compilation. Special thanks are due to Carolyn Long, U.S. Congressman Frank Horton, and Professor William E. Doll, Jr. I would also like to express my gratitude to Ellen Morin and the Fulton Public Library, and to the staff of Penfield Library, State University of New York at Oswego.

ROBERT EMMET LONG

August 1984

I. U.S. PUBLIC SCHOOLS: THE OFFICIAL INDICTMENT

EDITOR'S INTRODUCTION

Nineteen eighty-three has been called "The Year of the Great Debate" in American education, since it was in that year that a large number of reports appeared, all censuring the public schools and calling for immediate reform. The National Science Foundation issued its report *Educating Americans for the 21st Century,* which expressed alarm at declining standards in the teaching of mathematics and science. The Education Commission of the States released its findings, entitled *Action for Excellence,* which was highly critical of U.S. secondary school education. The Task Force of the Business-Higher Education Forum, in *America's Competitive Challenge: the Need for a National Response,* voiced concern that the deterioration of quality in the schools and colleges was jeopardizing America's ability to compete in the increasingly technological international marketplace. The year also saw the publication of studies by well-known scholars, such as John Goodlad's *A Place Called School,* which added to the weight of evidence that the schools had failed in their mission, or at least fallen far short of "excellence."

Three of the most widely known reports of "The Great Debate of 1983" are reprinted here—*A Nation at Risk, High School,* and *Making the Grade. A Nation at Risk: the Imperative for Educational Reform,* the report of the National Commission on Excellence in Education, is far from dispassionate. It strikes a note of urgency and crisis, and its language is sometimes rhetorical. Just as America was urged to improve its educational system following Soviet advances in space technology, so *A Nation at Risk* calls upon the country to reform its schools or face national defeat in the competition for foreign markets in a post-industrial, technological age. *A Nation at Risk* proposes a new core curriculum for all high-school students whose "new basics" would include four years of English, three of mathematics, three of science, three of social studies, and six months of computer science. It compares the level of competence of American high schools with those of other industrialized countries and urges an adoption of their rigorous standards.

The second article in this section is a reprinting of "An Agenda for Action," the final chapter of the report of the Carnegie Foundation for the Advancement of Teaching, *High School: A Report on Secondary Education in America*. Like *A Nation at Risk*, this report endorses a *single track* and a common core curriculum for *all* students that would include a two-year science requirement, a two-year mathematics sequence, and a foreign language requirement. Much more than *A Nation at Risk*, however, the Carnegie Report is concerned with upgrading the teaching profession itself.

The third article is the Twentieth Century Fund's *Making the Grade*, a report that discusses the role of the federal government in education and calls for termination of federally funded bilingual education programs. It endorses a master-teacher program and merit pay for teachers, and also calls for an overhaul of the educational system, in which particular attention would be given to the teaching of mathematics and science, English, and foreign languages. Like the other reports, *Making the Grade* stresses a "back to basics" approach to education.

A NATION AT RISK:
THE IMPERATIVE FOR EDUCATIONAL REFORM[1]

Introduction

Secretary of Education T. H. Bell created the National Commission on Excellence in Education on August 26, 1981, directing it to examine the quality of education in the United States and to

[1]Reprint of a Report to the Nation and the Secretary of Education by the National Commission on Excellence in Education, April 1983. U.S. Department of Education. 1983.

make a report to the Nation and to him within 18 months of its first meeting. In accordance with the Secretary's instructions, this report contains practical recommendations for educational improvement and fulfills the Commission's responsibilities under the terms of its charter.

The Commission was created as a result of the Secretary's concern about "the widespread public perception that something is seriously remiss in our educational system." Soliciting the "support of all who care about our future," the Secretary noted that he was establishing the Commission based on his "responsibility to provide leadership, constructive criticism, and effective assistance to schools and universities."

The Commission's charter contained several specific charges to which we have given particular attention. These included:
• assessing the quality of teaching and learning in our Nation's public and private schools, colleges, and universities;
• comparing American schools and colleges with those of other advanced nations;
• studying the relationship between college admissions requirements and student achievement in high school;
• identifying educational programs which result in notable student success in college;
• assessing the degree to which major social and educational changes in the last quarter century have affected student achievement; and
• defining problems which must be faced and overcome if we are successfully to pursue the course of excellence in education.

The Commission's charter directed it to pay particular attention to teenage youth, and we have done so largely by focusing on high schools. Selective attention was given to the formative years spent in elementary schools, to higher education, and to vocational and technical programs. We refer those interested in the need for similar reform in higher education to the recent report of the American Council on Education, *To Strengthen the Quality of Higher Education*.

In going about its work the Commission has relied in the main upon five sources of information:
• papers commissioned from experts on a variety of educational

issues;

• administrators, teachers, students, representatives of professional and public groups, parents, business leaders, public officials,
and scholars who testified at eight meetings of the full Commission, six public hearings, two panel discussions, a symposium, and
a series of meetings organized by the Department of Education's
Regional Offices;

• existing analyses of problems in education;

• letters from concerned citizens, teachers, and administrators
who volunteered extensive comments on problems and possibilities in American education; and

• descriptions of notable programs and promising approaches in
education.

To these public-minded citizens who took the trouble to share
their concerns with us—frequently at their own expense in time,
money, and effort—we extend our thanks. In all cases, we have
benefited from their advice and taken their views into account;
how we have treated their suggestions is, of course, our responsibility alone. In addition, we are grateful to the individuals in
schools, universities, foundations, business, government, and communities throughout the United States who provided the facilities
and staff so necessary to the success of our many public functions.

The Commission was impressed during the course of its activities by the diversity of opinion it received regarding the condition
of American education and by conflicting views about what should
be done. In many ways, the membership of the Commission itself
reflected that diversity and difference of opinion during the course
of its work. This report, nevertheless, gives evidence that men and
women of good will can agree on common goals and on ways to
pursue them.

A Nation at Risk

Our Nation is at risk. Our once unchallenged preeminence in
commerce, industry, science, and technological innovation is being
overtaken by competitors throughout the world. This report is
concerned with only one of the many causes and dimensions of the
problem, but it is the one that undergirds American prosperity,

security, and civility. We report to the American people that while we can take justifiable pride in what our schools and colleges have historically accomplished and contributed to the United States and the well-being of its people, the educational foundations of our society are presently being eroded by a rising tide of mediocrity that threatens our very future as a Nation and a people. What was unimaginable a generation ago has begun to occur—others are matching and surpassing our educational attainments.

If an unfriendly foreign power had attempted to impose on America the mediocre educational performance that exists today, we might well have viewed it as an act of war. As it stands, we have allowed this to happen to ourselves. We have even squandered the gains in student achievement made in the wake of the Sputnik challenge. Moreover, we have dismantled essential support systems which helped make those gains possible. We have, in effect, been committing an act of unthinking, unilateral educational disarmament.

Our society and its educational institutions seem to have lost sight of the basic purposes of schooling, and of the high expectations and disciplined effort needed to attain them. This report, the result of 18 months of study, seeks to generate reform of our educational system in fundamental ways and to renew the Nation's commitment to schools and colleges of high quality throughout the length and breadth of our land.

That we have compromised this commitment is, upon reflection, hardly surprising, given the multitude of often conflicting demands we have placed on our Nation's schools and colleges. They are routinely called on to provide solutions to personal, social, and political problems that the home and other institutions either will not or cannot resolve. We must understand that these demands on our schools and colleges often exact an educational cost as well as a financial one.

On the occasion of the Commission's first meeting, President Reagan noted the central importance of education in American life when he said: "Certainly there are few areas of American life as important to our society, to our people, and to our families as our schools and colleges." This report, therefore, is as much an open letter to the American people as it is a report to the Secretary

of Education. We are confident that the American people, properly informed, will do what is right for their children and for the
generations to come.

The Risk

History is not kind to idlers. The time is long past when America's destiny was assured simply by an abundance of natural resources and inexhaustible human enthusiasm, and by our relative
isolation from the malignant problems of older civilizations. The
world is indeed one global village. We live among determined,
well-educated, and strongly motivated competitors. We compete
with them for international standing and markets, not only with
products but also with the ideas of our laboratories and neighbor-
hood workshops. America's position in the world may once have
been reasonably secure with only a few exceptionally well-trained
men and women. It is no longer.

The risk is not only that the Japanese make automobiles more
efficiently than Americans and have government subsidies for development and export. It is not just that the South Koreans recently built the world's most efficient steel mill, or that American
machine tools, once the pride of the world, are being displaced by
German products. It is also that these developments signify a re-
distribution of trained capability throughout the globe. Knowledge, learning, information, and skilled intelligence are the new
raw materials of international commerce and are today spreading
throughout the world as vigorously as miracle drugs, synthetic fer-
tilizers, and blue jeans did earlier. If only to keep and improve on
the slim competitive edge we still retain in world markets, we must
dedicate ourselves to the reform of our educational system for the
benefit of all—old and young alike, affluent and poor, majority
and minority. Learning is the indispensable investment required
for success in the "information age" we are entering.

Our concern, however, goes well beyond matters such as industry and commerce. It also includes the intellectual, moral, and
spiritual strengths of our people which knit together the very fab-
ric of our society. The people of the United States need to know
that individuals in our society who do not possess the levels of skill,

literacy, and training essential to this new era will be effectively disenfranchised, not simply from the material rewards that accompany competent performance, but also from the chance to participate fully in our national life. A high level of shared education is essential to a free, democratic society and to the fostering of a common culture, especially in a country that prides itself on pluralism and individual freedom.

For our country to function, citizens must be able to reach some common understandings on complex issues, often on short notice and on the basis of conflicting or incomplete evidence. Education helps form these common understandings, a point Thomas Jefferson made long ago in his justly famous dictum:

I know no safe depository of the ultimate powers of the society but the people themselves; and if we think them not enlightened enough to exercise their control with a wholesome discretion, the remedy is not to take it from them but to inform their discretion.

Part of what is at risk is the promise first made on this continent: All, regardless of race or class or economic status, are entitled to a fair chance and to the tools for developing their individual powers of mind and spirit to the utmost. This promise means that all children by virtue of their own efforts, competently guided, can hope to attain the mature and informed judgment needed to secure gainful employment and to manage their own lives, thereby serving not only their own interests but also the progress of society itself.

Indicators of the Risk

The educational dimensions of the risk before us have been amply documented in testimony received by the Commission. For example:

• International comparisons of student achievement, completed a decade ago, reveal that on 19 academic tests American students were never first or second and, in comparison with other industrialized nations, were last seven times.

• Some 23 million American adults are functionally illiterate by the simplest tests of everyday reading, writing, and comprehension.

• About 13 percent of all 17-year-olds in the United States can be considered functionally illiterate. Functional illiteracy among minority youth may run as high as 40 percent.

• Average achievement of high school students on most standardized tests is now lower than 26 years ago when Sputnik was launched.

• Over half the population of gifted students do not match their tested ability with comparable achievement in school.

• The College Board's Scholastic Aptitude Tests (SAT) demonstrate a virtually unbroken decline from 1963 to 1980. Average verbal scores fell over 50 points and average mathematics scores dropped nearly 40 points.

• College Board achievement tests also reveal consistent declines in recent years in such subjects as physics and English.

• Both the number and proportion of students demonstrating superior achievement on the SATs (i.e., those with scores of 650 or higher) have also dramatically declined.

• Many 17-year-olds do not possess the "higher order" intellectual skills we should expect of them. Nearly 40 percent cannot draw inferences from written material; only one-fifth can write a persuasive essay; and only one-third can solve a mathematics problem requiring several steps.

• There was a steady decline in science achievement scores of U.S. 17-year-olds as measured by national assessments of science in 1969, 1973, and 1977.

• Between 1975 and 1980, remedial mathematics courses in public 4-year colleges increased by 72 percent and now constitute one-quarter of all mathematics courses taught in those institutions.

• Average tested achievement of students graduating from college is also lower.

• Business and military leaders complain that they are required to spend millions of dollars on costly remedial education and training programs in such basic skills as reading, writing, spelling, and computation. The Department of the Navy, for example, reported to the Commission that one-quarter of its recent recruits cannot read at the ninth grade level, the minimum needed simply to understand written safety instructions. Without remedial work they cannot even begin, much less complete, the sophisticated training essential in much of the modern military.

These deficiencies come at a time when the demand for highly skilled workers in new fields is accelerating rapidly. For example:
• Computers and computer-controlled equipment are penetrating every aspect of our lives—homes, factories, and offices.
• One estimate indicates that by the turn of the century millions of jobs will involve laser technology and robotics.
• Technology is radically transforming a host of other occupations. They include health care, medical science, energy production, food processing, construction, and the building, repair, and maintenance of sophisticated scientific, educational, military, and industrial equipment.

Analysts examining these indicators of student performance and the demands for new skills have made some chilling observations. Educational researcher Paul Hurd concluded at the end of a thorough national survey of student achievement that within the context of the modern scientific revolution, "We are raising a new generation of Americans that is scientifically and technologically illiterate." In a similar vein, John Slaughter, a former Director of the National Science Foundation, warned of "a growing chasm between a small scientific and technological elite and a citizenry ill-informed, indeed uninformed, on issues with a science component."

But the problem does not stop there, nor do all observers see it the same way. Some worry that schools may emphasize such rudiments as reading and computation at the expense of other essential skills such as comprehension, analysis, solving problems, and drawing conclusions. Still others are concerned that an overemphasis on technical and occupational skills will leave little time for studying the arts and humanities that so enrich daily life, help maintain civility, and develop a sense of community. Knowledge of the humanities, they maintain, must be harnessed to science and technology if the latter are to remain creative and humane, just as the humanities need to be informed by science and technology if they are to remain relevant to the human condition. Another analyst, Paul Copperman, has drawn a sobering conclusion. Until now, he has noted:

Each generation of Americans has outstripped its parents in education, in literacy, and in economic attainment. For the first time in the history of our country, the educational skills of one generation will not surpass, will not equal, will not even approach, those of their parents.

It is important, of course, to recognize that *the average citizen* today is better educated and more knowledgeable than the average citizen of a generation ago—more literate, and exposed to more mathematics, literature, and science. The positive impact of this fact on the well-being of our country and the lives of our people cannot be overstated. Nevertheless, *the average graduate* of our schools and colleges today is not as well-educated as the average graduate of 25 or 35 years ago, when a much smaller proportion of our population completed high school and college. The negative impact of this fact likewise cannot be overstated.

Hope and Frustration

Statistics and their interpretation by experts show only the surface dimension of the difficulties we face. Beneath them lies a tension between hope and frustration that characterizes current attitudes about education at every level.

We have heard the voices of high school and college students, school board members, and teachers; of leaders of industry, minority groups, and higher education; of parents and State officials. We could hear the hope evident in their commitment to quality education and in their descriptions of outstanding programs and schools. We could also hear the intensity of their frustration, a growing impatience with shoddiness in many walks of American life, and the complaint that this shoddiness is too often reflected in our schools and colleges. Their frustration threatens to overwhelm their hope.

What lies behind this emerging national sense of frustration can be described as both a dimming of personal expectations and the fear of losing a shared vision for America.

On the personal level the student, the parent, and the caring teacher all perceive that a basic promise is not being kept. More and more young people emerge from high school ready neither for college nor for work. This predicament becomes more acute as the knowledge base continues its rapid expansion, the number of traditional jobs shrinks, and new jobs demand greater sophistication and preparation.

On a broader scale, we sense that this undertone of frustration has significant political implications, for it cuts across ages, generations, races, and political and economic groups. We have come to understand that the public will demand that educational and political leaders act forcefully and effectively on these issues. Indeed, such demands have already appeared and could well become a unifying national preoccupation. This unity, however, can be achieved only if we avoid the unproductive tendency of some to search for scapegoats among the victims, such as the beleaguered teachers.

On the positive side is the significant movement by political and educational leaders to search for solutions—so far centering largely on the nearly desperate need for increased support of the teaching of mathematics and science. This movement is but a start on what we believe is a larger and more educationally encompassing need to improve teaching and learning in fields such as English, history, geography, economics, and foreign languages. We believe this movement must be broadened and directed toward reform and excellence throughout education.

Excellence in Education

We define "excellence" to mean several, related things. At the level of the "individual learner," it means performing on the boundary of individual ability in ways that test and push back personal limits, in school and in the workplace. Excellence characterizes a *school or college* that sets high expectations and goals for all learners, then tries in every way possible to help students reach them. Excellence characterizes a *society* that has adopted these policies, for it will then be prepared through the education and skill of its people to respond to the challenges of a rapidly changing world. Our Nation's people and its schools and colleges must be committed to achieving excellence in all these senses.

We do not believe that a public commitment to excellence and educational reform must be made at the expense of a strong public commitment to the equitable treatment of our diverse population. The twin goals of equity and high-quality schooling have profound and practical meaning for our economy and society, and we cannot permit one to yield to the other either in principle or in practice. To do so would deny young people their chance to learn and live according to their aspirations and abilities. It also would lead to a generalized accommodation to mediocrity in our society on the one hand or the creation of an undemocratic elitism on the other.

Our goal must be to develop the talents of all to their fullest. Attaining that goal requires that we expect and assist all students to work to the limits of their capabilities. We should expect schools to have genuinely high standards rather than minimum ones, and parents to support and encourage their children to make the most of their talents and abilities.

The search for solutions to our educational problems must also include a commitment to life-long learning. The task of rebuilding our system of learning is enormous and must be properly understood and taken seriously: Although a million and a half new workers enter the economy each year from our schools and colleges, the adults working today will still make up about 75 percent of the workforce in the year 2000. These workers, and new entrants into the workforce, will need further education and retraining if they—and we as a nation—are to thrive and prosper.

The Learning Society

In a world of ever-accelerating competition and change in the conditions of the workplace, of ever-greater danger, and of ever-larger opportunities for those prepared to meet them, educational reform should focus on the goal of creating a Learning Society. At the heart of such a society is the commitment to a set of values and to a system of education that affords all members the opportunity to stretch their minds to full capacity, from early childhood through adulthood, learning more as the world itself changes. Such a society has as a basic foundation the idea that education is important not only because of what it contributes to one's career goals but also because of the value it adds to the general quality of one's life. Also at the heart of the Learning Society are educational opportunities extending far beyond the traditional institutions of learning, our schools and colleges. They extend into homes and workplaces; into libraries, art galleries, museums, and science centers; indeed, into every place where the individual can develop and mature in work and life. In our view, formal schooling in youth is the essential foundation for learning throughout one's life. But without life-long learning, one's skills will become rapidly dated.

In contrast to the ideal of the Learning Society, however, we find that for too many people education means doing the minimum work necessary for the moment, then coasting through life on what may have been learned in its first quarter. But this should not surprise us because we tend to express our educational standards and expectations largely in terms of "minimum requirements." And where there should be a coherent continuum of learning, we have none, but instead an often incoherent, outdated patchwork quilt. Many individual, sometimes heroic, examples of schools and colleges of great merit do exist. Our findings and testimony confirm the vitality of a number of notable schools and programs, but their very distinction stands out against a vast mass shaped by tensions and pressures that inhibit systematic academic and vocational achievement for the majority of students. In some metropolitan areas basic literacy has become the goal rather than the starting point. In some colleges maintaining enrollments is of greater day-to-day concern than maintaining rigorous academic standards. And the ideal of academic excellence as the primary goal of schooling seems to be fading across the board in American education.

Thus, we issue this call to all who care about America and its future: to parents and students; to teachers, administrators, and school board members; to colleges and industry; to union members and military leaders; to governors and State legislators; to the President; to members of Congress and other public officials; to members of learned and scientific societies; to the print and electronic media; to concerned citizens everywhere. America is at risk.

We are confident that America can address this risk. If the tasks we set forth are initiated now and our recommendations are fully realized over the next several years, we can expect reform of our Nation's schools, colleges, and universities. This would also reverse the current declining trend—a trend that stems more from weakness of purpose, confusion of vision, underuse of talent, and lack of leadership, than from conditions beyond our control.

The Tools at Hand

It is our conviction that the essential raw materials needed to reform our educational system are waiting to be mobilized through effective leadership:

• the natural abilities of the young that cry out to be developed and the undiminished concern of parents for the well-being of their children;

• the commitment of the Nation to high retention rates in schools and colleges and to full access to education for all;

• the persistent and authentic American dream that superior performance can raise one's state in life and shape one's own future;

• the dedication, against all odds, that keeps teachers serving in schools and colleges, even as the rewards diminish;

• our better understanding of learning and teaching and the implications of this knowledge for school practice, and the numerous examples of local success as a result of superior effort and effective dissemination;

• the ingenuity of our policymakers, scientists, State and local educators, and scholars in formulating solutions once problems are better understood;

• the traditional belief that paying for education is an investment in ever-renewable human resources that are more durable and flexible than capital plant and equipment, and the availability in this country of sufficient financial means to invest in education;

• the equally sound tradition, from the Northwest Ordinance of 1787 until today, that the Federal Government should supplement State, local, and other resources to foster key national educational goals; and

• the voluntary efforts of individuals, businesses, and parent and civic groups to cooperate in strengthening educational programs.

These raw materials, combined with the unparalleled array of educational organizations in America, offer us the possibility to create a Learning Society, in which public, private, and parochial schools; colleges and universities; vocational and technical schools and institutes; libraries; science centers, museums, and other cultural institutions; and corporate training and retraining programs offer opportunities and choices for all to learn throughout life.

The Public's Commitment

Of all the tools at hand, the public's support for education is the most powerful. In a message to a National Academy of Sciences meeting in May 1982, President Reagan commented on this fact when he said: "This public awareness—and I hope public action—is long overdue. . . . This country was built on American respect for education. . . . Our challenge now is to create a resurgence of that thirst for education that typifies our Nation's history."

The most recent (1982) Gallup Poll of the *Public's Attitudes Toward the Public Schools* strongly supported a theme heard during our hearings: People are steadfast in their belief that education is the major foundation for the future strength of this country. They even considered education more important than developing the best industrial system or the strongest military force, perhaps because they understood education as the cornerstone of both. They also held that education is "extremely important" to one's future success, and that public education should be the top priority for additional Federal funds. Education occupied first place among 12 funding categories considered in the survey—above health care, welfare, and military defense, with 55 percent selecting public education as one of their first three choices. Very clearly, the public understands the primary importance of education as the foundation for a satisfying life, an enlightened and civil society, a strong economy, and a secure Nation.

At the same time, the public has no patience with undemanding and superfluous high school offerings. In another survey, more than 75 percent of all those questioned believed every student planning to go to college should take 4 years of mathematics, English, history/U.S. government, and science, with more than 50 percent adding 2 years each of a foreign language and economics or business. The public even supports requiring much of this curriculum for students who do not plan to go to college. These standards far exceed the strictest high school graduation requirements of any State today, and they also exceed the admission standards of all but a handful of our most selective colleges and universities.

Another dimension of the public's support offers the prospect of constructive reform. The best term to characterize it may simply be the honorable word "patriotism." Citizens know intuitively what some of the best economists have shown in their research, that education is one of the chief engines of a society's material well-being. They know, too, that education is the common bond of a pluralistic society and helps tie us to other cultures around the globe. Citizens also know in their bones that the safety of the United States depends principally on the wit, skill, and spirit of a self-confident people, today and tomorrow. It is, therefore, essential—especially in a period of long-term decline in educational achievement—for government at all levels to affirm its responsibility for nurturing the Nation's intellectual capital.

And perhaps most important, citizens know and believe that the meaning of America to the rest of the world must be something better than it seems to many today. Americans like to think of this Nation as the preeminent country for generating the great ideas and material benefits for all mankind. The citizen is dismayed at a steady 15-year decline in industrial productivity, as one great American industry after another falls to world competition. The citizen wants the country to act on the belief, expressed in our hearings and by the large majority in the Gallup Poll, that education should be at the top of the Nation's agenda.

Findings

We conclude that declines in educational performance are in large part the result of disturbing inadequacies in the way the educational process itself is often conducted. The findings that follow, culled from a much more extensive list, reflect four important aspects of the educational process: content, expectations, time, and teaching.

FINDINGS REGARDING CONTENT

By content we mean the very "stuff" of education, the curriculum. Because of our concern about the curriculum, the Commission examined patterns of courses high school students took in 1964–69 compared with course patterns in 1976–81. On the basis of these analyses we conclude:

• Secondary school curricula have been homogenized, diluted, and diffused to the point that they no longer have a central purpose. In effect, we have a cafeteria-style curriculum in which the appetizers and desserts can easily be mistaken for the main courses. Students have migrated from vocational and college preparatory programs to "general track" courses in large numbers. The proportion of students taking a general program of study has increased from 12 percent in 1964 to 42 percent in 1979.

• This curricular smorgasbord, combined with extensive student choice, explains a great deal about where we find ourselves today. We offer intermediate algebra, but only 31 percent of our recent high school graduates complete it; we offer French I, but only 13 percent complete it; and we offer geography, but only 16 percent complete it. Calculus is available in schools enrolling about 60 percent of all students, but only 6 percent of all students complete it.

• Twenty-five percent of the credits earned by general track high school students are in physical and health education, work experience outside the school, remedial English and mathematics, and personal service and development courses, such as training for adulthood and marriage.

FINDINGS REGARDING EXPECTATIONS

We define expectations in terms of the level of knowledge, abilities, and skills school and college graduates should possess. They also refer to the time, hard work, behavior, self-discipline, and motivation that are essential for high student achievement. Such expectations are expressed to students in several different ways:

• by grades, which reflect the degree to which students demonstrate their mastery of subject matter;

• through high school and college graduation requirements, which tell students which subjects are most important;

• by the presence or absence of rigorous examinations requiring students to demonstrate their mastery of content and skill before receiving a diploma or a degree;

• by college admissions requirements, which reinforce high school standards; and

• by the difficulty of the subject matter students confront in their texts and assigned readings.

Our analyses in each of these areas indicate notable deficiencies:

• The amount of homework for high school seniors has decreased (two-thirds report less than 1 hour a night) and grades have risen as average student achievement has been declining.

• In many other industrialized nations, courses in mathematics (other than arithmetic or general mathematics), biology, chemistry, physics, and geography start in grade 6 and are required of *all* students. The time spent on these subjects, based on class hours, is about three times that spent by even the most science-oriented U.S. students, i.e., those who select 4 years of science and mathematics in secondary school.

• A 1980 State-by-State survey of high school diploma requirements reveals that only eight States require high schools to offer foreign language instruction, but none requires students to take the courses. Thirty-five States require only 1 year of mathematics, and 36 require only 1 year of science for a diploma.

• In 13 States, 50 percent or more of the units required for high school graduation may be electives chosen by the student. Given this freedom to choose the substance of half or more of their education, many students opt for less demanding personal service courses, such as bachelor living.

• "Minimum competency" examinations (now required in 37 States) fall short of what is needed, as the "minimum" tends to become the "maximum," thus lowering educational standards for all.

• One-fifth of all 4-year public colleges in the United States must accept every high school graduate within the State regardless of program followed or grades, thereby serving notice to high school students that they can expect to attend college even if they do not follow a demanding course of study in high school or perform well.

• About 23 percent of our more selective colleges and universities reported that their general level of selectivity declined during the 1970s, and 29 percent reported reducing the number of specific high school courses required for admission (usually by dropping foreign language requirements, which are now specified as a condition for admission by only one-fifth of our institutions of higher education).

• Too few experienced teachers and scholars are involved in writing textbooks. During the past decade or so a large number of texts have been "written down" by their publishers to ever-lower reading levels in response to perceived market demands.

• A recent study by Education Products Information Exchange revealed that a majority of students were able to master 80 percent of the material in some of their subject-matter texts before they had even opened the books. Many books do not challenge the students to whom they are assigned.

• Expenditures for textbooks and other instructional materials have declined by 50 percent over the past 17 years. While some recommend a level of spending on texts of between 5 and 10 percent of the operating costs of schools, the budgets for basal texts and related materials have been dropping during the past decade and a half to only 0.7 percent today.

FINDINGS REGARDING TIME

Evidence presented to the Commission demonstrates three disturbing facts about the use that American schools and students make of time: (1) compared to other nations, American students spend much less time on school work; (2) time spent in the classroom and on homework is often used ineffectively; and (3) schools are not doing enough to help students develop either the study skills required to use time well or the willingness to spend more time on school work.

• In England and other industrialized countries, it is not unusual

for academic high school students to spend 8 hours a day at school, 220 days per year. In the United States, by contrast, the typical school day lasts 6 hours and the school year is 180 days.
• In many schools, the time spent learning how to cook and drive counts as much toward a high school diploma as the time spent studying mathematics, English, chemistry, U.S. history, or biology.
• A study of the school week in the United States found that some schools provided students only 17 hours of academic instruction during the week, and the average school provided about 22.
• A California study of individual classrooms found that because of poor management of classroom time, some elementary students received only one-fifth of the instruction others received in reading comprehension.
• In most schools, the teaching of study skills is haphazard and unplanned. Consequently, many students complete high school and enter college without disciplined and systematic study habits.

Findings Regarding Teaching

The Commission found that not enough of the academically able students are being attracted to teaching; that teacher preparation programs need substantial improvement; that the professional working life of teachers is on the whole unacceptable; and that a serious shortage of teachers exists in key fields.
• Too many teachers are being drawn from the bottom quarter of graduating high school and college students.
• The teacher preparation curriculum is weighted heavily with courses in "educational methods" at the expense of courses in subjects to be taught. A survey of 1,350 institutions training teachers indicated that 41 percent of the time of elementary school teacher candidates is spent in education courses, which reduces the amount of time available for subject matter courses.
• The average salary after 12 years of teaching is only $17,000 per year, and many teachers are required to supplement their income with part-time and summer employment. In addition, individual teachers have little influence in such critical professional decisions as, for example, textbook selection.

• Despite widespread publicity about an overpopulation of teachers, severe shortages of certain kinds of teachers exist: in the fields of mathematics, science, and foreign languages; and among specialists in education for gifted and talented, language minority, and handicapped students.

• The shortage of teachers in mathematics and science is particularly severe. A 1981 survey of 45 States revealed shortages of mathematics teachers in 43 States, critical shortages of earth sciences teachers in 33 States, and of physics teachers everywhere.

• Half of the newly employed mathematics, science, and English teachers are not qualified to teach these subjects; fewer than one-third of U.S. high schools offer physics taught by qualified teachers.

Recommendations

In light of the urgent need for improvement, both immediate and long term, this Commission has agreed on a set of recommendations that the American people can begin to act on now, that can be implemented over the next several years, and that promise lasting reform. The topics are familiar; there is little mystery about what we believe must be done. Many schools, districts, and States are already giving serious and constructive attention to these matters, even though their plans may differ from our recommendations in some details.

We wish to note that we refer to public, private, and parochial schools and colleges alike. All are valuable national resources. Examples of actions similar to those recommended below can be found in each of them.

We must emphasize that the variety of student aspirations, abilities, and preparation requires that appropriate content be available to satisfy diverse needs. Attention must be directed to both the nature of the content available and to the needs of particular learners. The most gifted students, for example, may need a curriculum enriched and accelerated beyond even the needs of other students of high ability. Similarly, educationally disadvantaged students may require special curriculum materials, smaller classes, or individual tutoring to help them master the material presented. Nevertheless, there remains a common expectation: We must demand the best effort and performance from all students, whether they are gifted or less able, affluent or disadvantaged, whether destined for college, the farm, or industry.

Our recommendations are based on the beliefs that everyone can learn, that everyone is born with an *urge* to learn which can be nurtured, that a solid high school education is within the reach of virtually all, and that life-long learning will equip people with the skills required for new careers and for citizenship.

Recommendation A: *Content*

We recommend that State and local high school graduation requirements be strengthened and that, at a minimum, *all students seeking a diploma be required to lay the foundations in the Five New Basics by taking the following curriculum during their 4 years of high school: (a) 4 years of English; (b) 3 years of mathematics; (c) 3 years of science; (d) 3 years of social studies; and (e) one-half year of computer science. For the college-bound, 2 years of foreign language in high school are strongly recommended in addition to those taken earlier.*

Whatever the student's educational or work objectives, knowledge of the New Basics is the foundation of success for the after-school years and, therefore, forms the core of the modern curriculum. A high level of shared education in these Basics, together with work in the fine and performing arts and foreign languages, constitutes the mind and spirit of our culture. The following Implementing Recommendations are intended as illustrative descriptions. They are included here to clarify what we mean by the essentials of a strong curriculum.

IMPLEMENTING RECOMMENDATIONS

1.   The teaching of *English* in high school should equip graduates to: (a) comprehend, interpret, evaluate, and use what they read; (b) write well-organized, effective papers; (c) listen effectively and discuss ideas intelligently; and (d) know our literary heri-

tage and how it enhances imagination and ethical understanding, and how it relates to the customs, ideas, and values of today's life and culture.

2. The teaching of *mathematics* in high school should equip graduates to: (a) understand geometric and algebraic concepts; (b) understand elementary probability and statistics; (c) apply mathematics in everyday situations; and (d) estimate, approximate, measure, and test the accuracy of their calculations. In addition to the traditional sequence of studies available for college-bound students, new, equally demanding mathematics curricula need to be developed for those who do not plan to continue their formal education immediately.

3. The teaching of *science* in high school should provide graduates with an introduction to: (a) the concepts, laws, and processes of the physical and biological sciences; (b) the methods of scientific inquiry and reasoning; (c) the application of scientific knowledge to everyday life; and (d) the social and environmental implications of scientific and technological development. Science courses must be revised and updated for both the college-bound and those not intending to go to college. An example of such work is the American Chemical Society's "Chemistry in the Community" program.

4. The teaching of *social studies* in high school should be designed to enable students to: (a) fix their places and possibilities within the larger social and cultural structure; (b) understand the broad sweep of both ancient and contemporary ideas that have shaped our world; (c) understand the fundamentals of how our economic system works and how our political system functions; and (d) grasp the difference between free and repressive societies. An understanding of each of these areas is requisite to the informed and committed exercise of citizenship in our free society.

5. The teaching of *computer science* in high school should equip graduates to: (a) understand the computer as an information, computation, and communication device; (b) use the computer in the study of the other Basics and for personal and work-related purposes; and (c) understand the world of computers, electronics, and related technologies.

In addition to the New Basics, other important curriculum matters must be addressed.

6.   Achieving proficiency in a *foreign language* ordinarily requires from 4 to 6 years of study and should, therefore, be started in the elementary grades. We believe it is desirable that students achieve such proficiency because study of a foreign language introduces students to non-English-speaking cultures, heightens awareness and comprehension of one's native tongue, and serves the Nation's needs in commerce, diplomacy, defense, and education.

7.   The high school curriculum should also provide students with programs requiring rigorous effort in subjects that advance students' personal, educational, and occupational goals, such as the fine and performing arts and vocational education. These areas complement the New Basics, and they should demand the same level of performance as the Basics.

8.   The curriculum in the crucial eight grades leading to the high school years should be specifically designed to provide a sound base for study in those and later years in such areas as English language development and writing, computational and problem solving skills, science, social studies, foreign language, and the arts. These years should foster an enthusiasm for learning and the development of the individual's gifts and talents.

9.   We encourage the continuation of efforts by groups such as the American Chemical Society, the American Association for the Advancement of Science, the Modern Language Association, and the National Councils of Teachers of English and Teachers of Mathematics, to revise, update, improve, and make available new and more diverse curricular materials. We applaud the consortia of educators and scientific, industrial, and scholarly societies that cooperate to improve the school curriculum.

Recommendation B:
Standards and Expectations

We recommend that schools, colleges, and universities adopt more rigorous and measurable standards, and higher expectations, for academic performance and student conduct, and that 4-year colleges and universities raise their requirements for admission. This will help students do their best educationally with challeng-

ing materials in an environment that supports learning and authentic accomplishment.

IMPLEMENTING RECOMMENDATIONS

1.   Grades should be indicators of academic achievement so they can be relied on as evidence of a student's readiness for further study.

2.   Four-year colleges and universities should raise their admissions requirements and advise all potential applicants of the standards for admission in terms of specific courses required, performance in these areas, and levels of achievement on standardized achievement tests in each of the five Basics and, where applicable, foreign languages.

3.   Standardized tests of achievement (not to be confused with aptitude tests) should be administered at major transition points from one level of schooling to another and particularly from high school to college or work. The purposes of these tests would be to: (a) certify the student's credentials; (b) identify the need for remedial intervention; and (c) identify the opportunity for advanced or accelerated work. The tests should be administered as part of a nationwide (but not Federal) system of State and local standardized tests. This system should include other diagnostic procedures that assist teachers and students to evaluate student progress.

4.   Textbooks and other tools of learning and teaching should be upgraded and updated to assure more rigorous content. We call upon university scientists, scholars, and members of professional societies, in collaboration with master teachers, to help in this task, as they did in the post-Sputnik era. They should assist willing publishers in developing the products or publish their own alternatives where there are persistent inadequacies.

5.   In considering textbooks for adoption, States and school districts should: (a) evaluate texts and other materials on their ability to present rigorous and challenging material clearly; and (b) require publishers to furnish evaluation data on the material's effectiveness.

6.   Because no textbook in any subject can be geared to the needs of all students, funds should be made available to support text de-

velopment in "thin-market" areas, such as those for disadvantaged students, the learning disabled, and the gifted and talented.

7.   To assure quality, all publishers should furnish evidence of the quality and appropriateness of textbooks, based on results from field trials and credible evaluations. In view of the enormous numbers and varieties of texts available, more widespread consumer information services for purchasers are badly needed.

8.   New instructional materials should reflect the most current applications of technology in appropriate curriculum areas, the best scholarship in each discipline, and research in learning and teaching.

Recommendation C: Time

We recommend that significantly more time be devoted to learning the New Basics. This will require more effective use of the existing school day, a longer school day, or a lengthened school year.

Implementing Recommendations

1.   Students in high schools should be assigned far more homework than is now the case.

2.   Instruction in effective study and work skills, which are essential if school (and independent) time is to be used efficiently, should be introduced in the early grades and continued throughout the student's schooling.

3.   School districts and State legislatures should strongly consider 7-hour school days, as well as a 200- to 220-day school year.

4.   The time available for learning should be expanded through better classroom management and organization of the school day. If necessary, additional time should be found to meet the special needs of slow learners, the gifted, and others who need more instructional diversity than can be accommodated during a conventional school day or school year.

5.   The burden on teachers for maintaining discipline should be reduced through the development of firm and fair codes of student conduct that are enforced consistently, and by considering alterna-

tive classrooms, programs, and schools to meet the needs of continually disruptive students.

6.   Attendance policies with clear incentives and sanctions should be used to reduce the amount of time lost through student absenteeism and tardiness.

7.   Administrative burdens on the teacher and related intrusions into the school day should be reduced to add time for teaching and learning.

8.   Placement and grouping of students, as well as promotion and graduation policies, should be guided by the academic progress of students and their instructional needs, rather than by rigid adherence to age.

Recommendation D:
Teaching

This recommendation consists of seven parts. Each is intended to improve the preparation of teachers or to make teaching a more rewarding and respected profession. Each of the seven stands on its own and should not be considered solely as an implementing recommendation.

1.   Persons preparing to teach should be required to meet high educational standards, to demonstrate an aptitude for teaching, and to demonstrate competence in an academic discipline. Colleges and universities offering teacher preparation programs should be judged by how well their graduates meet these criteria.

2.   Salaries for the teaching profession should be increased and should be professionally competitive, market-sensitive, and performance-based. Salary, promotion, tenure, and retention decisions should be tied to an effective evaluation system that includes peer review so that superior teachers can be rewarded, average ones encouraged, and poor ones either improved or terminated.

3.   School boards should adopt an 11-month contract for teachers. This would ensure time for curriculum and professional development, programs for students with special needs, and a more adequate level of teacher compensation.

4.   School boards, administrators, and teachers should cooperate to develop career ladders for teachers that distinguish among the

beginning instructor, the experienced teacher, and the master teacher.

5.   Substantial nonschool personnel resources should be employed to help solve the immediate problem of the shortage of mathematics and science teachers. Qualified individuals including recent graduates with mathematics and science degrees, graduate students, and industrial and retired scientists could, with appropriate preparation, immediately begin teaching in these fields. A number of our leading science centers have the capacity to begin educating and retraining teachers immediately. Other areas of critical teacher need, such as English, must also be addressed.

6.   Incentives, such as grants and loans, should be made available to attract outstanding students to the teaching profession, particularly in those areas of critical shortage.

7.   Master teachers should be involved in designing teacher preparation programs and in supervising teachers during their probationary years.

Recommendation E:
Leadership and Fiscal
Support

We recommend that citizens across the Nation hold educators and elected officials responsible for providing the leadership necessary to achieve these reforms, and that citizens provide the fiscal support and stability required to bring about the reforms we propose.

Implementing Recommendations

1.   Principals and superintendents must play a crucial leadership role in developing school and community support for the reforms we propose, and school boards must provide them with the professional development and other support required to carry out their leadership role effectively. The Commission stresses the distinction between leadership skills involving persuasion, setting goals and developing community consensus behind them, and managerial and supervisory skills. Although the latter are neces-

sary, we believe that school boards must consciously develop leadership skills at the school and district levels if the reforms we propose are to be achieved.

2. State and local officials, including school board members, governors, and legislators, have *the primary responsibility* for financing and governing the schools, and should incorporate the reforms we propose in their educational policies and fiscal planning.

3. The Federal Government, in cooperation with States and localities, should help meet the needs of key groups of students such as the gifted and talented, the socioeconomically disadvantaged, minority and language minority students, and the handicapped. In combination these groups include both national resources and the Nation's youth who are most at risk.

4. In addition, we believe the Federal Government's role includes several functions of national consequence that States and localities alone are unlikely to be able to meet: protecting constitutional and civil rights for students and school personnel; collecting data, statistics, and information about education generally; supporting curriculum improvement and research on teaching, learning, and the management of schools; supporting teacher training in areas of critical shortage or key national needs; and providing student financial assistance and research and graduate training. We believe the assistance of the Federal Government should be provided with a minimum of administrative burden and intrusiveness.

5. The Federal Government has *the primary responsibility* to identify the national interest in education. It should also help fund and support efforts to protect and promote that interest. It must provide the national leadership to ensure that the Nation's public and private resources are marshaled to address the issues discussed in this report.

6. This Commission calls upon educators, parents, and public officials at all levels to assist in bringing about the educational reform proposed in this report. We also call upon citizens to provide the financial support necessary to accomplish these purposes. Excellence costs. But in the long run mediocrity costs far more.

America Can Do It

Despite the obstacles and difficulties that inhibit the pursuit of superior educational attainment, we are confident, with history as our guide, that we can meet our goal. The American educational system has responded to previous challenges with remarkable success. In the 19th century our land-grant colleges and universities provided the research and training that developed our Nation's natural resources and the rich agricultural bounty of the American farm. From the late 1800s through mid-20th century, American schools provided the educated workforce needed to seal the success of the Industrial Revolution and to provide the margin of victory in two world wars. In the early part of this century and continuing to this very day, our schools have absorbed vast waves of immigrants and educated them and their children to productive citizenship. Similarly, the Nation's Black colleges have provided opportunity and undergraduate education to the vast majority of college-educated Black Americans.

More recently, our institutions of higher education have provided the scientists and skilled technicians who helped us transcend the boundaries of our planet. In the last 30 years, the schools have been a major vehicle for expanded social opportunity, and now graduate 75 percent of our young people from high school. Indeed, the proportion of Americans of college age enrolled in higher education is nearly twice that of Japan and far exceeds other nations such as France, West Germany, and the Soviet Union. Moreover, when international comparisons were last made a decade ago, the top 9 percent of American students compared favorably in achievement with their peers in other countries.

In addition, many large urban areas in recent years report that average student achievement in elementary schools is improving. More and more schools are also offering advanced placement programs and programs for gifted and talented students, and more and more students are enrolling in them.

We are the inheritors of a past that gives us every reason to believe that we will succeed.

A Word to Parents and Students

The task of assuring the success of our recommendations does not fall to the schools and colleges alone. Obviously, faculty members and administrators, along with policymakers and the mass media, will play a crucial role in the reform of the educational system. But even more important is the role of parents and students, and to them we speak directly.

To Parents

You know that you cannot confidently launch your children into today's world unless they are of strong character and well-educated in the use of language, science, and mathematics. They must possess a deep respect for intelligence, achievement, and learning, and the skills needed to use them; for setting goals; and for disciplined work. That respect must be accompanied by an intolerance for the shoddy and second-rate masquerading as "good enough."

You have the right to demand for your children the best our schools and colleges can provide. Your vigilance and your refusal to be satisfied with less than the best are the imperative first step. But your right to a proper education for your children carries a double responsibility. As surely as you are your child's first and most influential teacher, your child's ideas about education and its significance begin with you. You must be a *living* example of what you expect your children to honor and to emulate. Moreover, you bear a responsibility to participate actively in your child's education. You should encourage more diligent study and discourage satisfaction with mediocrity and the attitude that says "let it slide"; monitor your child's study; encourage good study habits; encourage your child to take more demanding rather than less demanding courses; nurture your child's curiosity, creativity, and confidence; and be an active participant in the work of the schools. Above all, exhibit a commitment to continued learning in your own life. Finally, help your children understand that excellence in education cannot be achieved without intellectual and moral integrity coupled with hard work and commitment. Children will look to their parents and teachers as models of such virtues.

To Students

You forfeit your chance for life at its fullest when you withhold your best effort in learning. When you give only the minimum to learning, you receive only the minimum in return. Even with your parents' best example and your teachers' best efforts, in the end it is *your* work that determines how much and how well you learn. When you work to your full capacity, you can hope to attain the knowledge and skills that will enable you to create your future and control your destiny. If you do not, you will have your future thrust upon you by others. Take hold of your life, apply your gifts and talents, work with dedication and self-discipline. Have high expectations for yourself and convert every challenge into an opportunity.

A Final Word

This is not the first or only commission on education, and some of our findings are surely not new, but old business that now at last must be done. For no one can doubt that the United States is under challenge from many quarters.

Children born today can expect to graduate from high school in the year 2000. We dedicate our report not only to these children, but also to those now in school and others to come. We firmly believe that a movement of America's schools in the direction called for by our recommendations will prepare these children for far more effective lives in a far stronger America.

Our final word, perhaps better characterized as a plea, is that all segments of our population give attention to the implementation of our recommendations. Our present plight did not appear overnight, and the responsibility for our current situation is widespread. Reform of our educational system will take time and unwavering commitment. It will require equally widespread, energetic, and dedicated action. For example, we call upon the National Academy of Sciences, National Academy of Engineering, Institute of Medicine, Science Service, National Science Foundation, Social Science Research Council, American Council of Learned Societies, National Endowment for the Humanities,

National Endowment for the Arts, and other scholarly, scientific, and learned societies for their help in this effort. Help should come from students themselves; from parents, teachers, and school boards; from colleges and universities; from local, State, and Federal officials; from teachers' and administrators' organizations; from industrial and labor councils; and from other groups with interest in and responsibility for educational reform.

It is their America, and the America of all of us, that is at risk; it is to each of us that this imperative is addressed. It is by our willingness to take up the challenge, and our resolve to see it through, that America's place in the world will be either secured or forfeited. Americans have succeeded before and so we shall again.

HIGH SCHOOL: AN AGENDA FOR ACTION[2]

The world has changed, irrevocably so, and quality education in the 1980s and beyond means preparing all students for the transformed world the coming generation will inherit. To achieve this goal, a comprehensive school-improvement program must be pursued urgently. Without excellence in education, the promise of America cannot be fulfilled. We have identified twelve priorities that, taken together, provide an agenda for action.

I. *Clarifying Goals*

A high school, to be effective, must have a clear and vital mission. Educators must have a shared vision of what, together, they are trying to accomplish. That vision should go beyond keeping students in school and out of trouble, and be more significant than adding up the Carnegie course units the student has completed. Specifically, we recommend:
• Every high school should establish clearly stated goals—

[2]Excerpted from *High School: A Report on Secondary Education in America*, by Ernest Boyer, president of the Carnegie Foundation for the Advancement of Teaching. Copyright © 1983 by The Carnegie Foundation for the Advancement of Teaching. Reprinted by permission of Harper & Row, Publishers, Inc.

purposes that are widely shared by teachers, students, administrators and parents.

• School goals should focus on the mastery of language, on a core of common learning, on preparation for work and further education, and on community and civic service.

II. *The Centrality of Language*

The next priority is language. Formal schooling has a special obligation to help all students become skilled in the written and oral use of English. Those who do not become proficient in the primary language of the culture are enormously disadvantaged in school and out of school as well. The following recommendations are proposed:

• Elementary school should build on the remarkable language skills a child already has acquired. In the early grades, students should learn to read and comprehend the main ideas in a written work, write standard English sentences, and present their ideas orally.

• The English proficiency of all students should be formally assessed before they go to high school. A pre-high school summer term and an intensive freshman year remediation program should be provided for students who are deficient in the use of English.

• Clear writing leads to clear thinking; clear thinking is the basis of clear writing. Therefore, all high school students should complete a basic English course with emphasis on writing. Enrollment in such classes should be limited to twenty students, and no more than two such classes should be included in the teacher's regular load.

• The high school curriculum should also include a study of the spoken word. Speaking and listening are something more than the mere exchange of information. Communication at its best should lead to genuine understanding.

III. *The Curriculum Has a Core*

A core of common learning is essential. The basic curriculum should be a study of those consequential ideas, experiences, and traditions common to all of us by virtue of our membership in the human family at a particular moment in history. The content of the core curriculum must extend beyond the specialties and focus on more transcendent issues, moving from courses to coherence. The following are recommended:

• The number of required courses in the core curriculum should be expanded from one-half to two-thirds of the total units required for high school graduation.

• In addition to strengthening the traditional courses in literature, history, mathematics and science, emphasis should also be given to foreign language, the arts, civics, non-Western studies, technology, the meaning of work, and the importance of health.

Highlights of the core curriculum are as follows:

Literature: All students, through a study of literature, should discover our common literary heritage and learn about the power and beauty of the written word.

United States History: United States history is required for graduation from all the high schools included in our study, and it is the one social studies course uniformly required by most states. We favor a one-year United States history course that would build on the chronology of the emergence of America, including a study of the lives of a few influential leaders—artists, reformers, explorers—who helped shape the nation.

Western Civilization: Beyond American history lies the long sweep of Western Civilization. We recommend that all students learn about the roots of our national heritage and traditions through a study of other cultures that have shaped our own.

Non-Western Civilization: All students should discover the connectedness of the human experience and the richness of other cultures through an in-depth study of the non-Western world. Specifically, we suggest a one-semester required course in which students study, in considerable detail, a single non-Western nation.

Science and the Natural World: The study of science introduces students to the processes of discovery—what we call the scientific method—and reveals how such procedures can be applied to many disciplines and to their own lives. We suggest a two-year science sequence that would include basic courses in the biological and physical sciences.

Technology: All students should study technology: the history of man's use of tools, how science and technology have been joined, and the ethical and social issues technology has raised.

Mathematics: In high school, all students should expand their capacity to think quantitatively and to make intelligent decisions regarding situations involving measurable quantities. Specifically, we believe that all high schools should require a two-year mathematics sequence for graduation and that additional courses be provided for students who qualify to take them.

Foreign Language: All students should become familiar with the language of another culture. Such studies should ideally begin in elementary school, and at least two years of foreign language study should be required of all high school students. By the year 2000, the United States could be home to the world's fifth largest population of persons of Hispanic origin. It does seem reasonable for all schools in the United States to offer Spanish.

The Arts: The arts are an essential part of the human experience. They are not a frill. We recommend that all students study the arts to discover how human beings use nonverbal symbols and communicate not only with words but through music, dance, and the visual arts.

Civics: A course in American government—traditionally called civics—should be required of all students, with focus on the traditions of democratic thought, the shaping of our own governmental structures, and political and social issues we confront today.

Health: No knowledge is more crucial than knowledge about health. Without it, no other life goal can be successfully achieved. Therefore, all students should learn about the human body, how it changes over the life cycle, what nourishes it and diminishes it, and how a healthy body contributes to emotional well-being.

Work: The one-semester study of work we propose would ask how attitudes toward work have changed through the years. How do they differ from one culture to another? What determines the status and rewards of different forms of work? Such a curriculum might also include an in-depth investigation of one specific occupation.

• All students, during their senior year, should complete a Senior Independent Project, a written report that focuses on a significant social issue and draws upon the various fields of study in the academic core.

IV. *Transition: To Work and Learning*

The high school should help all students move with confidence from school to work and further education. Today, we track students into programs for those who "think" and those who "work," when, in fact, life for all of us is a blend of both. Looking to the year 2000, we conclude that, for most students, twelve years of schooling will be insufficient. Today's graduates will change jobs several times. New skills will be required, new citizenship obligations will be confronted. Of necessity, education will be lifelong. We recommend:

• The school program should offer a single track for all students, one that includes a strong grounding in the basic tools of education and a study of the core curriculum. While the first two years would be devoted almost exclusively to the common core, a portion of this work would continue into the third or fourth year.

• The last two years of high school should be considered a "transition school," a program in which about half the time is devoted to "elective clusters."

• The "elective cluster" should be carefully designed. Such a program would include advanced study in selected academic subjects, the exploration of a career option, or a combination of both.

• In order to offer a full range of elective clusters, the high school must become a connected institution. Upper-level specialty schools (in the arts or science or health or computers, for example) may be appropriate in some districts. High schools should also establish connections with learning places beyond the schools—such as libraries, museums, art galleries, colleges, and industrial laboratories.

There is also an urgent need to help students figure out what they should do after graduation. Therefore, we recommend:

• Guidance services should be significantly expanded. No counselor should have a case load of more than one hundred students. Moreover, school districts should provide a referral service to community agencies for those students needing frequent and sustained professional assistance.

• A new Student Achievement and Advisement Test (SAAT) should be developed, one that could eventually replace the SAT. The academic achievement portion of the test would be linked to the core curriculum, evaluating what the student has learned. The advisement section would assess personal characteristics and interests to help students make decisions more intelligently about their futures. The purpose is not to screen students out of options but to help them move on with confidence to colleges and to jobs.

The needs of the student for guidance are matched by the need of the school to be better informed about its graduates. To achieve this, the following is proposed:

• The United States Department of Education—working through the states—should expand its national survey of schools to include a sampling of graduates from all high schools at four-year intervals to learn about their post-high school placement and experience. Such information should be made available to participating schools.

V. *Service: The New Carnegie Unit*

Beyond the formal academic program the high school should help all students meet their social and civic obligations. During high school young people should be given opportunities to reach beyond themselves and feel more responsibly engaged. They should be encouraged to participate in the communities of which they are a part. We recommend:

• All high school students should complete a service requirement—a new Carnegie unit—that would involve them in volunteer work in the community or at school. Students could fulfill this requirement evenings, weekends, and during the summer.

• Students themselves should be given the responsibility to help organize and monitor the new service program and to work with school officials to assure that credit is appropriately assigned.

VI. *Teachers: Renewing the Profession*

The working conditions of teachers must improve. Many people think teachers have soft, undemanding jobs. The reality is different. Teachers are expected to work miracles day after day and then often get only silence from the students, pressure from the principal, and criticism from the irate parent. To improve the working conditions of the teachers, we propose the following:

• High school teachers should have a daily teaching load of four regular class sessions. In addition, they should be responsible one period each day for small seminars and for helping students with independent projects.

• Teachers should have a minimum of sixty minutes each school day for class preparation and record keeping. The current catch-as-catch-can "arrangement" is simply not good enough.

• Teachers should be exempt from routine monitoring of halls, lunchrooms, and recreation areas. School clerical staff and parent and student volunteers should assume such noninstructional duties.

• A Teacher Excellence Fund should be established in every school—a competitive grant program to enable teachers to design and carry out a special professional project.

• Good teachers should be given adequate recognition and rewards—from a student's "thank you" to cash awards and to active support from parents. Outstanding teachers also should be honored annually in every school district and, statewide, by the governor and the legislature, newspapers, and other businesses in each community.

• Teachers should be supported in the maintenance of discipline based on a clearly stated code of conduct.

Teachers' salaries should be increased. When teachers' salaries are compared to those of other professionals, the contrast is depressing. For many teachers, moonlighting has become essential. Salaries for teachers must be commensurate with those of other professions and with the tasks teachers must perform.

• As a national goal, the average salary for teachers should be increased by at least 25 percent beyond the rate of inflation over the next three years, with immediate entry-level increases.

Outstanding students should be recruited into teaching. We cannot have gifted teachers if gifted students do not enter the classrooms of the nation. When salaries and working conditions improve, prospects for recruiting talented young people will improve as well. We propose:

• Every high school should establish a cadet teacher program in which high school teachers identify gifted students and encourage them to become teachers. Such students should be given opportunities to present information to classmates, tutor other students who need special help, and meet with outstanding school and college teachers. Also some districts may wish to establish a magnet school for prospective teachers.

• Colleges and universities should establish full tuition scholarships for the top 5 percent of their gifted students who plan to teach in public education. These scholarships would begin when students are admitted to the teacher preparation program at the junior year.

• The federal government should establish a National Teacher Service, especially for those who plan to teach in science and mathematics. This tuition scholarship program would be for students in the top one-third of their high school graduating classes. Students admitted to the National Teacher Service would be expected to complete successfully an academic program and teach at least three years in the public schools.

The schooling of teachers must improve. There are serious problems with the education of our teachers. Many teacher training programs are inadequate. The accreditation of schools of education is ineffective. The careful selection of teacher candidates is almost nonexistent, and college arts and science departments fail to recognize the critical role they play in teacher preparation. The following is proposed:

• Prospective teachers should complete a core of common learning, one that parallels in broad outline the high school core curriculum proposed in this report.

• Every teacher candidate should be carefully selected. Formal admission to teacher training should occur at the junior year, the time when students begin a three-year teacher preparation sequence. Only students with a cumulative grade point average of

3.0 (B) or better and who have strong supportive recommendations from two professors who taught them in a required academic course should be admitted.

• Once admitted to the program, the teacher candidate should devote the junior and senior years to the completion of a major, plus appropriate electives. Every secondary school teacher should complete a sharply focused major in one academic discipline, not in education. During the junior and senior years, time also should be scheduled for prospective teachers systematically to visit schools.

• After grounding in the core curriculum and a solid academic major, prospective teachers should have a fifth-year education core built around the following subjects: Schooling in America, Learning Theory and Research, The Teaching of Writing, and Technology and Its Uses.

• The fifth year also should include classroom observation and teaching experience. This is the best way, we believe, to learn about students and to develop effective methods of instruction.

• In addition, the fifth year of teacher preparation should include a series of six one-day common learning seminars in which students meet with outstanding arts and science scholar-teachers who would relate the knowledge of their fields to a contemporary political or social theme. Such seminars would help provide the interdisciplinary perspective every high school teacher must acquire.

The continuing education of the teacher must be strengthened. We cannot expect a teacher trained twenty years ago to prepare students to live forty years into the future with no policy of systematic continued education for the teacher. Even the most dedicated teacher will fall behind, and students will learn how to live, not in the future, but in the past. School boards must accept lifelong learning as an essential condition for every teacher.

• A two-week Teacher Professional Development Term should be added to the school year, with appropriate compensation. This term for teachers would be a time for study, a period to improve instruction and to expand knowledge. The planning of such a term should be largely controlled by teachers at the school or district level.

• Every school district should establish a Teacher Travel Fund to make it possible for teachers, based on competitive application, to travel occasionally to professional meetings to keep current in their fields.

• Every five years, teachers should be eligible to receive a special contract—with extra pay to match—to support a Summer Study Term. To quality and compete for this extended contract, each teacher would prepare a study plan. Such a plan would be subject to review and approval both by peers and by the school and district administrations.

A career path for teachers should be developed. Two of the most troublesome aspects of the teaching profession today are the lack of a career ladder and the leveling off of salaries. The irony is that to "get ahead" in teaching, you must leave it. Good teachers must be recognized and move forward within the profession, not outside it. Our proposals for restructuring the teaching career are these:

• The credentialing of teachers should be separated from college preparation. To qualify for a credential, each candidate should submit letters of recommendation from members of the faculty in his or her academic major, from faculty in his or her education sequence, and from a teacher who has supervised his or her school internship.

• Before being credentialed, the candidate would also pass a written examination administered by a Board of Examiners to be established in every state. The majority membership on such a board should be composed of senior classroom teachers.

• After credentialing, a career path based on performance should be available to the teacher, moving from associate teacher to senior teacher.

• With each professional advancement, salary increases should be provided. Such increases would be in addition to cost-of-living and merit pay earned within the ranks.

• The evaluation of teacher performance should be largely controlled by other teachers who themselves have been judged to be outstanding in the classroom.

Skilled professionals should be recruited to teach part-time in the nation's classrooms. More flexible arrangements will be needed to permit highly qualified nonacademic professionals to teach.

Such "teachers" could serve in those fields where shortages exist—such as math and science—and provide enrichment in other fields as well. We recommend that:

• School districts should establish a lectureship program to permit qualified nonacademic professionals to teach on a part-time basis. Such teachers would devote most of their time to their regular jobs—in business or government or law or medicine—while also contributing significantly to education.

• School districts should look to recently retired personnel—college professors, business leaders, and others—who, after brief orientation, could teach part-time in high-demand subjects.

• School districts should enter into partnerships with business and industry to create joint appointments. In this way, two-member teacher teams could be created with one member of the team teaching in school for a year or two while the other works at a non-school job. Then the cycle could be reversed.

• In-and-out teaching terms should be established—permitting a professional to teach for one to three years, step out, and then return for another one-to-three-year term.

• A Part-Time Practitioner Credential should be created in every state to put in place the recommendations we propose.

VII. *Instruction: A Time for Learning*

Much about good pedagogy is familiar. There remain, however, some old-fashioned yet enduring qualities in human relationships that still work: contagious enthusiasm, human sensitivity, optimism about the potential of the students. Improving instruction requires a variety of changes. We make the following recommendations:

• Teachers should use a variety of teaching styles—lecturing to transmit information, coaching to teach a skill, and Socratic questioning to enlarge understanding. But there should be particular emphasis on the active participation of the student.

• For classroom instruction to be effective, expectations should be high, standards clear, evaluation fair, and students should be held accountable for their work.

• Textbooks seldom communicate to students the richness and excitement of original works. The classroom use of primary source materials should be expanded.

• States should ease their control over the selection of textbooks and transfer more authority to the district and local school. Teachers should have a far greater voice in selecting materials appropriate to their own subject areas.

VIII. *Technology: Extending the Teacher's Reach*

Technology, particularly computers, can enrich instruction. But educators are confused about precisely what the new machines will do. The strategy seems to be buy now, plan later. The absence of computer policy is itself a policy with major risks. A number of important steps should be taken to link computers to school objectives.

• No school should buy computers, or any other expensive piece of hardware, until key questions have been asked—and answered. Why is this purchase being made? Is available software as good as the equipment? What educational objectives will be served? Which students will use the new equipment, when, and why?

• In purchasing computers, schools should base their decisions not only on the quality of the equipment, but also on the quality of the instructional material available. School districts also should take into account the commitment of the computer company to work alone—or in collaboration with other companies—to develop instructional materials for schools.

• Every computer firm selling hardware to the schools should establish a Special Instructional Materials Fund. Such a fund would be used to develop, in consultation with classroom teachers, high-quality, school-related software.

• For technology to be used effectively, teachers must learn about the new equipment. Computer companies should provide technology seminars for teachers to keep them up-to-date on the uses of computers as a teaching tool.

• A National Commission on Computer Instruction should be named by the Secretary of Education to evaluate the software now offered for school use and propose an ongoing evaluation procedure that would be available to the schools. Outstanding teachers should comprise an important segment of such a panel.

• Federal funds should be used to establish ten Technology Resource Centers on university campuses—one in each major region of the nation. These centers would assemble, for demonstration, the latest technology. Also, federally funded regional networks should be developed to make computerized library services available to all schools.

• Schools should relate computer resources to their educational objectives. Specifically, all students should learn *about* computers; learn with computers; and, as an ultimate goal, learn *from* computers. The first priority, however, should not be hands-on experience, but rather educating students about the social importance of technology, of which the computer is a part.

Prospects for a technology revolution in education go far beyond computers. Through the use of television, films, and video cassettes, the classroom can be enormously enriched. In this connection, we recommend:

• School districts with access to a cable channel should use the facility for school instruction, and a district-wide plan of such use should be developed.

• All commercial television networks should set aside prime-time hours every week to air programs for education and thereby indirectly enrich the school curriculum.

• A National Film Library should be established with federal support. This resource center would secure outstanding film and television programs, both commercial and public offerings, index and edit them, and make them available for school use.

IX. *Flexibility: Patterns to Fit Purpose*

Our next priority is flexibility. There are many different high schools in the United States, with many different students. Greater flexibility in school size and the use of time will help schools achieve, more effectively, their educational objectives. The urgent need is not more time but better use of time. The following is proposed:

• The class schedule should be more flexibly arranged to permit larger blocks of instructional time, especially in courses such as

a laboratory science, a foreign language, and creative writing.
• Small high schools should expand their education offerings by using off-campus sites or mobile classrooms or part-time professionals to provide a richer education for all students.
• Large high schools, particularly those with over 2,000 students, should organize themselves into smaller units—"schools-within-schools"—to establish a more cohesive, more supportive social setting for all students.

Gifted and talented students represent a unique challenge if they are to realize their potential. Therefore, we suggest:
• Every high school should develop special arrangements for gifted students—credit by examination, independent study, and accelerated programs.
• A network of Residential Academies in Science and Mathematics should be established across the nation. Some academies might be within a densely populated district. Others might serve an entire state. A residential school may serve several states. Academies might be located on college campuses. Such schools should receive federal support, since clearly the vital interests of the nation are at stake.

Special arrangements are also needed for students at the other end of the education spectrum. Year after year, about one out of every four students who enroll in school drops out before graduation. This nation cannot afford to pay the price of wasted youth. We recommend:
• Federally supported remedial programs—most of which have been concentrated in the early grades—have demonstrated that improvements can be made in the academic achievement of even the most disadvantaged child. Therefore, the federally funded Elementary and Secondary Education Act (Title I) should be fully funded to support all students who are eligible to participate in this effective program.
• Every high school district, working with a community college, should have a reentry school arrangement to permit dropouts to return to school part time or full time or to engage in independent study to complete their education.

X. *The Principal as Leader*

What we seek are high schools in which the school community—students, teachers, and principals—sees learning as the primary goal. In such a community, the principal becomes not just the top authority but the key educator, too. Rebuilding excellence in education means reaffirming the importance of the local school and freeing leadership to lead. We make the following recommendations:

• The principal should be well prepared. The basic preparation should follow that of teachers.

• A principal should complete all requirements for licensing as a teacher and serve a year as an "administrative intern." At least two years as an assistant principal should be served before one could assume a full principalship.

• Principals and staff at the local school should have more control over their own budgets, operating within guidelines set by the district office. Further, every principal should have a School Improvement Fund, discretionary money to provide time and materials for program development and for special seminars and staff retreats.

• Principals should also have more control over the selection and rewarding of teachers. Acting in consultation with their staffs, they should be given responsibility for the final choice of teachers for their schools.

• In order to give principals time to reflect upon their work and stay in touch with developments in education, a network of Academies for Principals should be established.

XI. *Strengthening Connections*

High schools do not carry on their work in isolation. They are connected to elementary and junior high schools and to higher education. In the end, the quality of the American high school will be shaped in large measure by the quality of these connections. School-college relationships can be improved in a variety of ways:

• All states should establish a School-College Coordination Panel to define the recommended minimum academic requirements to smooth the transfer from school to public higher education.

• Every high school in the nation should offer a "university in the school" program and a variety of other arrangements—credit by examination, early admission and advanced placement—to permit able students to accelerate their academic programs.

• Each college or university should form a comprehensive partnership with one or more secondary schools.

Schools need the help of industry and business, and business needs the schools. The quality of work is linked to the quality of education. The following school-business partnerships are proposed:

• Businesses should provide help for disadvantaged students through volunteer tutorial and family counseling services and should support special school and part-time apprenticeship experience for high-risk students.

• Businesses should provide enrichment programs for gifted students, especially those in science and mathematics, and for those in the new technologies.

• Businesses should provide cash awards for outstanding teachers. In addition, they should consider establishing Endowed Chair Programs in the schools, and summer institute arrangements.

• Corporate grants should provide sabbaticals to outstanding principals and a discretionary fund for principals to work with teachers on creative programs. Further, large corporations should donate the use of their training facilities for a week or two each year to house an Academy for Principals.

• To help schools improve their physical plant and science laboratories, business should sponsor a facilities and equipment program. In addition, appropriate industries should conduct inventories of science laboratories and help upgrade school equipment.

XII. *Excellence: The Public Commitment*

Finally, school improvement is dependent on public commitment. How we as a nation regard our schools has a powerful impact on what occurs in them. Support for schools can take many forms, and it must come from many sources. Citizens, local school boards, state agencies and legislatures, and the federal government must work together to help bring excellence to our public schools. A number of steps are imperative:

• Parent-Teacher-Student Advisory Councils should be established at all schools. Further, a Parent Volunteer Program should be organized to tutor students, provide teacher aides, and other administrative, counseling, and clerical support.

• Parents should become actively involved in school board elections, attend meetings, and be willing to serve as members of the board.

• Boards of education should hold special meetings with representatives of the schools in their districts—principals and teachers—at least once a year.

• A network of community coalitions—Citizens for Public Schools—should be formed across the nation to give leadership in the advocacy of support for public education.

• The states should recognize that their overriding responsibility to the schools is to establish general standards and to provide fiscal support, but not to meddle. The state education law should be revised to eliminate confusing and inappropriate laws and regulations.

To achieve excellence in education the federal government also must be a partner in the process. In this report, we propose that funding of Title I of the Elementary and Secondary Education Act be increased to support all eligible students. We call for a National Teacher Service and a federally-funded network of Residential Academies in Science and Mathematics. We recommend that the federal government help create a National Film Library for schools and that a network of Technology Resource Centers be established with federal support to teach teachers about technology and its uses.

There is yet another urgent school need that calls for a national response. Many of our public schools have fallen into disrepair. Laboratory equipment is in poor shape. The situation is as alarming as the decay of our highways, dams, and bridges. Federal action is needed now to help meet an emergency in the schools. We propose:

• A new School Building and Equipment Fund should be established, a federal program that would provide short term, low interest loans to schools for plant rehabilitation and for the purchase of laboratory equipment.

No one reform can transform the schools. The single solution, the simple answer, may excite a momentary interest, but the impact will not last.

In this report we have tried to think inclusively and to search out interconnected solutions to the schools' interconnected problems. The result is something that is at once a yardstick to measure the need for reform and an agenda for action to bring about that reform.

Not every recommendation we present is appropriate for every school. Each institution will have its own agenda for renewal. What is important is that all high schools take steps to achieve excellence and that this effort be sustained.

We conclude this report on the American high school with the conviction that the promise of public education can be fulfilled and that, as a nation, we will meet the challenge.

MAKING THE GRADE[3]

The nation's public schools are in trouble. By almost every measure—the commitment and competency of teachers, student test scores, truancy and dropout rates, crimes of violence—the performance of our schools falls far short of expectations. To be sure, there are individual schools and school districts with devoted teachers doing a commendable job of educating their students, but too many young people are leaving the schools without acquiring essential learning skills and without self-discipline or purpose. The problem we face was succinctly summed up just three years ago by the President's Commission for a National Agenda for the Eighties when it reported that " . . . continued failure by the

[3]Excerpted from *Making the Grade: Report of the Twentieth Century Fund Task Force on Federal Elementary and Secondary Education Policy*, background paper by Paul E. Peterson. Copyright © 1983 by the Twentieth Century Fund. Reprinted by permission.

schools to perform their traditional role adequately, together with a failure to respond to the emerging needs of the 1980s, may have disastrous consequences for this nation."*

This Task Force believes that this threatened disaster can be averted only if there is a national commitment to excellence in our public schools. While we strongly favor maintaining the diversity in educational practices that results from the decentralization of the schools, we think that schools across the nation must at a minimum provide the same core components to all students. These components are the basic skills of reading, writing, and calculating; technical capability in computers; training in science and foreign languages; and knowledge of civics, or what Aristotle called the education of the citizenry in the spirit of the polity.

As we see it, the public schools, which constitute the nation's most important institution for the shaping of future citizens, must go further. We think that they should ensure the availability of large numbers of skilled and capable individuals without whom we cannot sustain a complex and competitive economy. They should foster understanding, discipline, and discernment, those qualities of mind and temperament that are the hallmarks of a civilized polity and that are essential for the maintenance of domestic tranquility in a polyethnic constitutional democracy. And they should impart to present and future generations a desire to acquire knowledge, ranging from the principles of science to the accumulated wisdom and shared values that derive from the nation's rich and varied cultural heritage.

These are admittedly formidable tasks that too few schools today come close to accomplishing. The Task Force believes that the schools must make a concerted effort to improve their performance and that there is a clear national interest in helping schools everywhere to do so. That interest can be asserted and dramatized most effectively by the federal government. The federal government, after all, is charged with providing for the security and well-being of our democratic society, which rest largely on a strong and com-

---

*President's Commission for a National Agenda for the Eighties, *A National Agenda for the Eighties* (Washington, D.C.: U.S. Government Printing Office, 1980).

petent system of public education. It is in the best position to focus
public attention on the vital importance of quality in our schools
and to support its attainment. The federal government should be
able to foster excellence in education, serving as a firm but gentle
goad to states and local communities without impeding or restrict-
ing state and local control of and accountability for the schools.

Excessive Burdens

Before putting forward our proposals for a new federal policy
on elementary and secondary schooling, we think it useful to identify what has gone wrong. Why, despite spending more per student than every other advanced nation, is there a growing gap
between the goals and achievements of our schools? Many developments—economic, demographic, social, political—have contributed, directly and indirectly. We have always demanded a
great deal of our schools, but never before have we demanded of
them as much as we have over the past thirty years. On one hand
we have charged them with being the melting pot, the crucible for
dissolving racial divisiveness, and on the other with sustaining,
and even exalting, ethnic distinctiveness.

The schools, moreover, have had to provide a wide array of
social services, acting as surrogate parent, nurse, nutritionist, sex
counselor, and policeman. At the same time, they are charged with
training increasing percentages of the nation's youth, including
large numbers of hard-to-educate youngsters, to improved levels
of competency so that they can effectively enter a labor market in
which employers are currently demanding both technical capability and the capacity to learn new skills. In essence, the skills that
were once possessed by only a few must now be held by the many
if the United States is to remain competitive in an advancing technological world.

Demographic changes as well as changes in attitudes toward
traditional mores and values have also had a marked influence.
The schools have had to cope with more children, and especially
more problem children, than ever before—those who are without
the rudiments of English and those who are unmotivated or prone
to violence, quite apart from those who are physically handi-

capped. Problems have also come about as a result of the ready availability of drugs, the growing number of family breakups and the increased permissiveness in those remaining intact, the distractions of television and of easily affordable video games, and the growth of underworld culture.

The difficulties of coping with these burdens have been compounded in some cities by inappropriate judicial intervention and by the spread of the trade-union mentality that has accompanied the bureaucratization and politicization of the schools. As a consequence, already large administrative staffs have burgeoned, and new rules and procedures have been promulgated, forcing classroom teachers to spend more time on paperwork and less on teaching. The rise in teacher and administrative unions has thus helped transform what had been a noble though poorly compensated profession into a craft led by collective bargaining organizations with a focus on bread-and-butter issues—wages, working conditions, and job security (for which read seniority).

The federal courts have been particularly criticized for playing so conspicuous a role. There is no doubt that they were active in enforcing the rights guaranteed by the Fourteenth Amendment, and that their activity was critical to ensuring those rights for many citizens. But the spectacle of judges, who had little knowledge—and no experience—of the intricacies of operating school systems, taking over responsibility was often harmful. More often than not, though, judges had no choice. They acted because politicians in state legislatures and Congress, in state houses and the White House, failed to act. In most jurisdictions no local political leadership emerged; cowardice rather than courage prevailed, creating a leadership vacuum that the courts filled.

The Federal Presence

In recent years the federal executive and legislative branches have enlarged their roles. In the view of some critics, federal intervention looms so large that it has not only overstepped constitutional limitations but bears responsibility for most of the failings of the schools. We consider these criticisms exaggerated. True, since 1965, with the passage of the Elementary and Secondary Education Act (ESEA), the executive branch has intervened, by law and by regulation, in many school activities, tilting the allocation of resources to compensatory education and affirmative action programs. But the achievements of some federal activities must be acknowledged. Its Title I program as well as Head Start have been particularly successful, especially among children in elementary schools where these programs were concentrated. Even affirmative action programs registered some success, although most were hampered by excessive federal manipulation. Federal involvement was underscored by the establishment of the U.S. Department of Education in 1979–80, but long before it was on the scene some observers claimed that the delicate balance of what had been a complicated but relatively efficient educational system had been needlessly upset by the federal presence.

Many other criticisms of the federal role in elementary and secondary education are warranted, but not the complaint that the federal government has violated its constitutional authority. This Task Force believes that educating the young is a compelling national interest, and that action by the federal government can be as appropriate as action by state and local governments. Certainly, federal intervention was not only appropriate but necessary in bringing about desegregation of the public schools, and in providing needed assistance to poor and handicapped children.

All too often, though, the nature of federal intervention has been counterproductive, entailing heavy costs and undesirable consequences. Direct federal outlays accounted, at their peak, for less than 10 percent of total annual spending on the schools, but by resorting to compulsory regulation and mandated programs, the federal government has swelled school bureaucracies, imposed dubious and expensive procedures, and forced state and local governments to reallocate substantial portions of their scarce revenues. What is more, its emphasis on promoting equality of opportunity in the public schools has meant a slighting of its commitment to educational quality.* Thus, the federal government

*Comment by Mr. Riles: The "slighting of its commitment to educational quality" by the federal government should not be blamed on the promo-

has not only had a pervasive influence on the spending of local school districts but has undoubtedly played a part in many of the other troubles of the schools.**

Despite all of its shortcomings, however, there is a need for a continued federal role, in part because equality and excellence are not mutually exclusive objectives. We think that both objectives should be vigorously pursued through a fresh approach, one that reflects the national concern for a better-educated America and that strikes a reasonable and effective balance between quality and equality. The federal government must continue to help meet the special needs of poor and minority students while taking the lead in meeting the general and overwhelming need for educational quality. Federal education policy must function, moreover, in ways that complement rather than weaken local control. This calls for a change in direction, replacing the current emphasis on regulations and mandates with a new emphasis on incentives.

The Federal Commitment

Even before there were public schools everywhere, the federal government expressed its commitment to education. The Northwest Ordinance of 1787 specified that land was to be set aside for education purposes in every town and rural area. In the words of the proviso to the ordinance, "Religion, morality, and knowledge being necessary to good government and the happiness of man-

tion of equality of opportunity. As previously stated in this report, Congress has historically "refrained" from addressing the issue of educational quality. I believe it is essential that both issues be addressed.

**Comment by Ms. Graham:* There have been many mistakes in federal education programs, much misplaced money, numerous stupidities. None should be justified. There have also been important achievements, particularly for children from low-income families through Title I of the Elementary and Secondary Education Act, through Head Start, and for young minority children in the South (especially areas affected by the 1954 *Brown* v. *Board of Education* desegregation decision). Both the mistakes and achievements are worthy of note. Given the conflicting mandates the public schools have been assigned, the tone of this document is more critical of their performance than I believe justified either by the evidence presented here or from other sources with which I am familiar. *Messrs. Hortas and Wentz* wish to associate themselves with Ms. Graham's comment.

kind, schools and the means of education shall forever be encouraged." Thus, soon after the nation's founding, its leaders recognized that the experiment in political democracy upon which they were embarking could not succeed without an educated citizenry.

Seventy-five years later, in the midst of the Civil War, Congress sought to enlist the aid of the nation's educational institutions in the Morrill Act, which granted land for the purpose of supporting colleges of agriculture and mechanical arts. In this century, Congress passed the Smith-Hughes Act, which provided federal support for vocational education, and the National Defense Education Act (NDEA), which, in the immediate aftermath of the Soviet Union's Sputnik, called for improved training in such critical subject areas as science, mathematics, and foreign languages.

Although Congress has from time to time acknowledged the essential need for public education and even for specific kinds of education, it has refrained, apparently deliberately, from addressing the issue of educational quality. This matter, with good reason, was left to the discretion of the states and localities. The control of public education, even though subject to constitutional restriction, is exercised by thousands of school boards and school superintendents within a legal framework set up by fifty different state legislatures. There has been no one place—and we do not think there should be—in which a national policy defines the correct school curriculum or the proper qualifications for teachers, or sets forth the precise duration of the school day or year. These are matters that traditionally have been left to lay citizens, reinforced by the advice and counsel of professional educators or schools of education. We believe it should remain that way.

The genius of our decentralized arrangements is that we have managed to forge a national education system that allows room for variations and even for disagreements. This is not to say that the Task Force is satisfied with the performance of local school districts. To the contrary, we believe that the vast majority must do much better. But because learning depends upon intangibles— the leadership provided by a school principal, the chemistry between teachers and students, the extent of parental involvement and support—we strongly favor leaving control over schooling at the local level. Good schools cannot be created by federal mandate. They grow from the ground up in complex and often idiosyncratic fashion. Most good schools have many characteristics in common, but there is no formula that can bring about their duplication because there is no one best way of providing a first-rate education.

Quality of Leadership

Because quality in education is easier to recognize than to define, some of the reluctance of Congress to face up to the issues is understandable. Educational quality cannot be legislated into existence. Still, Congress must not continue to be ostrichlike about the failings of primary and secondary school education. Its readiness to legislate on other aspects of education, whether in programs for the handicapped, or for all those whose English is limited or nonexistent, or for special interests—for example, the National Educational Association—that successfully lobbied for the establishment of the Department of Education, while ignoring declines in test scores, suggests to many Americans that quality in education is not a national goal. That false impression must be erased.

This Task Force calls on the executive and legislative branches of the federal government to emphasize the need for better schools and a better education for all young Americans. We have singled out a number of specific areas in which the federal government, mainly through a series of incentives, can act to improve that quality of education in the public schools. Most of our proposals are directed toward improving the quality of teaching, ensuring proficiency in English while developing fluency in foreign languages, and promoting ways to increase proficiency in mathematics and science. We then go on to discuss the nature and content of the federal role in education, what it can do to further quality as well as equality in schooling, and the extent of choice that ought to be made available to parents.

Quality of Teachers

The traditional commitment of teachers to quality education has been challenged by many forces, some that have affected all of society, others that are peculiar to the community of educators. The teacher—along with all other authority figures—does not appear to command the respect commonly accorded a generation ago. The complex organizational structure in which the classroom teacher now operates restricts independence and autonomy; as new organizational positions have proliferated, many of the best teachers have been "promoted" to better paying administrative positions, devaluing the status of the teacher. In addition, the organizations—the unions and professional associations—to which teachers belong have functioned to protect their weakest members rather than win rewards for their strongest. They have promoted the principle of equal pay or, at best, a differential pay scale that primarily takes into account educational background and seniority, thereby limiting the financial incentives available for rewarding superior professional work. The collective bargaining process, moreover, has not only made it difficult to encourage promising teachers or dismiss poor ones, it has forced many of the best to leave teaching for more financially rewarding work. The result is that the quality of teaching suffers.

Deterioration in quality is probably greatest in specialized subjects, most markedly in mathematics and science. Because of the constant need of industry for skilled personnel, teachers in these fields can easily find more profitable employment. This problem is not new, of course, but standardized salary schedules, reinforced by the collective bargaining process, have made for staff shortages in mathematics and science in many local school districts. School boards frequently resort to such stratagems as paying science and mathematics teachers overtime for extra work instead of directly facing up to the unions and to the need to increase salaries for specialized teachers in short supply.

Because the institutional arrangements and procedures governing teachers are so well entrenched, incremental changes in federal policy cannot by themselves dramatically improve the quality of instruction. The Task Force is convinced that what is required is a major federal initiative that unmistakably emphasizes the critical importance of quality teachers in our schools. *We propose the establishment of a national Master Teachers Program, funded by the federal government, that recognizes and rewards teaching excellence.*

Under our proposed program, the best teachers from every state would be awarded the accolade of Master Teacher and a monetary grant—say, $40,000 a year—above that of the ceiling for teachers' salaries for five years. Criteria for selection might be set by such established agencies as the National Endowment for the Humanities, the National Science Foundation, and other federal agencies, with the actual selections made by them after their canvassing of local advisers, including school boards and school administrators, teachers, and parents.

In maintaining Master Teachers in the program for five years, we propose that up to one full year should be devoted to professional improvement through graduate or similar work and that additional funds, for tuition or for the assistance of graduate students, should be made available for such purposes. The remaining four years would be spent teaching, with perhaps some of that time used to work with and provide help to other teachers.*

Rather than spell out the details of the proposed program, we have set down the guidelines we think should be followed. We recommend the adoption of an incentive approach, establishing clear criteria for teachers of exceptional merit and making the awards numerous enough to attract national attention and substantial enough for long enough to keep Master Teachers in the classroom.

Dissent by Ms. Yalow: I oppose the establishment of a Master Teachers Program. It would be expensive and would not address a real need, namely the shortage of teachers in chemistry, physics, and mathematics. I believe it would hurt morale in that a reward for a limited period to be followed by a period of reduced salary would be a retrogressive step. Moreover, I question whether it is necessary or desirable to give a "Master Teacher" a full year for "professional improvement." What is required is a salary structure that reflects competency and that would aid in recruitment of teachers in short supply. The goals of the proposed Master Teachers Program seem noble, but the mechanism suggested is highly unlikely to have the desired effect.

It is our view that the proposed program would help pave the way for reconsideration of merit-based personnel systems for teachers, which we believe would foster improvements in quality. Despite many surveys of public servants and professionals that have disclosed a strong preference for merit pay increases and promotions, school boards and legislators have almost always yielded to union demands for equal pay. Collective bargaining has served teachers and the public by improving working conditions and compensation, and we do not want to see it abandoned. But both the public and teachers would be even better served if the opposing sides in the bargaining process—the unions and local school boards—realized that merit-based systems and collective bargaining are not incompatible.

The Master Teachers Program will be expensive—just how expensive will depend on the number of awards made each year. At a minimum there should be at least one award for each congressional district, but we think that many more should be given. By the fifth year of the program, the cost could run as high as $5 billion.

The Task Force believes that such an expense is warranted. Good teachers are as valuable to the nation as new tanks or fighter planes or a new highway. By making so visible and costly a commitment, the federal government will be not only assuming leadership in the quest for educational excellence but also undertaking a major program to help achieve it.

The Primacy of English

Our political democracy rests on the conviction that each citizen should have the capacity to participate fully in our political life; to read newspapers, magazines, and books; to bring a critical intelligence to television and radio; to be capable of resisting emotional manipulation and of setting events within their historical perspective; to express ideas and opinions about public affairs; and to vote thoughtfully—all activities that call for literacy in English. Accordingly, *the Task Force recommends that the federal government clearly state that the most important objective of elementary and secondary education in the United States is the development of literacy in the English language.*

A significant number of young Americans come from homes where English is not the first language, and many now live in neighborhoods in an increasing number of states in which languages other than English are spoken. Although this nation has become more aware of the value of ethnic identities than it was during previous influxes of non-English-speaking immigrants, anyone living in the United States who is unable to speak English cannot fully participate in our society, its culture, its politics. This is not because of prejudice but because most Americans speak, write, and think in English. English is, after all, our national language.

We recommend, then, that students in elementary school learn to read, write, speak, and listen in English. As children advance in grade, these skills should be continually improved. By the time they finish high school, students ought to possess such advanced cognitive skills as reasoning, critical analysis, the ability to explain and understand complex ideas, and to write clearly and correctly.

Many different methods have been proposed for educating children who are not literate in English. It is not the role of the Task Force nor is it the responsibility of the federal government to instruct our schools and teachers on which pedagogy is most appropriate. The federal role, we believe, is to guarantee that all children have equal educational opportunity. Therefore, *the Task Force recommends that federal funds now going to bilingual programs be used to teach non-English-speaking children how to speak, read, and write English.** Local school districts may decide to teach children in more than one language or to teach them a language other than English. Although we believe that the failure to recognize the primacy of English is a grave error, that is their prerogative. The distinctive nature of the federal role, we believe, derives from the premise that all of us must be able to communicate with one another as fellow citizens.

Dissent by Mr. Hortas: It is unquestionable that all students must learn to speak, read, and write English in order to function in our society. Nonetheless, bilingual programs in which children are taught in English and in their native language are essential if we are to provide a healthy learning environment for children of limited English ability. Because local school districts cannot afford to underwrite such programs, I recom-

Accordingly, *the Task Force recommends that the federal government promote and support proficiency in English for all children in the public schools, but especially for those who do not speak English, or have only limited command of it.*

At the same time, the Task Force considers the ability to speak and read a second language a valuable resource for both the individual and the nation. Acquiring facility in a foreign language can help to improve a student's understanding and command of English and lead to the appreciation of the literature and culture of another people, which is clearly educationally desirable. It should also be an advantage in a business or professional career.

From a national perspective, young men and women with proficiency in foreign languages are sorely needed now that we are increasingly involved in competitive trade and investment with the rest of the world. More and more jobs will be available in government, industry, trade, commerce, and the universities for Americans who can converse with other people in their own languages and who can participate in strengthening our international ties.

This Task Force wants every American public school student to have the opportunity to acquire proficiency in a second language. Unfortunately, there is no practical possibility of obtaining this objective quickly. The neglect of foreign language study and instruction in the United States is of such long standing that we simply do not have enough language teachers to provide adequate training. Nevertheless, we propose that proficiency in a second language should be a long-term goal. We must begin a training program now if we are to achieve that goal in future decades.* The federal government can help in the training of language teachers and in encouraging and assisting in programs for students with proficiency in English to learn a second language that may or may not be a language spoken in their homes.

mend that the proposal on federal impact aid, set forth later in this report, be applied to bilingual programs. The academic achievements of children of limited English-speaking ability will be significantly greater if the child's first language skills are maintained and improved.

Comment by Mr. Hortas: Every public school student should start the study of a foreign language in elementary school, which is standard educational practice in the developed countries of the world. A knowledge of

Our aim is to see this second-language policy sponsored by the federal government and carried out by state and local governments. The immediate need is for a modest matching grant program to train language teachers. Even though it will take time and effort, we think that a comprehensive approach to the study of languages, in which fluency in English is primary but adequate training in a second language is also made available, is absolutely essential if the United States is to be a leader among nations in the next century.**

In the long run, these recommendations to ensure fluency in English are the only kind that make sense. The nation cannot afford a multiplicity of special language programs in every commu-

---

a second language at an early age will stimulate a better appreciation of our country's cultural pluralism. The achievement of proficiency in a second language must be a project for this decade, not for future generations.

Ms. Graham and Mr. Denny wish to associate themselves with Mr. Hortas's comment.

**Comment by Ms. Yalow*: I am in complete agreement with the Task Force recommendation about the essentiality of all Americans acquiring proficiency in English. In addition, it is desirable to develop a cadre with proficiency in foreign languages. Therefore, I accept that every American public school student should have the opportunity to acquire proficiency in a foreign language. But I really doubt the desirability of recommending that all high school students be required to study a foreign language. Is such competency really necessary for a farmer in Iowa, a coal miner in West Virginia, or a factory worker in the textile mills of the South? It might be highly desirable for a shopkeeper or a secretary in a bilingual community. The extent of competency, whether it should be ability to read, write, or speak fluently, should depend on personal and professional interests.

If there appears to be a severe shortage of foreign language teachers at present, perhaps this shortage would more easily be remedied by taking advantage of the large number of people in our country for whom English is not the first language and who have sufficient fluency in both English and the foreign language to be ideal as teachers. Often they do not have appropriate education courses or the right degrees. It is perhaps heretical to suggest that the education courses or degrees are not essential for teaching students to develop proficiency in a foreign language. Teachers without the right credentials but with competency in the foreign language and English could be employed on an adjunct basis if there are rules against their serving as regular teachers.

Mr. Wentz wishes to associate himself with Ms. Yalow's comment.

nity in which ethnolinguistic minorities are present in significant numbers. More important, school children to whom English is an alien language are being cheated if it remains unfamiliar to them; they will never swim in the American mainstream unless they are fluent in English. The best way to ensure the nation's linguistic resources is to make literacy in English the primary objective and to promote literacy in a second language as a valuable supplement to, not a substitute for, English.*

Science and Mathematics

At the turn of the twentieth century, there was no real need for widespread scientific literacy. Today, training in mathematics and science is critical to our economy. Our citizens must be educated in science if they are to participate intelligently in political decisions about such controversial issues as radiation, pollution, and nuclear energy. *The Task Force recommends that the federal government emphasize programs to develop basic scientific literacy among all citizens and to provide advanced training in science and mathematics for secondary school students.*

The schools must go beyond the teaching of basic science to give adequate training in advanced science and mathematics to a large enough number of students to ensure that there are ample numbers capable of filling the increasing number of jobs demanding these skills. The Reagan administration has proposed a $50 million scholarship program for students in mathematics and science, which we think is a step in the right direction. The more ambitious programs emerging from Congress move even further in that direction. Our preference is for an incentive program to augment the supply of teachers in science and mathematics as well as in foreign languages. Federal loans might be made available to prospective teachers who exhibit exceptional skills and who are

*Comment by Mr. Hortas: No bilingual program in the United States promotes another language as a *substitute for English*. In fact, intensive English instruction is a part of every bilingual program. Bilingual programs attempt to show that English is not, in and of itself, a superior or richer language than the student's native language. There is a greater social benefit in promoting and encouraging linguistic diversity than in calling for specious uniformity.

pursuing degree programs in areas of existing or anticipated shortages. Those who complete their educational programs might be forgiven up to 10 percent of the funds lent to them for every year of classroom teaching—for a maximum of five years.

Better Education for All

In proposing new federal measures to stimulate national interest in improving the quality of public education, we urge that they not come at the expense of children from low-income families or of children suffering from one or another disability. In recent years the federal education effort has concentrated on the needs of special categories of students—those from low-income homes, the handicapped, the non-English-speaking—because states and local governments failed to meet national educational objectives for them. By furnishing special services to the handicapped and by addressing the educational needs of the poor, the federal role has had much the same influence as it had in desegregating the schools. Without such intervention, many states and most local school boards would not have done what clearly needed doing.

But if categorical programs have their uses, critics argue that there are not only too many of them but that many of these proliferating programs are poorly designed. They go on to argue that, while minorities may not have been effectively organized at state and local levels to secure needed programs two decades ago, the political organization and sophistication of such groups have so increased—in part because of federal assistance—that they no longer need the extensive federal protection that they once did. Although this may be the case in many large cities, the political power of minorities is far less potent in most school districts.

Perhaps the most persuasive reason for federal support of categorical programs is that, even under favorable political conditions, few local school systems have the will to concentrate their resources on the minority of students with special needs. Moreover, recent political and economic conditions have been anything but favorable for local governments. The cost of educating children with special needs has forced many school districts to resort to imposing taxes on productive members of the community without providing immediate benefits in return. Business firms along with residents in higher income brackets may choose to leave communities where the tax burden for educating the children of poor, needy residents is relatively heavy. Accordingly, *the Task Force supports continuing federal efforts to provide special educational programs for the poor—and for the handicapped.*

We applaud the steps taken by Congress to simplify regulatory restrictions and to reduce the overlap among many programs. In enacting legislation acknowledging the responsibility of the federal government for groups with special needs, *the Task Force believes that the guiding principle should be that categorical programs required by the federal government should be paid for from the federal treasury.* These categorical programs are not special-interest legislation serving particular groups at the expense of the nation as a whole. To the contrary, compensatory programs and education for the handicapped concentrate limited resources on specific populations and in particular areas where the need for better education is especially urgent, thereby providing the equality of opportunity essential for the well-being of our democracy. Their cost, then, should be assumed by the federal government, not by states or localities, although local school districts must take the responsibility for the effective provision of special help.

The Task Force also recommends that "impact" aid, originally aimed at helping cushion the burden imposed on local school facilities by the children of military personnel, be reformulated to focus on school districts that are overburdened by substantial numbers of immigrant children. During World War II, the influx of the military into particular communities placed unusual burdens on local school districts; currently, when cities and regions compete vigorously for defense spending, the military is often a boon to local economies. Under today's conditions, we believe it fitting that federal impact aid should be used when large numbers of aliens and immigrants, many of whom are poor, place a special burden on local school districts. Given the Supreme Court decision reaffirming the right of children of illegal aliens to equal educational opportunities, the federal government has an obligation to temporarily assist states and localities facing added costs for educating these children, who usually need special help.

A related problem is the plight of localities in economic distress—mainly in the nation's central cities but also in impoverished rural areas, where there is an undue concentration of low-income groups, where high unemployment persists, and where there is a clear and urgent need for better education of the young. *The Task Force thus urges that federal attention and assistance go to depressed localities that have concentrations of immigrant and/or impoverished groups as well as those that are already making strong efforts to improve their education performance.* Quantitative measures of needs are available, grants can be flexible, and targets can be specific.

Educational Research

Proponents of the cabinet-level Department of Education predicted that its establishment would provide federal leadership for the public schools. Since it was set up, that prophecy has not been fulfilled, partly because initially the department had to take responsibility for a set of questionable and intrusive policies, partly because its role was downgraded with the change of administrations. This Task Force did not spend much time examining the function and performance of the Department of Education. Some members took the position that it was largely irrelevant; others thought that it would be better to restore it to a restructured Department of Health and Human Services, which might give it a stronger political influence; still others believed that its activities should be split up among various federal agencies.

But in the course of our deliberations, we had many opportunities to appreciate the value of the department's information and analysis on the state of our public schools. It does not seem necessary to keep the Department of Education in being simply because it has responsibility for information gathering and research, but federal responsibility for those activities ought to be maintained. Federal agencies have long had experience in the field and are superbly situated for collating data from the states. Whatever the fate of the department, we urge that the collection of data remain a federal responsibility.

Ever since it was established in 1867, the federal Office (now Department) of Education had gathered such basic data as the average number of pupils in daily attendance in the nation's schools, the number of teachers and other school employees, and the cost of educational services. More recently, the federal government has undertaken broad surveys of school practices, pupil performance, and the consequences of schooling for adult life. It has also funded the development of new curricula, studies of the effects of various educational innovations, and basic research on the processes of human learning. Currently, two agencies of the Department of Education bear much of this responsibility for research—the National Center for Education Statistics gathers information and data, and the National Institute of Education supports research and development. (Other federal agencies, such as the Census Bureau and the National Science Foundation, along with private foundations, also sponsor education research.) The results of data collection and research have proven useful in identifying areas of progress or emerging difficulties; sometimes they have pointed toward possible solutions; and sometimes they have served to focus the national debate on the schools.

Research on questions of educational quality can have symbolic as well as substantive value. For example, the study of the effects of school segregation undertaken by James Coleman for the Office of Education in 1965 focused public attention on the perniciousness of racism. Subsequent studies stimulated and informed public debate over such critical questions as the effects of school desegregation on "white flight," the results of compensatory education programs, and the relative merits of public and private schools. Current national concern with the quality of public education, particularly at the high school level, has been stimulated in part by findings of such federally sponsored projects as the National Assessment of Educational Progress.

The Task Force recommends federal support for a number of specific activities:

• The collection of factual information about various aspects of the education system itself. Such data gathering is traditional, uncontroversial, and essential if policies are to be developed on the basis of accurate information. Because collecting this information seems so routine, and because it has no particular "constituency," it is often starved for resources and is always vulnerable to the government's periodic efforts to "reduce paperwork." We urge that collection of this information be made mandatory.

• The collection of information about the educational performance of students, teachers, and schools across the nation. Although the National Assessment of Educational Progress has done useful work and should be continued and strengthened, current federal efforts to appraise the quality of American education are inadequate. We urge the federal government, for example, to collect and disseminate information available from routine tests. Nearly every elementary school student regularly takes tests of performance and achievement in various skills and subjects, many of them prepared by private agencies and administered by school systems. The majority of states require high school students to take "competency" tests; college-bound students take a battery of tests developed by the Educational Testing Service and the American College Testing Service. All of this data should be collected and made accessible to researchers.

Other information would be useful too. In addition to knowing how many high school juniors are "taking mathematics," for example, it would be enlightening to know how many years of mathematics they have previously taken, what their courses have covered, and what kind of training and qualifications their teachers possess.

• Evaluation of federally sponsored education programs. Most federal education programs have some form of built-in evaluation, but all too often these are superficial, self-serving, or (especially when the results are critical) not readily accessible. A good rule of thumb, the Task Force believes, is that whenever the federal government conducts an educational program, whether it is a simple transfer of resources to college students or an attempt to foster a major pedagogical change in elementary schools, a "report card" on the effectiveness of that program should be made public.

• Fundamental research into the learning process. The more that is known about how youngsters learn, the better they can be taught. Learning is an immensely complicated affair, and progress has been made on it in recent years, partly with federal support.

But the federal government spends a pittance on such research compared with its support for basic research into health, agriculture, the physical sciences, and weaponry. More money is needed, enough to enlist able scholars in the process—as designers of research agendas, as researchers, as "peer reviewers" of research proposals, and as evaluators of research findings.

Unfortunately, the National Institute of Education and other federal agencies have too often allowed their interests and resources to be diverted into peripheral topics, into fruitless quests for "quick fixes," or into catering to particular educational interest groups. So if the federal government is to be given primary responsibility for educational research, it must adopt sensible ground rules and safeguards to assure that its research is sound and comprehensive, and it must be supported in these efforts through the political process.

Provision of Choice

Although elementary and, to a considerable extent, secondary education in the United States is compulsory, it does not have to be public school education. American parents, who traditionally have insisted on a say in their children's schooling, can turn to private schools when they are not satisfied with public schooling—and some 10 percent of the school-age population attends private schools today. But the vast majority of children attend public schools, and it is critical that their parents be able to influence the quality of schooling.

Public schools are governed by local school boards, whose members in most districts are elected and are generally responsive to the parent-teacher associations (PTAs) whose members helped elect them. In many districts, PTAs or comparable parent groups play a constructive role, raising extra money for the schools and building community support for them. That role is a rarity in many urban districts, where community spirit is often lacking and where local schools are subject to the directives of higher authorities, who are frequently insensitive to community concerns.

The major choice available to parents opting for the public school system is their selection of a community in which to live.

In large metropolitan areas subdivided into numerous small- to medium-sized suburbs, parents have a great deal of choice among many different—and different quality—public schools. A significant measure of the market value of a house is the prevailing opinion on the quality of the schools where it is located.

The biggest drawback to these options is the cost to the family. To send a child to a good public school often means paying more for a house or apartment. Private school tuition is extremely costly and must be paid over and above the taxes paid for local public schools. Family income thus limits choice. Only 4.8 percent of the nonpublic elementary school population came from families with incomes of less than $5,000 a year, compared with the 13.2 percent of the public school population. At the other end of the scale, 18.2 percent of elementary nonpublic school pupils came from families with incomes of $25,000 or more, compared with only 8.9 percent of public school pupils.

Many proposals have been made in recent years to give parents more of a voice in choosing where their children are educated. Among them are tax credit plans and tuition vouchers. The Task Force does not endorse such proposals or recommend a major redefinition of the relationship between public and nonpublic schools. We believe that the provision of free public education must continue to be a public responsibility of high priority, while support of nonpublic education should remain a private obligation. Yet we recognize that some children have not been able to learn in the present setting of public education. We cannot ignore, for example, students who repeatedly fail city or state competency examinations or fail in other ways to attain their academic capacity. Rather than having such students either held back time and time again or promoted year after year to new levels of remediation, *the Task Force recommends the establishment of special federal fellowships for them, which would be awarded to school districts to encourage the creation of small, individualized programs staffed by certified teachers and run as small-scale academies.** Eligibility for these fellowships, available to no more

*Comment by Mr. Denny: I fully support the position taken by the Task Force on the provision of choice and our position not to support such ideas as tax credit plans and tuition vouchers. I also support the recommenda-

than 5 percent of public school enrollment, should be jointly determined by local, state, and federal school officials. Such an experiment, designed to benefit those who have been unable to learn in public schools, might provide the intensive and encouraging environment that these students need, and would free up the substantial resources now being spent on remediation with so little to show for it.**

tion for the establishment of special federal fellowships for students who cannot learn in the present setting of public education. But I would also like such a fellowship program to offer support for especially able students who live in school districts where quality educational opportunities do not exist in the public schools. Such a program should follow the recommendation of the Task Force in providing fellowships to public school districts to encourage the creation of programs staffed by certified teachers and run as small-scale academies.

**Comment by Ms. Graham*: Although I agree with this proposal because it has much potential merit, I want to point out the danger that such a program could lead to resegregation without significant remediation.

Comment by Mr. Finn: This fellowship proposal is a variation on the idea that has sometimes been called "literary vouchers," an idea that I find interesting and potentially worthwhile for those youngsters having the least success in ordinary public schools. As formulated by the Task Force, however, it makes little or no use of the remarkable educational resource already present in some 18,000 private schools in the United States. Moreover, it cannot fairly be regarded as a substitute for or an alternative to various plans that have been advanced to assist those who would like to send their children to private schools but cannot afford to do so. While welcoming the Task Force's general endorsement of the principle of educational choice, I deeply regret the unwillingness of my colleagues to regard the nongovernmental schools already attended by one child in ten as a full and legitimate element of the nation's educational enterprise and as a particularly important resource in achieving the Task Force's vigorously stated goal of improved educational quality.

Comment by Ms. Yalow: I do not support a fellowship or tuition scholarship program for either the gifted or educationally retarded student. There are few schools or school districts, particularly in urban or suburban regions, which are so small as to make impracticable the setting aside of special classes for each of these groups. I believe the mixing in the same class of students with vastly differing abilities in the name of equality has been a retrogressive step. All students cannot learn at the same rate or acquire the same degree of competency. There is no a priori reason why a public school cannot provide a learning environment equal to that of a private school. Segregation according to ability as previously was done would assure each child an opportunity to develop in accordance with that

Leadership in Education

While the federal role in promoting equality of opportunity and educational quality in the nation's schools is significant, elementary and secondary education in the United States must primarily remain a responsibility of state and local governments. A state-supported, locally administered system of public schools has successfully survived numerous challenges for more than one hundred years. By and large, this decentralized system of education has served more pupils, has provided a broader range of services, has proved more flexible in response to changing conditions, and has moderated class and group antagonisms more successfully than have the school systems of most other industrial nations.

But even though state and local governments should continue to bear the major responsibility for the provision of educational services, it is increasingly important that the federal government emphasize the pressing need for a high-quality system of education open to all Americans, regardless of race or economic position. Toward this end, the Task Force has put forward a coordinated policy of overall federal support for American schools that simultaneously asserts the national interest in quality schools and in equal access to education, with assistance for those with special needs.

To attain improvement in quality, we have proposed a number of new programs designed to strengthen teaching in curricular areas where national needs are especially great. To spur equal access to education, we recommend that current programs for special-needs students be supplemented by programs that will support school districts with large numbers of poor and immigrant pupils as well as districts that are experiencing fiscal difficulties. In addition, we have recommended that federal funding be provided to local school districts as an incentive to encourage new ways to help failing students.

ability. The fact that parents are turning to private schools is a measure of the inadequacy of public schools. Any available funding should go to support of special programs in the public school system and not to removing students from that system.

In all of these programs, it must be kept in mind that equality of educational opportunity cannot be separated from educational quality. The nation is best served by offering our young people the most rigorous educational experience that we can. The federal government has a responsibility to help overcome the unevenness of state efforts. It will have to provide compensatory assistance, for some time to come, to those who are in need of special help, especially for students who must achieve English-language proficiency. But that does not mean abandoning a single standard of excellence. There cannot be a white standard or a black standard or a Hispanic standard when measuring educational performance.

The Task Force is aware that some of its proposals are costly. But we should be able to afford the price of a commitment to educational excellence. This nation's young people are our most precious and potentially our most productive asset, provided that we invest wisely in educating them. In our view, support for our program by Congress and the White House will demonstrate the value that they attach to better schooling for all.

Our proposed new approach for federal education policy will, we believe, stimulate a national reawakening of interest in educational excellence. But carrying out this policy requires our nation's political leaders to take an active part in supporting needed programs. It is no longer a cause that requires political courage. All across the country parents are demanding more of the schools, and in many cases the schools are already responding. We think the time is past due to offer a better education to all Americans. What it takes now is the political will to bring it about.

II. RESPONSE TO THE REFORM REPORTS

EDITOR'S INTRODUCTION

A recurring theme in the many responses to the reform reports is the problem of reconciling "quality" in education with "equity," or equal access to educational opportunity. The proposals for uniformly rigorous standards mention their concern with the needs of all students, but show more concern for the needs of those who will go on to college and join the professions. They generally do not consider the effect that the curricular changes would have upon the less able students from disadvantaged circumstances who might well drop out of school, creating an underclass of educationally deprived citizens. In the first article in this section, "Arming Education," an editorial from *The Nation, A Nation at Risk* is attacked for its exclusive concern with educating the elite, and disregard for the needs of the disadvantaged. The editorial is particularly scornful of the militarist language of *A Nation at Risk*, which betrays its conception of education as a training ground for competition in the market place.

In the second article, "Just Among Us Teachers," reprinted from *Phi Delta Kappan*, Harry N. Chandler questions whether all students should take the same courses in science, mathematics, and foreign languages, when such a program would not be appropriate to those not going on to college. He asks whether the merit pay idea could be fairly implemented, and wonders how such an overhaul of the quality of education could be accomplished in our current economic circumstances. In the third article, "A Nation at Risk: Another View," also from *Phi Delta Kappan*, James Albrecht addresses many of the same issues, and argues that *A Nation at Risk* identifies the welfare of the college-bound as the sole criterion of a school's success.

In a third article from *Phi Delta Kappan* that takes a more comprehensive view of the reform reports, Harold Howe II, a former U. S. Commissioner of Education, turns to the question of financing, and wonders whether the financial burden of such a commitment to excellence can be sustained over a period of years. Moreover, Howe finds little understanding on the part of the authors of the reports, most of whom were businessmen, of the realities of the schools. They reveal no interest, he points out, in vocational training or in the special needs of inner-city schools and minority groups, and have only a vague sense of the diversity of the country's 16,000 local school systems.

In the final article in this section, "The Schools Flunk Out," from *The New York Review of Books,* Andrew Hacker surveys eight different studies and reports and finds all of them lacking. Their proposals for merit pay and master teacher programs seem to him to offer too little; the disparity between opportunities for advancement and compensation for those in industry and teaching are so great that the marginal bonuses they envision would be inadequate to attract the best and brightest to the profession. Like Howe, Hacker argues that the reports stress test scores as a proof of superior education, focus narrowly on education as a means of social advancement, and lack a broader vision of education as a source of personal enrichment for all.

ARMING EDUCATION[1]

The root problems of American education can be found in "A Nation at Risk," the report of the National Commission on Excellence in Education, but they are not the ones named by the commissioners. Those seventeen august educators, plus a token parent, toiling under a $785,000 grant and a mandate from the Department of Education, zeroed in on the length of the school day, the average load of homework, and the teaching of the "new basics" (computer science, for example) as subjects for remedial action. No doubt there is room for improvement in such areas. But as they appear on the national report card, they sound more like

[1]Reprint of an editorial from *The Nation.* 236:594-5. My. 14, '83. Copyright 1983 by The Nation. Reprinted by permission.

effects than causes of the "tide of mediocrity" the commissioners see engulfing the country. And what is wrong with education turns out to be less a matter of school administration than of social and political direction.

Some problems pop up at first glance, as the study frames the educational malaise in the terms of an unremitting militarism. "We have been committing an act of unthinking, unilateral educational disarmament," the report says. Marching right along: "If an unfriendly foreign power had attempted to impose on America the mediocre educational performance that exists today, we might well have viewed it as an act of war." Out come the big guns: "Our very future as a Nation and a people" is at risk.

Seen that way, education is just another line item in the national security budget: MX, Pershing 2, more homework, $C^3 I$, summer sessions. Upgrading the educational infrastructure is indistinguishable from modernizing the missile command. Throughout, education is conceived of as an instrument (or weapon) to be used to secure "America's place in the world." There's a war on—against the Japanese, who "make automobiles more efficiently than Americans," against the South Koreans and "the world's most efficient steel mill," against the West Germans and their high-quality machine tools.

The fiercest competitor, of course, is the Soviet Union: American students are found to score lower on most achievement tests than they did "26 years ago when Sputnik was launched." What with the proliferation of frilly subjects such as driver ed, training for adulthood, and foods and cooking, American students are in danger of losing the high-tech race to their Russian counterparts.

The problems that appear at second glance are, if anything, more insidious. In the paragraph of lip service the commissioners pay to matters "beyond . . . industry and commerce," they assert that "a high level of shared education is essential to a free, democratic society and to the fostering of a common culture." What that means, shorn of its piety, is that education is another kind of instrument for demobilizing uncommon cultures that threaten the peace and undermine the reign of the free democrats who happen to dominate society.

Education Secretary Terrel Bell set up the commission two years ago to prove a political point that President Reagan and like-minded conservatives had been making for some time: public schooling in America has been seriously subverted by liberal theorists of educational permissiveness and of racial (and cultural) integration. The experts came up with a bunch of statistics detailing the educational mess, which was easy, since it is plain enough for anyone who ventures inside an inner-city grade school, or even a glassy, grassy suburban high school, to see.

But their proposals could not break free of the political confines inherent in the commission's mandate. "It's a rerun of Vietnam," one educator (who was not on the commission) said last week. "Instead of sending in Marines to beat peasants, they want to send in a small number of adults to pacify a large number of unruly children. Unfortunately," he concluded, "the kids' capacity for resistance is greatly underestimated by the occupying power."

Every generation seems to get the educational mess it deserves; at least, it gets the response it provokes. The turmoil of the 1960s gave birth to educational reforms that were experimental, undisciplined, even chaotic—but innovative and enriching as well. The values and the attitudes of the Reagan years are repressive, conformist, and competitive. The reforms prescribed for this case are managerial and instrumental, and they are more likely to augment the tide of mediocrity than reverse it.

JUST AMONG US TEACHERS[2]

My first impressions and reactions to the report of the National Commission on Excellence in Education, *A Nation at Risk: The Imperative for Educational Reform,* have been altered by the unexpected response it has generated. Politicians at all levels have expressed alarm about the findings of the report; syndicated col-

[2]Reprint of an article by Harry N. Chandler, secondary school teacher in McMinnville, Oregon, and education editor of the *Journal of Learning Disabilities. Phi Delta Kappan.* 65:181-2. N. '83. Copyright © 1983 by Phi Delta Kappan.

umnists, from Mike Royko to James Kilpatrick, have written about it; and the report has received the "five-minute, in-depth" treatment on television news broadcasts, as well as generating discussion on the public radio program, "All Things Considered." Educational organizations, from the American Association of School Administrators to the National Education Association and the American Federation of Teachers, have issued position papers on the report; meanwhile, civic organizations ranging from chambers of commerce to church groups have sought speakers who can explain its implications for business, religion, and the larger society.

The Commission's report has something for everybody. Perhaps that's why it didn't just fade away, as did the comments of the Twentieth Century Fund Task Force and those of the National Task Force on Education for Economic Growth. Even John Goodlad's recently released study has been seen as a footnote to the Commission's statement that U.S. schools are generally worthless. *A Nation at Risk* briefly and condescendingly states that some schools and teachers do well. The report also insists that schools should be locally financed and controlled. Then it states that the federal government should spend money on special programs for special students. The reader can almost hear Commission members compromising frantically to include everyone's viewpoint. *U.S. News & World Report* has listed education as one of the five major domestic issues in the 1984 election campaign.* The National Commission's report supplies ammunition for all politicians, regardless of their leanings.

As a teacher I'm pleased that education is receiving national attention. I would be more pleased if the attention and attendant debate centered on a more respectable, data-based document. That *A Nation at Risk* is a mass of opinion pretending to be fact is not surprising; after all, the Commission members were not, for the most part, public school educators, nor was the report meant to be of value to educators. It is a political document.

Among the 18 Commission members, there was only one public school teacher. There were also two principals and a lone su-

*"Tomorrow," *U.S. News & World Report,* 8 August 1983, p. 11.

perintendent—who was included, I hope, for his educational background and not just for his Hispanic surname. The other Commission members came from business and from that part of educational management which is hardly distinguishable from industry.

By contrast, when the "Grace Commission" (President Reagan's private-sector survey on cost control) was formed to study how the federal government did business, the 1,300 members of that group came "mostly from business."** Apparently U.S. business can be trusted to study the way the federal government conducts its own business and the way it regulates the very businesses whose representatives are studying this issue—but U.S. education cannot be trusted to see itself clearly.

Now the organizations of educators are warning their members not to respond defensively by pointing out the many ambiguities and errors in *A Nation at Risk*. These organizations are right, of course. After all the publicity about the terrible teachers in second-rate schools, who would believe us anyway? But since this article is just among us teachers, I will dwell on some of the weaknesses in the Commission's report. Readers will be able to spot many others on which I will not waste space (among them, accepting out-of-date Scholastic Aptitude Test scores as valid indicators of educational quality and comparing U.S. schools to those of other cultures).

The Commission assumes that a monolith called "U.S. education" exists, that it is mediocre throughout, and that all regions of the nation need, desire, and can pay for the same type of schooling. The Commission pays lip service to local control, but it recommends an educational program for the nation that does not take regional differences into account. Perhaps led by futurists among its members, the Commission makes a further assumption: that the states are united, not just in a political union but in a common acceptance of technology and its applications to daily life. However, it is not necessarily true that what the Commission sees as proper education for the year 2000 will also be perceived as proper by the citizens of Manhattan, of Yamhill County, of Minneapolis, and of Plaquemines Parish.

**"Nobody Has Any Guts' in Washington," *U.S. News & World Report*, 25 July 1983, pp. 53–56.

In one of its many inconsistencies, the report says that schools are "routinely called on to provide solutions to personal, social, and political problems" that other institutions cannot resolve—and then blames schools and teachers for America's economic problems and charges them with solving those problems. Here we can detect the Commission's view of the purpose of schooling: schools must become instruments of national policy. Although this view is never stated, it dominates *A Nation at Risk,* which clearly emphasizes throughout the notion that effective schools turn out well-trained, highly competitive workers for business and industry.

The Commission asserts that its formula for reforming the schools is appropriate for all students, yet what it has recommended is really a college-preparatory curriculum. I don't disagree with emphasizing the "five new basics" (English, mathematics, science, social studies, and computer science), but I wouldn't place money on the idea that all students (and their parents) want that many academic courses in that much depth. The "diluted" curriculum of today—if it exists at all—is more the product of legislative mandates than of educational theory. And legislative mandates in a democracy presumably reflect the public will.

I am sure that at least 80% of all students can learn what the Commission wants them to learn, if teachers know how to teach this content well and if the necessary support services and materials are supplied. But I also know that, by the time they reach high school, many students are taking full responsibility for all decisions related to their schooling. One such decision might be to drop out if the school offers too few alternatives. It is true that many students are already deciding to do "the minimum work necessary for the moment, then coast through life." I deplore this decision, but I would not outlaw it as a possible democratic choice, especially in a society in which many teenage (and adult) idols—with the help of the business community—preach via records, television programs, and movies the quick and easy pursuit of happiness. *A Nation at Risk* not only emphasizes academic excellence as the road to higher education and thus to commercial or scientific success, but the report also implicitly denigrates those youths and adults who do not—or *cannot*—choose that road. The curriculum that the Commission recommends would be of value to anyone. But some students—perhaps a majority of them—also want to spend some time studying such things as art, auto repair, metal working, music, or food preparation.

It is useless to counter that parents should teach these skills, that they should be covered in private lessons after school, that they should be studied in technical schools after graduation from high school, or that the public schools cannot teach these skills well. If students are not at least exposed to these skills in school, they may lack both the motivation and the opportunity to learn them elsewhere. Moreover, if the schools can teach academics well, they can also teach—or learn to teach—the vocational and artistic basics effectively. The Commission's stand on this matter does great damage to that most democratic of U.S. institutions, the comprehensive high school.

Another problem with *A Nation at Risk* is that it terms the eight years before high school "crucial," but it devotes only one paragraph to schooling during the elementary and middle years. Schools serving these age groups are seen as prologues to high school, not as enterprises important in themselves and just as deserving of support as their secondary counterparts. The Commission report does not even mention kindergarten, preschool, or such early childhood compensatory programs as Head Start. Some of the recommendations in the report do apply to grades 1 through 8, but the Commission clearly regards older students—the ones preparing for college—as the most important age group. This attitude reflects the general stance of our supposedly child-centered society: those individuals who hold political or economic power tend to value children only when they are old enough to function as independent consumers and workers. Clearly, politicians appoint commissions to validate preconceived ideas.

Another preconceived idea that runs throughout *A Nation at Risk* is the notion that professional teachers are of little value. The Commission advocates the use of "nonschool personnel" from industry and higher education to teach science and mathematics, and it suggests that methods courses in teacher training institutions should be replaced by "subject-matter" courses. (What are the appropriate subject-matter courses for a primary teacher?)

Indeed, the Commission seldom misses an opportunity to take a shot at teachers, and this shotgun approach works; it attracts attention and does not require a scholarly consideration of actual school conditions. Firing into a group of terrorists and their hostages will kill some of the guilty, if you don't care about the innocent. In fact, the Commission's blasts *have* hit some of the guilty. There *are* poor teachers who, through administrative incompetence or union strength, remain in classrooms. There *are* some education courses that benefit only the instructor (who is paid to teach them). One reason it is difficult to argue publicly with the Commission's report is that parts of it are at least partly true.

However, even those parts have a "yes, but" attached to them:
• Teacher salaries are too low. Yes, but where do we get the money to improve them?
• We need more direct teaching time in the classroom. Yes, but is increasing the length of the school day and school year the most effective way to resolve this problem?
• School board members should be more interested in education, instead of functioning solely as fiscal watchdogs. Yes, but they ran for election on the promise of cutting school budgets.
• Parents should play a more active role in their children's education. Yes, but that is difficult to do in this era of high unemployment and divorce rates, when so many families are under stress.
• Teachers need more than just intrinsic rewards for doing an effective job. Yes, but how can we determine fairly which teachers should receive merit pay or promotions?
• Students should take education more seriously. Yes, but educators have been trying to get them to do that for years. Any practical suggestions?

Meanwhile, the Commission's recommendations are going to cost money—and the Commission says that these extra funds should come from local governments, which are already facing tax revolts. Thus many of the Commission's suggestions can only be implemented in communities with heavy concentrations of upwardly mobile, middle-class citizens who think as the Commission members do. This is because the Commission report is much like a brainstorming session, where one comes up with as many solutions to a problem as possible without examining the problem (to see if it is real) or the solutions (to see if they are practical).

The Commission chooses to ignore one fact that teachers cannot forget: we are members of a larger society, and, although we like to think that we have great influence on our students—and, through them, on U.S. culture—we face stiff competition for children's time and attention. But we teachers will try to implement as many of the Commission's recommendations as we can, since *A Nation at Risk* reflects the mood of the country and we teachers are experts at responding to the country's mood. Indeed, we teachers will *have* to change, because educational philosophy in the U.S. (what little we know of it) is so fragmented that we have no shared professional ideal with which to stave off even the most idiotic suggestions for reform; because educational psychology (what little we understand of it) is so at odds in its findings that we have no proven methodology to fall back on in the face of attacks; and because our own craft (carried out independently in isolated cubicles) has given us few strong bonds beyond our unions, which are too absorbed in internecine warfare to defend us.

Therefore, we will try to change, even though by robbing Peter to pay *all* we will end up weakening education in other disciplines or at other grade levels. We will once again rush headlong into ill-conceived but widely advertised innovations that will hang like millstones from the curriculum long after the Commission and its report have been forgotten. Because we are teachers and we really do want to teach well, we will also spend long hours in stuffy rooms with stuffy committees, trying to decide whether we have done what is best.

A NATION AT RISK: ANOTHER VIEW[3]

I have argued elsewhere that *A Nation at Risk* contains within it the seeds of immense mischief, and I am by no means certain that quiet, polite, rational discourse will abort those seeds. In fact, I believe many have already begun to sprout.

[3]Reprint of an article by James E. Albrecht, professor of school administration at the University of Northern Iowa, Cedar Falls, Iowa. *Phi Delta Kappan*. 65:684-5. Je. '84. Copyright © 1984 by Phi Delta Kappan. Reprinted by permission.

In embracing the report of the National Commission on Excellence in Education, the public and the media also embrace, in effect, the unequivocal indictment of the quality of education in U.S. high schools set forth in that document. Ignoring James Conant's observation that there is no such thing as a typical American high school, the Commission would have us believe that a school is a school is a school. Hence, it is easy for the public, especially those who have no children in the schools, to generalize that what's wrong with one school is wrong with all (or very nearly all) and that what's supposed to be good for one must therefore be good for all. Logicians may decry such thinking, but many people who should know better nevertheless hold to it. Ultimately, the focus shifts from the local school to a muddy abstraction labeled American Education.

Given this situation, the list of quick fixes designed to set the schools right again has immense appeal, especially to governors, legislators, and state agencies—all eager to gain political advantage. For school boards, eager to make local schools better, the list is particularly seductive. And who among them can resist? For this is no ordinary list. It carries the imprimatur of the federal government of the United States of America. Thus board members and others believe that they know what must be done. They believe that the government has spoken. Perhaps only Moses came to a task so formidably armed.

Faced with such a juggernaut, many superintendents and principals are unable to exert effective leadership. Commission recommendations put forward by school boards and politicians are hard for school officials to resist. When they do, their resistance is inevitably dismissed as "defensiveness," a charge often elaborated in editorials in the state and local media. When school leaders must divert their energy from productive activity to warding off harmful and foolish recommendations, however well-intentioned, education suffers.

But the fascination of the public and the media with *A Nation at Risk* has created another problem: it has blunted and obscured the carefully researched, thoughtful, and imaginative reports of Ernest Boyer, John Goodlad, and Theodore Sizer. An alarming proportion of the public and even of the media (if they even know these reports exist) believe that they are essentially footnotes or appendices to *A Nation at Risk*. Though all three of these reports recommend school improvements that differ sharply from those recommended by the National Commission, their suggestions have not caught on with the general public. Indeed, many people who have not read these longer and more substantive reports believe that they only lend additional support to the solutions set forth in *A Nation at Risk*. They believe that the verdict has been delivered and the issue settled. All you need to know about education is in the report of the Commission on Excellence.

The tragedy of all this is that the real keys to improving education—involving students more actively in the learning process and paying more attention to the cultivation of higher thought processes—are difficult to get on the public agenda, which is now cluttered with the detritus of *A Nation at Risk*.

Few educators believe that all is well in the nation's schools. Clearly, all is *not* well. But what is not well will not be made so by the prescriptions of the Commission on Excellence.

Perhaps the most troublesome feature of the report, however, is the tone of urgency it sounds. *A Nation at Risk* is, as much as anything, a call to action. The nationalistic rhetoric of the report makes deliberate and thoughtful consideration of its recommendations seem somehow unpatriotic. "History is not kind to idlers," the commissioners tell us. Yet it seems to me that a more accurate reading of history clearly suggests that history is not kind to the impetuous, the irresponsible, and the unthinking. But action is what we're getting—though much of it, particularly from political bodies, is unquestionably harmful.

In the face of these realities, I have a gnawing concern, one shared by many secondary school principals. A friend of mine who is a principal captured it perfectly. He said, "We have now found a way to legitimize chasing kids out of school." I'm afraid he may be exactly right. More homework, more testing, more time, more "hard" courses required, higher grading standards, tougher discipline—more of everything *for every student*. No more mediocrity!

At a time when our dropout rate is inching upward, when more hard-to-educate youngsters attend our schools than ever before, the Commission's emphasis on *rigor* presents to both educators and the public a welcome diversion. Those students who drop out of school can now be explained away: they are, for whatever reasons, unwilling or unable to meet the new and rigorous standards demanded by society. The schools are therefore absolved.

But there's more. The Commission on Excellence implicitly reestablishes the welfare of the college-bound as the criterion of a school's success. That notion is reinforced by the relationship alleged by the Commission to exist between education and our nation's economic competitiveness. Though that relationship, which ignores the pivotal roles played by assorted government and corporate policies, is clearly tenuous, it has already created in many schools a counterfeit "high-tech" emphasis. The zeal of the Commission in rectifying our "act of unthinking, unilateral educational disarmament" leads it to claim that "all children by virtue of their own efforts" can manage the sort of education that the nation's future will require—the sort of education endorsed by the Commission.

Thus it comes together: a school is a school, and a student is a student. What is alleged to be good for the college-bound must be good for all, and that means more science, more math, more computers—*for everyone*.

Such an emphasis will only hasten the disenfranchisement of the inarticulate, those whose children are already unsuccessful and demoralized in our schools. Only rarely now is a voice raised to question the impact of stiffer academic requirements on these children. And even those voices, I believe, will be increasingly intimidated, then muted, by the powerful message of *A Nation at Risk*.

For those who believe that 1983 was a vintage year for educators, to use Ernest Boyer's term, my concern may seem misplaced. Before we rejoice in the 1983 vintage, however, I suggest that we wait until the wine is poured, and that will be some years hence. Simply to be put high on the national agenda is not an occasion for celebration.

EDUCATION MOVES TO CENTER STAGE:
AN OVERVIEW OF RECENT STUDIES[4]

A wave of reports and studies of American schools has inundated educators and policy makers in 1983. Although these documents, which have attempted to define the educational problems of the nation and suggest solutions, were expected, their arrival has resulted in a totally new environment for thinking about educational issues in the U.S. Suddenly corporate barons, Presidential candidates, university presidents, governors, and legislative leaders in the Congress and state capitols have mounted a crusade to improve the schools. This newfound enthusiasm for doing something about education is heady wine for most educators, who became accustomed in the Seventies to an atmosphere characterized by reduced funds for schools and media attention focused on their shortcomings, without much commitment to their improvement.

The reasons that national leaders are interested in the schools are numerous and complex. A few of them will have to suffice for the purpose of this discussion.

• Frustration over the diminishing capacity of the U.S. to compete in worldwide markets has awakened new interest in the old idea that the quality of human resources is a key element in the efficiency of the nation's economy. Better schools that produce better-educated workers are thought to be the way to outsell the Japanese and the Germans.

• Another version of the same idea applies to our defense establishment and national security. How can we keep ahead of the Soviets if their youths are better educated than ours? This view is a replay of the Sputnik scenario of the late Fifties. In its more extreme form it has distinctly chauvinistic overtones.

• Dissatisfaction with American education has coalesced because of disillusionment with the resolution of civil rights issues in the schools and because of widespread concern about declining test

[4]Excerpted from an article by Harold Howe II, former U. S. Commissioner of Education and senior lecturer in the Harvard Graduate School of Education, Cambridge, Massachusetts. *Phi Delta Kappan.* 65:167-72. N. '83. Copyright © 1983 by Phi Delta Kappan. Reprinted by permission.

scores. Today a typically pragmatic American reaction seems to have distilled from these negative views: let's stop complaining about our education problems and do something about them. The reports and studies of recent months have been instrumental in emphasizing this theme.

Despite the widespread knowledge of these national studies of education, it may be useful to make a few general observations about them.

• Little attention has been paid to the valuable efforts of individual scholars. At least two such works (being published this fall by Basic Books) carry powerful insights that augment the more visible national reports. One is Diane Ravitch's history of American education from 1945 to 1980, *The Troubled Crusade*; it offers a perspective on educational issues in the U.S. that transcends any analysis that has appeared in the major reports. A second book, by Sara Lawrence Lightfoot, is titled *The Good High School: Portraits of Character and Culture*. This work is a marvelous analysis of the actual operation of selected schools in all their human complexity. In discussing curriculum, organization, and other structural elements, it takes the *people* in schools into account, a factor that is almost completely ignored by most of the national studies. Reading these two books adds important background information to the reports that have appeared to date.

• Many additional reports are yet to come. The National Science Board's Commission on Precollege Education in Mathematics, Science, and Technology has already issued an "Interim Report to the National Science Board" (January 1983) and will have published its final report before this article appears in print. The Committee on Economic Development, an organization that represents business interests, has appointed a special Subcommittee on Business/Education Relationships, together with a staff and a group of advisors, to prepare a report that will reflect business interests in education. The report will focus on the cost of educational failure and on the needs of business. At its initial meeting, the subcommittee decided to take a careful look at strategies for improving teacher supply and teaching quality. The final report may not be published for two years, but the group intends to publish interim findings. In addition, many states have launched their own studies of education that will augment the national reports. Governors, state departments of education, and legislatures have all taken a renewed interest in education.

• Various national education organizations, such as the American Association of School Administrators and the National Association of Secondary School Principals, are issuing interpretive materials about some of the national studies. Critiques of the studies have already appeared in newspaper articles and magazines. It may take a year or two before anyone completes a comprehensive study of the studies, however.

• One example of the recent criticism of the studies can be found in the *New York Times* (Connecticut edition) of June 5, in which Charles Fowler, superintendent of schools in Fairfield, Connecticut, analyzes *A Nation at Risk,* the report of the National Commission on Excellence in Education, and finds it "mediocre." And Fred Hechinger, writing in the August 2 *New York Times,* observes: "This outpouring of concern is a welcome sign of public awareness after years of indifference. But the mass of proposals and the contradictory remedies could well neutralize each other. A confused public may grow impatient with all the talk and countertalk and tune out again. . . . "

Unattended Issues

1. *The costs of improving education.* The most glaring omission from the new studies of the shortcomings of education and recommendations for reform is any detailed estimate of attendant costs and how they are to be met. The single largest area of additional cost will certainly be the compensation of teachers. The studies all recognize the recent substantial decline in teaching salaries relative to other fields of work; less often do they recognize the subsidy provided U.S. schools for many years by able women who worked at low pay because women were not accepted in other professions. This subsidy has been slowly withdrawn in the last 15 years, as the women's movement has moved toward equity in employment for females. Add to this the calls for extending the school day and year, for attracting more able people to the teaching profession, and for creating merit pay arrangements, and a

very rough estimate suggests that at least $20 billion to $30 billion *a year* in new funds will be needed to put the schools on an upward course. There will be a multitude of additional costs, of course, for science equipment, computers, and a variety of other purposes.

The division of the new costs of excellence among federal, state, and local funding sources remains largely unexplored, although the last 15 years have brought major change and progress in our thinking about educational finance. Funding the costs of excellence will remain the most difficult of all the issues raised by the wave of recommendations regarding the reform of schooling. My observations on this vital matter are as follows.

• It seems unlikely that the federal government will assume the costs of paying teachers, even though it might help substantially with their training and retraining and with equipping schools. State and local governments will have to carry the financial load of teachers' salaries and share this load in a fashion that is both politically viable and fair to taxpayers. If the federal government were to become involved, it would have to take into account the relative fiscal capacity of the states to improve teacher compensation.

• The self-interest of business in improving education has led to vigorous participation by corporate leadership in helping the schools; however, business leaders have not yet issued any clear call to the business community to support increased taxes at state and local levels. Most businesses still regard taxes for schools as a cost of doing business that can affect their competitive position—not as an investment in the future. A few corporate leaders have a more enlightened attitude toward cost and tax issues, but whether they can succeed in bringing a strong response from businesses generally is still an open question.

• The current antipathy in the U.S. toward any form of added taxation is so strong that it bodes ill for the political success of extra funding for educational reform. State governors appear most likely to provide strong leadership that can change this attitude. Such leadership has already emerged in Mississippi, North Carolina, and several other states. But it is not yet clear whether governors can actually interest Americans in paying higher taxes.

• New technology may be able to cut the costs of education and make it more efficient. This is no certainty, of course; many problems and even dangers attend the pursuit of these goals. But the combination of computers with sound and video in increasingly flexible and inexpensive formats to provide effective learning is worth serious trial and exploration. Technology *could* result in making education a less labor-intensive enterprise and so reduce costs. We can expect no short-term solutions to cost problems through technology, however; time and substantial investments will first be required.

2. *A narrow focus on the high school and on cognitive elements in education.* It could be argued that the best national investment in improved education would be the establishment of a *universal* system of preschools and kindergartens by every state and school district in the U.S., but this argument is not strongly presented in the recent studies. Instead, the studies focus primarily on the shortcomings of secondary schools—and of high schools more than of junior high schools. In my opinion, the increases in both single-parent families and full-time working mothers indicate the need for more emphasis on early childhood services for children.

Thoughtful educators have long claimed that early adolescents have been badly served by the junior high schools. But the national studies that have emerged so far are more concerned with the curriculum and the teaching in grades 9 through 12. School districts using the reports and studies as an exploratory agenda for action would be wise to assess their sixth-, seventh-, and eighth-grade practices.

I do not mean to say that high schools don't need attention. They do, particularly in the cities. I have already mentioned the high dropout rates characteristic of inner-city schools, but they have numerous other problems—some of which are identified in the various studies—that suggest changes in course requirements, teaching practices, use of time, and the like to repair weaknesses in cognitive learning. These studies pay very little attention, however, to the noncognitive elements of schooling—those practices that build student morale and motivation and that ultimately make possible more demanding cognitive work.

Many of the recent reports (Goodlad, Sizer, and Boyer excepted) give one the feeling that children and youths in schools are mere receptacles into which information and skills can be dumped, so that the graduates of our system will be useful to society. Indeed, the psychological assumption that seems to underlie many recommendations is that the mind is like a muscle that can be improved by strenuous exercise. This view of learning has long been discredited, and it won't do any good to revive it in the name of rigor or economic productivity or national security. A school in all of its human complexity is, next to the home, the most important institution in a young person's life. If a youngster sees school as an unfriendly place that provides the protection of anonymity but offers little in the way of personal attention and recognition, no amount of added emphasis on new curricula will succeed.

In the early 1970s several national commissions examined the problems of adolescents in America and tried to promote understanding of some of the dilemmas they faced. Surprisingly, today's studies make no reference to the important findings of these groups.* The reports of the Seventies, with their attention to the meaning and value of life in the teenage years, would add an important dimension to today's narrow focus on the cognitive. Schools are legitimately concerned with developing positive student attitudes and behaviors, and the atmosphere and human relations of a school—in class and out—relate strongly to this important objective.

3. *The unfinished equity agenda.* All the recent reports and studies recognize in general terms that disadvantaged and minority students have special needs, but they all stop with such generalities. *A Nation at Risk* urges the federal government to do something about these needs, but it doesn't say what. *Action for Excellence* gives this subject only the most general treatment, grouping women and minorities in one sentence of its recommendations for action. The reports fail to mention school desegregation, and they give precious little attention to the demographic facts that are all too clear: the proportion of Hispanics, Asians, and blacks in U.S. schools will increase rapidly in the next 15 years, and most of these groups will concentrate in the cities. These omissions gave rise to my earlier recommendation for a new

*See in particular James S. Coleman et al., *Youth, Transition to Adulthood: Report of the Panel on Youth of the President's Science Advisory Committee* (Chicago: University of Chicago Press, 1974).

section of Title I devoted to high schools. Naturally, existing funding for elementary schools from that program should not be reduced.

San Francisco, St. Louis, and Chicago recently made imaginative moves to reduce racial isolation in their schools—all without the necessity for lengthy, disruptive trials and court orders. Instead, consent decrees were the basis for the settlement of suits. One would think that these events, which occurred while the major study groups were conducting their reviews, might have attracted attention as positive moves that recall the principles of the *Brown* decision. But that landmark of American freedom isn't mentioned, either. Clearly there is little remaining commitment to the idea that separate and unequal schools are unacceptable and not enough commitment to equal opportunity to elicit clear and specific recommendations on how these crucial goals are to be pursued.

One of the dangers inherent in all the recommendations for more demanding courses and higher standards is that these more rigorous requirements will be insensitively applied and will force more young people out of school altogether. There is no adequate safety net today for a boy or girl who does not finish high school, and those who are recommending tougher standards for a high school diploma have not suggested one. Yet the first hurdle for any job applicant is still, "Do you have a high school diploma?" It is possible to raise academic standards in high schools without rejecting large numbers of young people, but the difficulties of doing so are insufficiently recognized in many of the new reports.

4. *Neglect of vocational education.* Vocational education is given almost no attention in the new studies, which is surprising in view of the fact that the studies focus primarily on the secondary school years, where most vocational offerings concentrate. Does this omission imply that all is well with vocational education and that it should keep on doing what it has been doing? Or does it perhaps suggest that there just isn't much interest in vocational education, because it is not seen as very significant? I don't know the answers to these questions, but one possible implication may be that the business world is more interested in having job applicants with well-developed learning skills and responsible work

habits than prospective employees with technical training for particular jobs that may no longer exist. If this is so, then many vocational programs will be challenged by the new emphasis on higher-order learning skills.

5. *Is there a tendency to cheapen educational goals?* Business and political leaders (and some educators) justify their desires for major changes and higher investments in American education by maintaining that these changes are needed to compete with the Japanese and to hold off the Soviets. Surely a better-educated populace will help with both of these problems, and surely these problems are important, say our leaders. So why not let them dominate our motives for improving schools?

However, a careful reading of the various reports reveals that their authors conceived of broader and more timeless goals for the schools. *A Nation at Risk* mentions "civility" and "prosperity and security" in its opening paragraphs; it speaks of "intellectual, moral, and spiritual strengths," and it advocates a "learning society . . . that affords all members the opportunity to stretch their minds to full capacity. . . . "

But I still have a nagging concern about the emphasis of the reports on materialistic motives as a basic platform for educational reform. At the very least, we must remain alert to the danger that such goals can push aside other important educational issues. How do we bring up a generation that will truly make peace with our enemies, identify and change the unfairness in our economic system, and be willing to see other societies as more than just competitors?

We know that education has deeper purposes than merely to prepare people for jobs. We are aware that to define the mission of the schools along narrowly utilitarian lines would be to misperceive the purposes of schooling. But if preparation for work is not the only aim of education, it is nonetheless a very important aim. And surely education for economic growth is a worthwhile goal around which to organize our efforts to rally the American people in the cause of improving the nation's schools.

I'd find this statement more palatable if its first sentence were at the beginning of the report and if its last sentence were qualified in some fashion. But perhaps I am merely quibbling; it may be ungracious to question the motives of education's new friends in

high places. Most educators probably feel that the best strategy
is to ride the new wave of interest in education without questioning its values and motives. Nonetheless, my vague worries persist. . . .

THE SCHOOLS FLUNK OUT[5]

Having been through the mill ourselves, we all feel entitled to
expound on education. So, too, we believe that the schools belong
to us, and hence we have the right to set them straight. The past
year has been one for sounding alarms, mainly by a number of
task forces and commissions, titles taken by committees to suggest
vital issues are at stake. The National Commission on Excellence
in Education, appointed by Secretary of Education T. H. Bell, set
the general tone. Its report, *A Nation at Risk,* opened with the
now familiar warning that "the educational foundations of our society are presently being eroded by a rising tide of mediocrity."
The Education Commission of the States, created to counsel governors, released its report, *Action for Excellence,* "with an unusual
sense of urgency," because "a real emergency is upon us." The
Twentieth Century Fund followed with *Making the Grade,*
which forecast "disaster" unless we make "a national commitment
to excellence in our public schools." And the National Science
Board's *Educating Americans for the 21st Century* called for
"academic excellence by 1995." Something must be in the air,
when four independent panels choose "excellence" as their common denominator.

All four reports concentrate on public education, from kindergarten through high school. Lay and religious private schools,
which currently enroll one-ninth of all pupils, are apparently seen
as in good shape. Nor is much concern shown about the colleges,
compared with the clamor of a dozen years ago. The call today

[5]Reprint of an article by Andrew Hacker, professor of political science at Queens College, City University of New York. *The New York Review of Books.* 31:35–40. Ap. 12, '84. Copyright © 1984 by The New
York Review of Books. Reprinted by permission.

is for a more rigorous approach to learning, beginning as early as possible. *Educating Americans,* for example, recommends that first graders spend ninety minutes every day on mathematics and science. The reports also share a singleness of purpose. Nowhere is it avowed that learning may be pursued for its own sake, or that there may be reason to esteem a cultivated mind. A nation facing peril has no time for such asides. Rather, the concentration on "excellence" means that we must upgrade "the design and delivery of education" (*Action for Excellence*) if we hope to "keep and improve the slim competitive edge we still retain in world markets" (*A Nation at Risk*).

So the stakes are economic, with our living standards in the balance. (Interestingly, the reports say little about the relation of education to our military capability.) Other nations are outpacing us because they are, yes, smarter. The only way to preserve our position is to enlarge our pool of trained intelligence. These arguments can have a persuasive ring given this country's decline in so many ways. Even so, there remains the question of whether reorganizing the schools will improve our competitive position. And even if such a connection can be shown, we must ask how far we want to recast our assumptions about the aims of education.

Not surprisingly, the Japanese are held up as a model. Their students attend classes 220 days a year, against 180 for ours. An ordinary high school there devotes three times as many hours to studying science as do our best schools with full science programs. Moreover, their graduation rate is 95 percent, while ours is an embarrassing 73 percent. (True, they allow students to leave earlier; and of those who stay, fewer go to college.) On our side of the Pacific, less than a third of high school graduates have taken intermediate algebra; half last studied science in the tenth grade; and two-thirds do less than an hour of homework on an average night. According to *Action for Excellence,* the majority of our seventeen-year-olds cannot "write a letter correcting a billing error." All the reports point to the decline in Scholastic Aptitude Test scores. *A Nation at Risk* concludes that American students are "coasting" through "a cafeteria-style curriculum in which the appetizers and desserts can easily be mistaken for the main courses."

We are already into the era of the "technologically sophisticated workplace," whether the products be goods, services, or information. However, most employers report that the people they have had to hire "had basic skill deficiencies in a majority of job categories" (*Action for Excellence*). It is not just secretaries who cannot spell. Equipment operators cannot understand the diagrams in instruction manuals. According to *Action for Excellence,* the only way to upgrade our labor force is to "establish firm, explicit, and demanding requirements concerning discipline, attendance, homework, grades . . . " for all students in all schools. *A Nation at Risk* calls for three years of mathematics and science for all students, along with at least a semester of computer science, plus more hours of instruction and a longer school year. *Making the Grade* would also like to see all students "acquire proficiency in a second language," and possibly a third for those who do not speak English at home. *Action for Excellence* would have every boy and girl know how to "use elementary concepts of probability and statistics" and "distinguish problems whose genesis is in basic mechanics, physics, or chemistry." *Educating Americans* adds that "algorithmic thinking is an essential part of problem solving." It also urges bilingual training; in its case, however, that means "two computer languages."

While the reports stress that education must be improved if we are to catch up with our competitors, they also profess a broader goal: excellence for everyone. *Educating Americans* specifically states that "academic or educational excellence . . . does not mean the provision of high quality education to only a small group of highly talented youth." Of course, this is the American way of discourse. A panel addressing a general audience cannot conclude that the nation's work force needs, say, 25 million people with sophisticated skills, and then propose that we provide such training for only that number. The democratic ideology dictates that algorithmic thinking must reach rural Wyoming and inner Chicago. The panelists omit saying that what they are proposing is both unprecedented and radical. Equal opportunities for everyone may be our accepted rhetoric. However, as a practical matter, we have never sought to close the gaps between different classes of schools. At best, some cities have special public schools that permit students from modest backgrounds to press ahead. By the same token, state and municipal universities have offered talented students a similar chance. However, the fact remains that high quality schooling, as defined by the educators themselves, at best reaches about a third of young Americans. Nor is this solely a matter of spending money. Expanding the number of people with comparable qualifications can threaten those in comfortable positions. We can already see this happening with the impending oversupply of lawyers and physicians.

The reports are highly critical of teachers, especially on grounds of competence. *Educating Americans* states that half of those hired as science instructors are "unqualified," meaning not incomplete credentials but deficiencies in knowledge. Of course, picking on teachers is easy, not least for class reasons. They are the most marginal of middle-class professionals, with their union and civil-service affiliations reducing an already shaky status. Young people who choose teaching have tended to come from the bottom of their college classes, enrolling in often sterile courses on education instead of in classes with more substance. Hence the complaint that we have been staffing our schools with "C"-level graduates for too long; a nation aiming at excellence will need "A"- and "B"-grade people in its children's classrooms.

So it is curious that the commissions show no more than passing interest in who our teachers are or why we end up with the ones we do. Teaching school is our largest profession, with approximately two million members in the public sector, of whom two-thirds are women. Because enrollments have been decreasing, there has been little recent hiring, so the typical teacher is now thirty-seven and has had thirteen years in the classroom. Salaries in 1982 averaged $17,360 for ten months of work, which would come to $20,830 if teachers taught—and were paid for—the entire year. Whether "C" quality or not, teachers are close to a minimum wage, by the standard of middle-class salaries. On the other hand, a majority of the women are married and belong to two-income households, as do most of the men. Indeed, 73 percent of the married male teachers have working wives, one of the highest proportions among the professions.[*]

[*]National Education Association, *Status of the American Public School Teacher* (1982).

All the panels say they support across-the-board raises to attract better teachers. At the same time, they do not pursue the matter, doubtless because they realize that raises of $5,000 to $10,000 multiplied would be very costly. So they settle instead for keeping the stars in the system. *Action for Excellence* urges "extraordinary rewards for extraordinary teachers," suggesting that not many will display that luster. *Making the Grade* would appropriate federal funds to create a class of "Master Teachers." All the panels favor differentials in pay, presumably based on merit, although none hints at how quality would be rated. Nor do they consider that each teacher's salary—construed as an evaluation—would be in public records available to parents and others.

There are few signs that the commission members made an effort to find out what goes on in some actual classrooms. It is customary, with such bodies, that the signatories review memorandums prepared by salaried staffs. The principal members of the panels were public officials and business executives, along with college professors and school superintendents. Three of the four groups thought to include a teacher, in one case from Beverly Hills. *A Nation at Risk* lists "site visits" to a dozen or so schools, but does not say who made those trips or what they did there. The panelists who signed *Making the Grade* call for terminating bilingual education without having seen such instruction in action. A Hispanic member of the commission felt obliged to file a footnote explaining how it really works.

It is probably too much to hope that commission members would take off time to sit in on some typical classes. Still, if they couldn't manage this, the next best thing would have been to examine some of the research done by John Goodlad, a professor and former dean of education at the Los Angeles campus of the University of California. While *A Place Called School* officially appeared at the same time as the task force and commission reports, the overall study began in 1975, and various of its findings have been available for several years. "Most of the efforts to improve schools," Goodlad writes, "founder on ignorance of the ways schools function." He and his associates approached thirty-eight public schools and secured permission to observe more than one thousand classes in grades one through twelve. In addition, they surveyed some twenty-seven thousand parents, teachers, and students. Most of the schools were middle class, although not more than a handful were in well-to-do districts. In only one or two did discipline or truancy present major problems.

Goodlad presents a disquieting picture. In its essentials, education has not changed since it moved indoors. Students sit at desks for five or more hours every day, listening to an adult. (The author calls this "frontal" teaching.) Education, he found, consists largely "of a teacher standing or sitting in front of a class imparting knowledge to a group of students. Explaining and lecturing constituted the most frequent teaching activities." In addition to listening (or not, as is often the case), pupils sit doing assignments, such as "filling in blank spaces in short narratives." This regimen remains much the same from kindergarten through the senior year.

Is anything wrong with this picture? After all, teachers know things that students don't, which means the former have to talk while the latter listen. The trouble with all that classroom sitting is that most young people are not natural scholars; they don't see the purpose in what they have to learn, or at least in the way it is presented. This is not to say that Goodlad found students resentful or rebellious. The majority dutifully attend and even do their lessons. Still, on the whole, they come unwillingly, as they have since Shakespeare's time. They realize "there is no choice" and that "society requires it . . . as part of growing up." So they cool it by keeping "the classroom experience relatively low in emotional drain in order to preserve energy for other things." When teachers were polled, they said their major regret was "lack of student interest." What they face, in fact, is a form of passive resistance.

Insofar as students find being in the building congenial, it is because school is their main social center where they make and meet with friends. When Goodlad's student informants were asked to cite the "one best thing" about their school, "my friends" and "sports" led the list, with "classes I'm taking" and "teachers" well at the rear. Needless to say, many perform well in the academic side and continue doing so in college. But usually it is their success they enjoy rather than the substance of their studies.

All of us agree that there are things youngsters should be learning. Beyond the elementary skills, the curriculum consists

largely of "subjects"—English, social studies, science, and so on—
that we are told form the groundwork of what an educated person
ought to know. But after reading *A Place Called School,* I am no
longer so sure. For what the schools teach is a very special brand
of knowledge, evolved by educators and tailored to textbooks and
segmented lessons. It is pretty dreary stuff, usually presented,
Goodlad notes, in a "flat emotional tone."

To this it may be replied that we need better teaching, to be
gained perhaps by attracting faculty with more varied training.
However, here Goodlad warns that "talk of securing and maintaining a stable corps of understanding teachers is empty rhetoric"
unless we lighten their classroom load. Even with its long vaca-
tions, teaching is one of our most demanding professions. You are
on center stage every hour of the day, obliged to hold the attention
of up to thirty students. In the elementary grades it is a single
group, which makes the job considerably easier. However, by
junior high school, you may have 150 or more students passing
through your room. One teacher told Goodlad, "It is the sheer
emotional drain of interacting with 173 students each day that
wears me down."

Still, we say we want teachers who will be both inspired and
inspiring, who can make chemistry and Chaucer come alive, as we
may recall happening in some of our own classes. I'm not sure
what reforms will bring more high-quality instruction to the nation's classrooms. Getting teaching candidates with higher test
scores or college grades would be desirable but is hardly a guarantee. In fact, we should not overestimate the number of adults who
have an aptitude for getting through to children. Certainly, we
won't get the best from teachers if they are on the verge of burning
out. At my own loftier level, I am in a classroom only eight hours
a week; and I don't have to monitor the cafeteria, confer with parents, or coach the debating team. *A Place Called School* acknowledges that teachers want better pay. What they would also like are
college schedules.

Theodore Sizer also concentrates on teaching. He makes an
excellent complement to Goodlad, because he gives us detailed accounts of real classrooms in action. To gather material for
Horace's Compromise, Sizer visited more than fifty high schools

himself in 1981 and 1982. The eponym of his title is not Horace Mann, but a semifictitious "Horace Smith," an English teacher at a suburban school who advises the theater club and moonlights at a liquor store. Sizer follows him throughout an average day, starting at 7:30 AM teaching *Romeo and Juliet* and ending close to midnight with papers uncorrected. The "compromises" are really the corners Horace must cut to fit everything in. Like using last year's class notes, or recycling paragraphs on college recommendations.

We observe about a half dozen other teachers, also "composites," but the class sessions Sizer describes are as realistic as any I have read. We can actually see and hear how some teachers hold their students' attention; or, in other cases, we read on helplessly as a class turns into chaos. "Martha Shiffe" certainly knows her subject, tenth-grade biology, but her class is a disaster. She writes *phylum chordata* and *superclass tetrapoda* on the board, but no one copies them down. Students giggle, pass notes, or gaze into the air. ("One girl took out her compact, popped the mirror open, and went over her face in detail, squinting at each incipient blemish.") Nor is this a problem school, but one "in a pleasant area of a small city." Do we really want to impose

CHORDATA

and

TETRAPODA

on all four million of our nation's fifteen-year-olds?

The star teacher in Sizer's book is "Sister Michael," a seventy-two-year-old nun who analyzes a Graham Greene story with fourteen seniors in a Catholic high school. She calls on every member of the group, posing questions admitting of no easy answers, orchestrating the replies into a disciplined discussion. ("The words a student used in this classroom were important. There was no sloppy language in Sister Michael's domain.") But it is doubtful if she will serve as a useful model for enlivening biology, or indeed for most teachers with larger and less carefully selected classes. (Sizer was headmaster at Andover, and feels easiest in seminar settings.)

Horace's Compromise makes clear that the first attribute of a good teacher is to be able to evoke the respect of an assorted group

of students. This talent can come in varied forms; we all recall
good teachers who had very different styles. Unfortunately, too
many people who take up teaching lack this capacity. (The class
element figures here as well; they are often the first in their families to enter a profession, so they tend to play it safe.) Knowledge
of a subject just isn't enough to stir youngsters who have been
deskbound since 7:30 AM. None of the commissions confronted this
issue, preferring to believe that pupils will learn a lot more if demanding standards are set. They have it the wrong way around.
Teachers who are first admired for their personal qualities end
up getting better performances, because their students make extra
effort. Some of the most successful teaching Sizer saw was done
by athletic coaches.

One rather sour note runs through all the commission reports.
So far as I can ascertain, almost all of the members are in their
forties or older, and they take pains to differentiate themselves
from the generation currently in school and recent graduates. *A
Nation at Risk* quotes one analyst, Paul Copperman, as saying
that "for the first time in the history of our country, the educational skills of one generation will not surpass, will not equal, will not
even approach, those of their parents." The commissions are in
fact indicting an entire generation: upward of eighty million
young Americans born during the baby-boom years of 1946
through 1964. The members of this cohort, a third of our current
population, are now between the ages of twenty and thirty-eight,
ranging from the group just completing college to those becoming
candidates for responsible positions. In the eyes of the commissions, this is largely a lost generation: indulged by their parents
and spoon-fed by the schools.

This charge calls for close examination. Let us assume that
many of today's middle-aged Americans—say, those between for-
ty-five and sixty—went through a more rigorous academic regimen. Has this been an especially able generation? If the United
States has "fallen behind" in various fields, they were in or very
close to presiding positions. Moreover, except for those who entered technical professions, there are few signs that adults who
studied calculus or physics at school can claim the "scientific
literacy" they now wish instilled in youngsters. And just for the

record, it would be interesting to know how many of the commissioners continue to be competent in another language. Or of those who spent four years studying literature, how many curl up with Jane Austen or John Donne in their spare time? John Goodlad suggests that what we were made to learn at school may have less impact on our later life than we would like to think. For support, he directs our attention to an ambitious study that looked up members of a high school class fifteen years after graduation. There was "little in the data to suggest that the high school curriculum contributed to job competence or satisfaction, late participation in civic and political activities, or life enjoyment."

Still, there is the fact that SAT scores have been declining ever since the baby-boom generation began taking the tests. Nor does the expanded pool of candidates explain the drop, because even students from well-regarded schools are among those doing poorly. Equally disturbing, high school graduation rates are actually declining. Between 1972 and 1982, the proportion of students who failed to finish high school rose from 23 percent to 27 percent. Attrition rates for 1982 ran from 37 percent in Mississippi to 11 percent in Minnesota, with large states like New York (34 percent) and California (31 percent) high in the dropout category.*

Unfortunately, none of the panels made a serious effort to ascertain why this has been happening. *Making the Grade* recites a familiar litany: "the ready availability of drugs, the growing number of family breakups and the increased permissiveness in those remaining intact, the distractions of television and of easily affordable video games, the growth of underworld culture." Well, yes. But the real fact that must be faced is that today's youngsters differ markedly, in character and constitution, from their counterparts in earlier generations. This revolution must be understood in connection with any discussion of education.

More students in the past tended to acquiesce to authority, and dutifully did their assignments. By and large, they were anxious to become adults, and looked for cues offered by that world (such as how to appear "mature"). At the turn of the century, immigrant children sat silently in classrooms, often with little idea of what

*US Department of Education, *State Education Statistics* (January 1984).

was going on, and most left for work as soon as the law allowed. High schools were elite institutions: in New York in 1910, altogether 2,477 students got diplomas, less than 3 percent of their age group. Even as late as 1948, only 54 percent completed high school nationwide. Through the 1950s—the Eisenhower era—students who stuck it out at school performed pretty much as expected.

How does it happen, then, that so many of today's students seem such a sloppy crew? One answer is that young people nowadays are less members of their own families than citizens in a nation of their own. A generation ago, we used the term "adolescence" to refer to that painful period in which teen-agers prepared for adulthood. Today that word is seldom heard. We speak instead of "youth," a span that runs from about the age of twelve often into one's thirties. This youthful nation stands apart from the adult world. It has a language and sensibilities of its own, holding a skeptical view toward adult authority.* In a curious way, the reports acknowledge this. While they criticize students and teachers, at no point do they hold parents responsible for their children's poor performance, in what amounts to an admission that parents have little influence over their own offspring.

Of course, there are still plenty of "good students," or students who can meet that standard if they are so inclined. Howard Gardner has described how they cope with the system:

Children skilled in the ways of school are accustomed to the presentation of problems and tasks, often out of context, and learn to tackle these assignments just because they are there. Children learn to look for clues, to devise steps and strategies, and to search doggedly for answers that are not known.**

On the whole, most pupils whose parents have been to college can get through their assignments with a minimum of strain. It is not that their parents help them with homework, but rather that middle-class households share enough of the academic culture so that they adapt relatively easily to what is required in the classroom.

Another dimension of the dropout problem, ignored by the reports, is that the rate for boys is considerably higher than for girls.

*See Andrew Hacker, "Farewell to the Family," *The New York Review*, March 18, 1982.
**Frames of Mind (Basic Books, 1983), p. 357.

The most common reasons boys give for quitting school are "poor grades," "couldn't get along with teachers," or simply, "school wasn't for me." Almost 15 percent had been expelled or suspended at least once. Another Education Department study, of students who did graduate, found that 40 percent of the girls had mostly A's and B's, while only 26 percent of the boys did that well. Of the students now going on to college, there are 108 women for every 100 men; and for the first time they out-numbered men among those receiving bachelors' and masters' degrees.*

By and large, girls submit more readily to a classroom setting, where they take better notes and turn in assignments to their teachers' liking. (They also put in more time doing homework at both the school and college levels.) Of course, many boys make good records, especially among the science and mathematics students. But on the whole, more boys lack the makeup for twelve or more years of sustained sitting. It seems hardly necessary to add that society will feel the side effects as more women move ahead of men in educational attainment.**

Despite the dropout statistics, all four commissions call for mandatory courses considerably more demanding than those required now. (*Educating Americans,* for example, wants "technological reasoning" taught to all eighth-graders.) Interestingly, none of the reports alludes to an earlier effort of this sort. Remember the "New Math"? It was instituted across the nation after the Soviets outpaced us with Sputnik in 1957. University

---

*See the following documents published by the National Center for Education Statistics: *High School and Beyond: Sophomore Cohort Follow-Up* (April 1983); *Digest of Education Statistics* (May 1982); *Earned Degrees Conferred by US Colleges and Universities* (January 1984). Part of the undergraduate imbalance can be explained by the fact that several hundred thousand young men of college age enlist in the armed forces.

**See Matilda Butler, *Education, the Critical Filter: A Statistical Report on the Status of Girls and Women in Elementary and Secondary Education* (US Government Printing Office, 1979). The imbalance is even more pronounced in the black community, where women have come to hold a higher proportion of white-collar and professional positions, due largely to their educational attainments. US Bureau of the Census, *Detailed Occupation and Years of School Completed by Age, for the Civilian Labor Force by Sex, Race, and Spanish Origin* (1983).

mathematicians said they knew why we were behind: our high school graduates lacked an understanding of mathematical theory. Students should not merely memorize equations, but begin with the foundations of the discipline. So elementary and high school teachers were sent to summer courses to master the New Math. Within a year, virtually every child in the nation was being taught "set theory" and "number fields." Teaching theory may have been a fine theory, but in the classrooms it didn't work. Not only could most students not follow what was going on, but the New Math also obstructed learning ordinary arithmetic.* Indeed, it was close to the time that test scores started going down. The New Math was dropped; and mathematical theory is now generally reserved for the few college students who are concentrating on the subject.

Do we really want to try to teach everyone subjects that only some need to know? At this point, we have no evidence that factory workers who have taken high school physics are more effective at their jobs or show more concern for the quality of their product. The opposite may be the case. One need not share George Gilder's overall outlook to see some sense in something he wrote several years ago:

Contrary to widespread belief, academic attainments are of little real importance in performing most jobs. What education is required can be given selectively to motivated workers, who learn rapidly for some clear purpose. Most skills in the United States economy are learned on the job and well under half require the knowledge entitled in a high school diploma. . . . Unschooled peasants in Taiwan, Singapore, South Korea, and Japan build television sets, automobiles, electronic devices, semiconductor chips, and musical instruments that compete successfully in American markets.**

Indeed, it is hard to pin down ideology here. Gilder, a supply-side conservative, opposes the emphasis on formal education because it creates a nonproductive class which raises barriers against other kinds of talents. In his view, a Korean immigrant working by his wits contributes more to the economy than a dozen MBAs. To this it may be added that scientific training is not the only factor in becoming number one. The Japanese turn out well-engineered

*Despite its unfortunate title Morris Kline's *Why Johnny Can't Add* (St. Martin's Press, 1973) provides an excellent post-mortem on the New Math.
***Wealth and Poverty* (Basic Books, 1981), pp. 147–148.

products. But part of their appeal is that they are also pleasing to behold. (We ought not to forget that Japan has always honored art, even to their serving food in floral configurations.) The Japanese are also superb at sales, without slapping a single back, tailoring their approaches to the needs and customs of a hundred different nations. This does not mean that schools should teach international sales and industrial design. Clever management and the widespread desire to make good are the critical factors in Japanese success. Stressing deficiencies in our schools can deflect attention from shortcomings in areas occupied entirely by adults.

Despite their professions of egalitarianism, all the reports end up hedging their bets. Thus while *A Nation at Risk* asks that we "demand the best effort and performance from all students, whether they are gifted or less able, affluent or disadvantaged," it does not assume that all will rise to the challenge. Accordingly, the National Commission on Excellence in Education goes on to propose that "placement and grouping . . . should be guided by the academic progress of students." In other words, tracking. And, as a contingency plan, it also suggests "alternative classrooms, programs, and schools" for "continually disruptive students." The only problem is that once pupils are grouped by performance or progress, or segregated in special schools, few in the slow lanes ever manage to catch up.

Educating Americans takes tracking even further, calling for the establishment of 2,000 "exemplary" elementary and secondary schools specializing in mathematics and science. These would enroll the top 2 percent of the students in the nation's public schools many if not most to be chosen at an early age. (North Carolina has taken the lead already, with a boarding school concentrating on science and mathematics.) *Making the Grade* offers a parallel proposal, recommending federal stipends for two million students who "have been unable to learn in public schools." These scholarships would enable them to attend a series of "small-scale academies" which would presumably start up once public money was available. Given the tone of the Twentieth Century Fund report—it charges that we have given too much attention to "equality of opportunity"—it seems unlikely that much of this money would go to youngsters from inner-city schools. Middle-class parents who think they have gifted children would be the ones more likely to file for the scholarships.

In this connection, we frequently hear of exceptional youngsters who need—and deserve—special educational treatment. It is one thing for parents to believe that they have talented offspring. It is quite another to have public policy based on this premise. Should we have special schools or classes for children identified as gifted? A lot of people seem to think so, including members of the US Senate, which now has a "Children's Caucus," presided over by Connecticut's liberal senator Christopher Dodd. At a recent hearing fourteen-year-olds told how boring they found the public-school classes they had to attend. ("I feel gifted children are a natural resource that is being wasted," testified a girl from Dodd's home state. "We are America's future, won't you invest in us?" pleaded a lad from the Pacific Northwest.) Senator Dodd estimated that the nation has 2.5 million of these outstanding youngsters, of all classes and races, half of whom have never been discovered.*

Of course a society should search for people with unusual talents, whether they are five or fifty-five. However, youngsters identified as "gifted" are children who master schoolwork more quickly than their peers. (Those who show artistic talent early are a different case, because they are often average classroom students.) I agree that it must be boring to have to sit listening to lessons you already understand. John Goodlad offers the suggestion that these youngsters work on a regular basis with their classmates who need help. In doing so, they would discover that explaining things to others can be considerably more difficult than simply understanding it yourself and is a skill worth developing in its own right. (They might find they have a flair for it and decide to become teachers.)

Still, what we are talking about is precocity: youngsters who absorb adult knowledge faster than their age-mates. Anyone who has been a teacher has had students who performed at extraordinary levels. But having acknowledged this, I must add that those of us who have been teaching long enough to encounter those stu-

*The New York Times, November 14, 1983. See also David Elkind, The Hurried Child: Growing Up Too Fast Too Soon (Addison-Wesley, 1981).

dents one or two decades later will testify that in most cases the brilliance has worn off. Indeed, there is no evidence that precocious children as a group go on to contribute more to society than those whose talents emerge later. Examine any Amherst College reunion class or one from the Bronx High School of Science. They may be solid citizens and respectably intelligent; but hardly a payoff for the investments lavished on them. Every society has people of merit who should be discovered and encouraged. But in trying to identify the meritorious at an early age, we too often end up with the precocious, and they are quite a different group.

Ernest Boyer disputes the view that the schools should be skewed to the supposed needs of the work force. In *High School* he asks that we make liberal education a universal goal. "People who cannot communicate are powerless," he writes. "People who know nothing of their past are culturally impoverished." The United States will simply be a better place if its inhabitants are literate, thoughtful, and share "a core of common learning." His book, which acknowledges Goodlad's findings, is ostensibly based on month-long visits at fifteen public high schools, with enrollments ranging from fewer than three hundred to more than five thousand. It is not clear from the text how far Boyer participated in this fieldwork, since he had a staff of twenty-three "observers" who wrote up reports.

But *High School* is less a research project than Boyer's own book. A former commissioner of education and currently head of the Carnegie Foundation for the Advancement of Teaching, he takes learning seriously. Literature and history head his list of required subjects, and he feels science sequences should "distinguish between the training of generalists and specialists." But his most emphatic recommendation is that the schools should show students how to write. Boyer believes that "clear writing leads to clear thinking; clear thinking is the basis of clear writing." He would have all pupils take at least one course demanding much written work, with the classes sufficiently small so teachers can comment on each assignment. *High School* skirts the question of the extent to which good writing can be "taught," and this is probably just as well. My own experience has been that writing is often self-taught. If frequent papers are assigned and criticized, however, students become more coherent and emerge with styles of their own. Insofar as this is so, the need is less for brilliant teachers than for reasonably competent ones with time to read those stacks of themes. I might add that aides and assistants will not do; students deserve to hear from the teachers of their class.

Boyer also holds that "the school program should offer a single track for all students." This prescription may make sense in some suburban settings where almost everyone goes to college. But he does not tell us how single-track instruction will succeed in schools with youngsters at different levels of preparation. In fact, this dilemma was put to one of Boyer's own observers by the principal of a big-city school: "Our students range from National Merit winners to kids who can hardly read and write. Some go to Harvard and others are mechanics. It's just crazy to think that one curriculum can serve them all." If we set "a core of common learning" as our goal, then it must reach those "kids who can hardly read and write." Boyer is right in refusing to write off children from sub-literate homes. Still, America is not a classless society; class segregation is evident in our schools, a fact Boyer does not directly confront. His argument would be stronger had *High School* depicted a few classrooms where the offspring of executives sit next to children from welfare families. But of all the books under review his is the only one that tries to define how education can contribute to a more interesting and thoughtful life—and not just a more competitive one.

Apart from the account of "Sister Michael" in *Horace's Compromise,* the books and reports avoid discussing private schools. This could be construed as a commitment to public education, or—more likely—an admission that the private schools as a subject are too hot to handle. For example, honesty might require evaluating some religious schools as mediocre. Also the issue of public aid is one few people wish to raise. And there is the fact that many private schools serve as class preserves, where some of the authors or commissioners may have sent their children.

Still, the parents of 11 percent of America's youngsters choose to pay for private education. This sector has changed a lot in recent years and can best be sorted out with a few statistics. In 1981, the most recent year for figures, 5 million children attended private schools, down from 5.2 million in 1971. However, this 5 percent drop was less than half the 11 percent decline in public enrollments. Consequently, in 1981 the private share was in fact higher than it had been a decade earlier.

Whereas Catholic schools once stood well in the lead in enrollments, this is no longer the case. Between 1971 and 1981, their student population fell by 21 percent. And in the last twenty years, 40 percent of their high schools and 27 percent of elementary schools have actually closed. In 1981, Catholic schools still drew 63 percent of all private students, but this is down from 77 percent in 1971.* This trend seems likely to continue, if only because the fees needed for survival are well above what most parents are willing to pay. One reason is that over three-quarters of Catholic schoolteachers are now lay people who are paid competitive salaries. We cannot expect many successors to "Sister Michael" in the future. Public funds, if they ever arrived, would be too little and too late.

However, lay schools and those under other religious sponsorships are growing, despite the decline in the number of school-age children. The former enroll about 800,000 students and the latter slightly more than one million. The leading religious sponsors are Lutherans, Baptists, and Seventh-Day Adventists; almost no research has been done on what happens in these schools. Some started as "Christian Academies" during public desegregation, and others continue for lower-middle-class parents who put a premium on discipline and religious instruction. Most old-line secular boarding schools are flourishing, but their overall enrollments are not high. The big expansion has been among day schools, catering to upper-middle-class families, not only in cities but also in the suburbs. Many suburban public schools have lost their elite veneer, because of the broader base on which they now draw. In many two-income households, private tuitions absorb much of the second check even before the college years.

The most comprehensive study of public and private education was published by James Coleman in 1982. His survey, *High School Achievement,* drew mainly on Catholic schools for the pri-

*National Center for Education Statistics, *The Condition of Education: A Statistical Report* (1982).

vate side. (His sample included some with other sponsorships, but
not enough for generalized findings.) Students at the Catholic
schools came away with higher test scores in every academic subject, and this was also the case with children from low-income and
single-parent homes. Indeed, the Catholic schools showed a smaller gap between poorer and better-off youngsters, leading Coleman to remark that they "come closer to the American ideal of the
'common school' educating all alike, than do the public schools."
Moreover, they accomplish this with slightly larger classes.

But the big variable, of course, is "selection bias": the public
schools must take every pupil who walks in the door. Coleman
shows that Catholic enrollments are more varied than people tend
to think, with 15 percent nonwhite and 9 percent non-Catholic.
Even so, only 22 percent of their students had family incomes under $16,000, compared with 37 percent in the public schools. Hav-
ing fewer pupils from the lowest economic group can make a huge
difference and may account for most of the variations in the test
scores.

Unfortunately, Coleman and his colleagues did not interview
any parents, settling for information the children put on forms.
What does appear, however, is that the Catholic schools are selective not simply in that they can expel unruly students, but that the
low-income parents who apply have a notably strong desire for
something better for their children. One index of this is that Catholic pupils spend more time on homework and less watching television, both suggestive of parental discipline. Of course, most poor
families—which produce most of the dropouts—can hardly afford
to send their children to private schools. Indeed, few send their
children to "magnet" schools in the public system or take advantage of voluntary busing programs. None of the books or reports
under review here proposes what might be done for youngsters
from low-income homes where adult determination is lacking.

Taken together, the books and reports devote surprisingly little space to financing their proposals or to potential sources of support. From the demographic standpoint, their proposals come at
a time when the constituency for improved education seems shaky.
As a proportion of the total population, school-age children and
their parents are at an all-time low. Between 1960 and 1982, the

proportion of Americans aged six through seventeen dropped by 22 percent, and parents as a group fell by 24 percent From 1970 to 1980, elementary and high school enrollments declined in all but ten of the states. The United States is a "mature" society now, and most calls on public funds involve adult wants and needs.

Adult Americans vary in their feelings about children, so it would be unwise to generalize. At one extreme are retirement communities that don't want youngsters around, even for short stays. Many people who are middle-aged and older feel they have paid their share of taxes and school fees for education and don't want to start again. At the same time, the schools no longer en-counter the hostility they did when "progressive" tendencies were under attack. Paul Peterson, in an essay appended to *Making the Grade,* indicates that school bond issues are doing rather well. During the 1970s, almost half of them went down to defeat; now the passage rate is up, at 73 percent, about where it was in the 1960s when children were in style. Of course there are not as many offerings now, and these have fewer frills attached. Peterson also points out that the baby-boom offspring are themselves be-coming parents. Since they are an outsize group, the number of children in the country will be on the rise once again. However, their reproduction rate will be nothing like that of a generation ago.

Each year, the Census conducts its "fertility survey," in which it asks women how many children they "expect" to have in the fu-ture. In the past, a majority generally said three or four; now most say one or two. Indeed, among young women who have not yet had children, as many as 31 percent say they do not expect to have any ever.* Their views may of course change, as may the circum-stances of their lives. Nevertheless, the fact remains that childless-ness—not merely the postponement of childbearing—is on the rise. The main reason is that children are expensive, given the ex-periences and outfitting parents feel obliged to provide. Women contemplating lifetime careers may also be thinking twice; in such projections they frequently find that no time is the "best time" to have children. And the availability of abortion means the number, or none at all, can be planned.

*Bureau of the Census, *Fertility of American Women* (April 1983).

Public education lacks the kind of constituency it had when birth rates were high and schools were linked to social mobility, especially in the expanding suburbs. The last infusion of funds involved special programs for handicapped children. While this was a cause no one could object to, such classes have proved very costly. (One effect of their small size has been to reduce, at least on paper, figures for pupil-teacher ratios.) Another problem is that public enrollments are becoming increasingly nonwhite, with the consequence that some citizens cease identifying with the schools.

As matters now stand, I can detect no visible sentiment for raising education's share of federal or local outlays. Nor does it seem likely that fears of economic decline will spur support for increasing teachers' salaries in any serious way, or reducing the size of classes or work loads. Some states are already raising graduation requirements, and it will be interesting to see if the result will be more knowledgeable students, an increase in attrition, or a combination of the two. Indeed, the current debate over education, like so many before it, illuminates the symbolic uses of our schools. We project onto them nostalgia for a past that only partially existed, plus blueprints for a future we may not entirely want; and our fantasies about them are underpinned by the belief that here is a subject in which anyone can be an expert.

At this point, all we can say with certainty is that no one really knows how far classroom education contributes to the kind of people we ultimately become. But if the schools leave a lot to be desired, the quality of educational commentary has declined even further. We no longer have commanding figures like John Dewey and Robert Hutchins, who, in their different ways, tried to create a vision of an educated citizenry whose members would have some chance at something that could be called the good life. That this goal, however nebulous, is all but absent from current books and reports is far more disconcerting than our lag in teaching algorithms to restless teenagers.

III. ISSUES

EDITOR'S INTRODUCTION

The third section of this compilation addresses some of the most prominent issues raised in the reform reports and in the books and articles that have followed: the erosion of the curriculum, bilingual education, merit pay and master teacher plans, the U. S. schools compared with those of other countries, and tuition tax credits for private schools.

The first three articles deal with the dilution of secondary school curriculum. In "The Schools We Deserve," Diane Ravitch, a specialist in education reform movements writing in *New Republic,* diagnoses the causes of the dilution of the secondary school curriculum. As electives replaced a hard-core curriculum of basic courses, the touchy problem of "tracking" students— assigning them to different achievement levels—was evaded. The most able students selected the more challenging courses and prepared themselves for college, while the less able chose electives in guitar-playing and bachelor living, and graduated without basic skills. In this way, they "tracked" themselves, an arrangement, Ravitch points out, that reflects the country's uncertainty about education—whether it is important to ensure quality education for all or only for some. In the following article from *USA Today* "Meeting the Needs for a High-Technology America," Robert P. Henderson points out that the deterioration of the science curriculum has had damaging consequences for industry. He notes that Japan, with only half the population of the U.S., graduates more engineers annually. The neglect of science education in American schools has reached the point at which only a small number of students study chemistry or physics. In "In Math & Science, an 'F,'" Jeremiah Baruch, writing in *Commonweal,* extends Henderson's argument, pointing out that the U. S. now ranks behind the Soviet Union, West Germany, and Japan in scientific literacy. He describes pending legislation that is designed to lure mathematicians and scientists into the teaching profession.

The next four articles take up the politically sensitive question of bilingual education, funded by the federal government in response to Hispanic and other ethnic group demands for recognition of their cultural heritages. Tom Bethell, a Washington editor of *Harper's* magazine, indicts the bilingual education programs in over ninety different languages as a boondoggle. In the following article Tomás Arciniega, an Hispanic educator writing in *Educational Research Quarterly*, believes that a termination of bilingual education would have disastrous consequences for Hispanic students, whose drop-out rate is already 85 percent. Abigail Thernstrom, in "Bilingual Mis-education," from the *New Republic*, updates the controversy in her discussion of the Reagan administration's effort to cut back on bilingual education programs. Bringing the issue further up to date is Senator S. I. Hayakawa's proposal before Congress, discussed in his address "Bilingual Education Improvement Act" from *Vital Speeches of the Day*. Senator Hayakawa would prefer instruction in English as a Second Language (ESL), favors making bilingual education optional, and would have an amendment added to the constitution declaring English the official language of the country.

Merit pay and master teacher plans are the subject of the next two articles. Dorothy Wickenden's piece "Merit Pay Won't Work" from the *New Republic* notes that merit pay schemes of various kinds have been tried in the schools in the past and have failed. "Education Reform: Merit Pay and Master Teacher Plans," an address by Albert Shanker reprinted from *Vital Speeches of the Day*, is one of many articles skeptical of the merit pay plan put forward by the Reagan administration. Shanker's address, however, is particularly notable, since, as president of the American Federation of Teachers, he expresses the viewpoint of teachers themselves.

The next article takes up the frequently discussed issue of how well U. S. schools compare with those of other countries. Torsten Husén, a specialist in international scholastic testing writing in *Phi Delta Kappan*, discusses the problem of verifying achievement when schools in different countries vary widely in the number and quality of students they admit and teach. American schools, he notes, do less well on international test scores than those in France,

England, and Germany, but the European schools have more selective admission policies. European and Soviet education is pursued with greater rigor for selected students, but education in
Japan is astonishing in the performance it demands of all students.

The final articles deal with tuition tax credits to private
schools which have met with particular opposition from liberals,
who regard them as an attack on the egalitarian commitment of
public education. John Merrow's article "The Tuition Tax
Dodge," reprinted from *New Republic*, points out the many flaws
in the proposal. An editorial from the Catholic magazine *America*
supports tuition tax credits, however, and a further defense is
presented in Thomas Sowell's article "Tuition Tax Credits: A Social Revolution" from *American Education*.

THE SCHOOLS WE DESERVE[1]

"To the casual observer, American education is a confusing
and not altogether edifying spectacle. It is productive of endless
fads and panaceas; it is pretentiously scientific and at the same
time pathetically conventional; it is scornful of the past, yet pain-
fully inarticulate when it speaks of the future." This strikingly
contemporary observation was made by the educational philoso-
pher Boyd Bode in *The New Republic* in 1930. Since then, American schools have lurched from crisis to crisis, and their internal
confusion and aimlessness remain intact.

During the past half-century, the schools have been persistent-
ly battered by controversy and crisis, much of it growing out of
efforts to redirect the purposes of the schools. In the 1930s, heated
pedagogical battles between progressive educators and traditional-
ists were decided when the progressives secured dominance in the
nation's teachers' colleges and professional educators' associations.
In the postwar 1940s, the schools were handicapped by critical

[1]Reprint of an article by Diane Ravitch, professor of history and education at Teachers College, Columbia University. *New Republic*. 184:23–27. Ap. 18, '81. Copyright © 1981 by the New Republic. Reprinted
by permission.

shortages of teachers and buildings, low teacher salaries, and the advent of the baby boom generation. In the early 1950s, the schools were attacked by a variety of critics—from those who objected to the anti-intellectualism of the latest progressive fad, known as "life adjustment education," to the reactionary vigilantes who wanted to cleanse the schools of "subversive" teachers and textbooks. The orbiting of Sputnik in 1957 marked a new crisis, when Americans discovered the costs of neglecting science, mathematics, and foreign languages in the secondary schools. Meanwhile, the prolonged struggle against racial inequality, both before and after the *Brown* decision, provided a recurrent source of strife. And then, in the mid-1960s, schools were again under fire, this time because of student protests and reformers who advocated such innovations as open classrooms, schools-without-walls, experiential learning, deschooling, and other arrangements whose common denominator was greater student choice and diminished adult authority.

The vast and variegated educational system that we have today, with all its virtues and flaws, is largely the product of policies shaped by responses to these events. In assessing the rising tide of criticism of the past five years, it is important to recall that the schools have tried to do, and for the most part have done successfully, what was demanded of them. Every nation gets the schools that it deserves, and we have today a system that reflects our own conflicts about the relative importance of different social and educational values.

For the past generation no goal has been more important to educational policy-makers than expanding access to educational opportunity for all youth. Whether one looks at high school graduation rates or college enrollment, it is clear that remarkable progress has been made. At mid-century, about 50 percent graduated from high school; the figure today is 85 percent. From 1968 to 1978, black enrollment grew from 6.4 percent to more than 10 percent of all college students, and the proportion of females increased from 39 percent to 48 percent. For the first time in our history, access to higher education is universal. A recent study by the College Board found that one-third of post-secondary institutions are "open-door," accepting all applicants regardless of their academic credentials; more than half are "selective," accepting only those who meet their qualifications, but nonetheless accepting most or all of those who apply for admission; and just eight percent are "competitive," accepting only a portion of qualified applicants. As college enrollments shrink in the years ahead, the number of competitive institutions will drop.

Yet having pursued the goal of increased participation so single-mindedly and successfully, educators are greeted not with laurels but with brickbats. While the schools were devising ways to retain students by meeting demands for "relevance," the pendulum began to swing, and a new critique of the schools emerged, which assumed mass education as a given but focused on the issue of quality. If there was a single event that precipitated the new public mood, it was the revelation in 1975 that scores on the Scholastic Aptitude Test for college entry had slipped steadily for 10 years. Other pieces of what seemed to be a jigsaw puzzle began to fall into place. At opposite ends of the country, angry parents sued the local school district for granting a high school diploma to their functionally illiterate children (both lost). The National Assessment of Educational Progress released a survey which showed that eight percent of 17-year-old whites were functionally illiterate, as well as a shocking 42 percent of 17-year-old blacks (since 75 percent of black students graduate from high schools, the diploma apparently had become merely a certificate of attendance for a substantial minority). There was a growing recognition that automatic promotion from grade to grade, regardless of attainment, had contributed to masking learning deficiencies and that the high school diploma no longer represented any particular level of proficiency. One response to the accumulation of bad news was the adoption of state-mandated minimum competency tests, which spread from one state (Arizona) in 1976 to 38 states in 1980, a spontaneous national movement without a spokesman or a national organization to promote it.

An extraordinary thing has happened to achievement levels since the mid-1960s. SAT scores, which had been a consistent measure of verbal and mathematical skills, have dropped dramatically. Median verbal scores have fallen from a high of 478 in 1963 to a new low of 424 in 1980; in the same period, mathematical scores fell from 502 to 466. On both tests girls' scores dropped more sharply than those of boys. The first reaction to the score drops was to attribute them to the fact that large numbers of minorities, females, and low-income students joined the college-bound pool during this time of expansion. But in fact the composition of the test-takers has been fairly stable since 1970, and the score drops have been even more extensive since then. It is more telling that the number and proportion of high-scoring students have fallen precipitously; the number of seniors who scored over 650 fell from 53,800 (5.3 percent) in 1972 to 29,000 in 1980 (2.9 percent). The shrinkage of the top-scorers has proceeded steadily since the mid-1960s and obviously is unrelated to the overall composition of the test-taking group.

When the College Board's blue-ribbon panel to investigate the causes of the score decline released its findings in 1977, it rounded up the usual suspects: the decline of the family; working mothers; television; the trauma of a decade of Vietnam, civil disorders, and Watergate; drugs; and sex-role stereotyping. When it came to describing the responsibility of schools for the score declines, the panel noted that "There have unquestionably been changes over the past 10 to 15 years in the standards to which students at all levels of education are held. Absenteeism formerly considered intolerable is now condoned. An 'A' or 'B' means a good deal less than it used to. Promotion from one grade to another has become almost automatic. Homework has apparently been cut about in half." It pointedly concluded, too, that "less thoughtful and critical reading is now being demanded and done," and "careful writing has apparently about gone out of style." After much sociological wandering, the panel came to a simple conclusion: the retreat from thoughtful reading and careful writing may explain a good deal about declining verbal skills, and it suggests changes that are within the reach of the school.

The unusual attention paid to the SAT provoked claims that there was something peculiar about the test itself and that it was somehow out of phase with the times. Unfortunately for this thesis, the SAT declines were reflected in other standardized tests. Researchers Annegret Harnischfeger and David E. Wiley analyzed other major tests, including the American College Test (which many colleges use instead of the SAT), the Iowa testing program (used statewide in Iowa and elsewhere), and the Minnesota Scholastic Aptitude Test (administered to more than 90 percent of Minnesota high school juniors). They found strikingly consistent patterns of decline: rising achievement levels until the mid-1960s, then a steady decline which accelerates as students reach higher grades and which is particularly pronounced in verbal areas. The only exception to the overall downward trend was in the subject-matter achievement tests of the SAT and the ACT science test. Rather than being contradictory, this phenomenon suggested a bifurcation between the top students and everyone else, with the best students doing exceptionally well and the others falling further behind.

Although Harnischfeger and Wiley were careful to insist that the score declines had many causes, they nonetheless argued that substantial enrollment declines in traditional subjects "parallel closely the test score decline patterns." They reported that fewer students were taking regular English, American history, math, and science courses, although the advanced college-preparatory courses did not experience a comparable dropoff in enrollment. Once again, the best students were taking the courses they needed, while everyone else was—doing what? Not enrolling in vocational or business courses, which also showed declines. Apparently the schools offered fewer instructional programs and more work-study options.

Last year the Gannett newspapers sent an investigative team into two dozen schools. Like Harnischfeger and Wiley, they discovered pervasive dilution of the secondary school curriculum. They described schools in which high school credit was offered for such courses as astrology, marriage simulation, cheerleading, student government, child care, and mass media. The average public school, they observed, had three hours each day of instructional time, compared to more than four hours in the average nonpublic school. In one junior high school they visited, the typical student spent two hours and 12 minutes in an academic class.

Concern about enrollment trends in science, mathematics, and foreign languages has provoked some scathing commentaries on the state of curricular requirements. The President's Commission on Foreign Language and International Studies complained in 1979 that "Americans' incompetence in foreign languages is nothing short of scandalous, and it is becoming worse." The commission pointed out that "only 15 percent of American high school students now study a foreign language—down from 24 percent in 1965. The decline continues." It also noted with alarm that only one out of 20 high school students studies a foreign language beyond the second year, while four years' study is considered necessary for competence. Equally shocking is the tiny number of Americans in high school or college who learn the languages of such major powers as Russia, China, or Japan. In fact, the number of Russian language students in American secondary schools dropped sharply, from 27,000 in 1965 to 11,000 in 1976.

Last fall a report sponsored by the National Science Foundation and the Department of Education warned of "a current trend toward virtual scientific and technological illiteracy. . . ." America's scientists continue to be internationally preeminent in research and publication, but the American people are increasingly ignorant about science and technology. Again the theme of bifurcation appears: "Those who are the best seem to be learning about as much as they ever did, while the majority of students learn less and less." Will important national decisions be made by a scientific elite, or will there be a broad enough diffusion of scientific knowledge for citizens to understand vital, science-related issues?

And there have been persistent complaints about students' writing ability. Few high school students have ever had systematic writing instruction of the sort that involves thinking through a topic, preparing multiple drafts, receiving written and oral comments from the teacher, and revising papers after the teacher returns them. Recognizing that a national problem exists, many colleges have introduced remedial writing classes. People often mistakenly assume that such classes are a response to rising numbers of minority students. At one major state university, more than half the freshman class this year is enrolled in a remedial writing course. This fall Bard College in New York will try a different approach. All incoming Bard freshmen will have to participate in an intensive three-week "Workshop in Language and Thinking" before regular classes begin. For six days a week, eight hours a day, students will learn how to read, write, and organize ideas. They will prepare a written assignment each day, which will be returned with a critique the following day. The Bard workshop is more concentrated and individualized than most such courses and avoids taking time away from regular college studies, permitting the student to improve his or her skills before beginning first-semester courses.

Well, then, what's going on here? How is it that some students finish high school with few skills and less knowledge, that others arrive at college underprepared for college-level work, while a small minority of the same graduating class has been remarkably well educated in their special fields of interest? This diverse range of outcomes actually is consistent with the changes that have been introduced in schools, especially public schools, during the past 15 years or so. In response to student demands for greater flexibility, colleges began to lower their entrance requirements in the mid-1960s, and high schools followed their lead by abolishing certain course requirements. (After all, goes the argument, if you don't need a foreign language to get into college, why should high schools require you to take one?) As requirements fell, the notion of a common curriculum was undermined. To maintain student interest, courses in traditional subjects were fragmented into electives and mini-courses, particularly in the "soft," humanistic areas like English and history, and requirements in the "hard" subjects like mathematics, science, and foreign language were eased or eliminated. In a time of rapidly proliferating electives, every felt need produced pressure for a new course, for values education, moral education, death education, consumer education (to name but a few), in addition to such old standbys as career education, sex education, drug education, and driver education. Inasmuch as the curriculum is a zero-sum game, with only a certain number of hours each day, every course added to a student's schedule displaces some other course. The proliferation of new courses and the easing of requirements meant that students could substitute a fun course like "mass media" for a demanding course in literature, and many evidently did.

With the authority of the common curriculum under challenge, it became difficult for educators to justify, or even to remember how to justify, any given course content. Why should students read Melville or e.e. cummings or Milton? Why did they need to know anything about the Greeks or Romans? Why learn a foreign language? If they weren't going to become scientists, why should they be compelled to study science? Wouldn't they be just as happy, happier even, if they never studied chemistry or physics or algebra or geometry? In many high schools the requirements and the common curriculum collapsed like eggshells. This meant that, after meeting minimal state-imposed requirements, students could practically design their own program. The best students, those with the highest motivation and purpose, continued to take advanced college-preparatory courses; the average and below-average students, who might have learned more if the expectations of the school had been clear and consistent, found that they could easily navigate around courses that appeared too challenging.

Uncertainty about what students should study reflected uncertainty about why they should study, and this self-doubt undermined the teachers' sense of purpose and authority. This confusion, quite understandable in a time of student unrest and societal permissiveness, made it increasingly difficult for teachers to impose demands on students, which in turn led to lower teacher expectations. Truancy began to rise as did discipline problems, like drug use during the school day. Homework and essays, once staples of schooling, fell into disfavor. Students didn't like to do the "extra" work, and teachers were relieved of reading and grading the 100 or more papers that would be turned in by their different classes. Part of a major new study by James Coleman, comparing public and private schools, documents how little time most public high school students spend on homework. Three out of four students do one hour or less each school night, while one of four does less than one hour each week. Not surprisingly, the students with the least homework watch the most television.

Homework may seem insignificant as an educational issue, but it does matter. Homework provides the necessary time for thoughtful writing and serious reading, time that is rarely available during school hours. Can the large majority who spend an hour or less each day on homework have time to read a novel or to write a short story? It seems not only unlikely but impossible. Homework matters, too, because of the importance of what is called "time-on-task." The phrase is educationese for the common-sense proposition that educational performance is directly related to the amount of time spent learning. Researchers have observed that a large part of the school day is consumed by changing of classes, interruptions, announcements, and disciplinary problems, and that a large part of the time even in good classrooms is not instructional time. Anything that extends the amount of time spent learning is likely to improve student performance. This does not suggest any particular method of teaching, since students can be fully engaged in individual or small group projects, but it does suggest the value of homework in stretching out the amount of learning time available to the student. It also explains why absenteeism, class-cutting, and disruptive behavior in the classroom rob students of precious learning time.

The dilemma of American education has persisted since the founding of public schools in the early 19th century. What kind of schooling is most appropriate for a democratic society? American educators championed a common school education, in the belief that it would promote equality, fraternity, and social progress. Common schools usually meant what we now consider elementary education and, even today, no one doubts that the curriculum for young children should be more or less the same for all. The problem arises as children become adolescents and their interests, talents, and abilities begin to diverge. It would be unrealistic and unsound to advocate that all young people should study the same things at the same time, in lockstep fashion, since the quick learners will find the pace too tedious and the slow learners will find it too fast. The solution to the problem of individual differences has been to establish different programs, depending on students' ability. This has taken various forms, but two especially. The first is tracking, which is determined by the students' apparent educational or occupational destinies, such as college-preparatory, vocational, and general. Because of its anti-democratic implications, tracking has been in disfavor. The second approach has been ability-grouping—dividing children into classes or learning groups based on ability, while having everyone learn the same subject-matter. Ability-grouping is still used in many schools, but in some, such as in Washington, DC, it was banned by the courts as racially discriminatory. (The acting superintendent of the DC schools recently complained that the black middle class pulled their children out of the District's public schools when ability-grouping was discontinued.) So the schools today try variants on these approaches, but find it particularly tempting to move toward lowering requirements and expanding electives. That way, the school doesn't have to have any policy of separating students by ability, but can rely on the students to do the sorting themselves.

But is it democratic for schools to permit students to decide whether they should or should not learn those things that every informed citizen should know? It is not clear why educators, more than any other profession, should become ensnared to the point of confusion by the word "democratic." Under that mantle, responsible authority has been attacked as authoritarianism, and students have been allowed to choose between an education of value and something decidedly less. Perhaps the message that schools send, when they suggest that there is no core of vital knowledge and skills, is that students can elect not only what to study but whether to come to school.

Whenever it is suggested that the schools can strive for a higher level of universal education, the refrain is quickly heard that some students don't have the brains or the inclination to study such things as history, literature, science, mathematics, foreign languages, and the arts. The challenge that has not been met is to present the same subject matter through a variety of teaching techniques and to make it immediate and valuable to all. This may be an impossible dream, but it is a dream worth pursuing. According to reports about Japan and France, universal quality education is not beyond imagination. In *Japan as Number One*, Ezra Vogel writes of a national education system that has produced a highly literate public, knowledgeable about international affairs and about the intricacies of scientific issues like nuclear power and pollution. And Paul Gagnon, a French historian at the University of Massachusetts, has written about widespread popular support in France for "the right to culture." The technological society, Gagnon notes, with its threat of alienation and boredom and its promise of extended leisure time, makes indispensable to everyone "a personal culture, a furnished mind, practiced senses, skilled hands." All French adolescents, not just the select few, receive an education by the age of 15 or 16 that is the equivalent of what an American student covers by the end of the sophomore year in college.

Despite our dissatisfaction, we will not soon transform our educational system. It is not that it can't be done. The problem is that we lack consensus about whether there should be a common curriculum, whether there are knowledge and skills that everyone should have. If we believed that it was important to have a highly literate public, to have a public capable of understanding history and politics and economics, to have citizens who are knowledgeable about science and technology, to have a society in which the powers of verbal communication are developed systematically and intentionally, then we would know what we wanted of our schools. Until we do, we get the schools we deserve, which accurately reflect our own confusion about the value of education.

MEETING THE NEEDS FOR A HIGH-TECHNOLOGY AMERICA[2]

Persons qualified to teach technical subjects in our primary and secondary grades are even scarcer than well-educated students. The state of our schools and the quality of students have become a matter of grave concern. These concerns have been expressed from many segments of our nation. Probably none, however, have been more outspoken than the high-technology industry, since the knowledge base of that industry is rapidly eroding. The dynamics of all our knowledge-based institutions have, over the past two decades, shifted away from math and science, thus weakening the historical relationship between education and

[2]Reprint of an article by Robert P. Henderson, chairman of the board of Itek Corporation, Lexington, Kentucky. *USA Today*. 112:47–49. N. '83. Copyright © 1983 by Society for the Advancement of Education. Reprinted by permission.

the industrial economy. At the college and university level, this has resulted in an insufficient number of scientists and engineers to satisfy demand. More importantly, it has resulted in the undermining of the foundation of all higher education—our primary and secondary public school systems.

Spokesmen for high technology have been vocal because they have been affected the most by the erosion of our knowledge institutions, a weakening which contributed to a shortfall of about 25,-000 engineers in 1981. This shortage has worsened for several years. The end of the tunnel is now darker than ever before. Demand will continue to outpace supply as new technologies develop and the flow of high-technology products to the consumer market continues its rapid increase. The marriage of computers and communications, the advent of robotics, the evolution of products based on VLSI circuitry—all will require new human technological resources.

If they are not available, this country will continue to lose markets to its overseas competitors. It is common knowledge that Japan, a country with half our population, graduates more engineers each year than the U.S. Having abundant human resources is one reason why, in four short years, from 1974 to 1978, Japan captured one-third of the market for one of today's most important computer parts—the 16K random access memory chip. That product was invented in the U.S. for a market in which we were dominant, but it quickly went the way of color television sets and automobiles.

It does not appear enough engineers will be available. A recent survey of projected demand for electronic engineers alone indicated that the shortfall in this discipline would exceed 123,000 by 1985—and this assumes an almost 12% per year increase in engineering graduates. The long-term forecast is even more dismal. Between now and 1991, because of changing demographics, this country will experience a decline of nearly one-third in the number of high school students. This is not a projection; these future students have already been born.

With increasing requirements for scientists and engineers, and with a decreasing student body, our total educational system has to change to accurately reflect the market for college graduates.

This is not happening now. In a nation with a surplus of lawyers, 35,000 more are added each year. The current output of elementary teachers is another example. Unless we make this change, we will continue to direct students to careers for which there are no jobs. This change can be made.

Two and one-half decades ago, we were faced with this same challenge in a different way. The Soviets achieved the most dramatic engineering accomplishment of that time with the launch of Sputnik I. Two months later, America's first earth satellite exploded on its launch pad. Our prestige plunged to new lows. American educators responded admirably to the clamor for increased education in science and engineering; and for a short time—but for a short time only—it was sufficient.

The Downgrading to Technology

Only 66 years separated Orville Wright's first flight and Neil Armstrong's first giant step to the lunar surface from Apollo II. What extraordinary technological advances were achieved in this short period! Yet, by 1970, with the fulfillment of John F. Kennedy's challenge to this nation, science and engineering had been downgraded in our list of national priorities.

Why did this happen? In a word: Vietnam. The mid-1960's saw a move away from technology. At this time, much of the technology was defense-oriented, and defense was associated with Vietnam. Since Vietnam was bad, technology was bad. Students shied away from technology and became social workers, teachers, or lawyers. College directed their faculties and facilities to the liberal arts and, in the minds of many, technology is still an area to be looked at with acrid skepticism. Less than one out of 20 of all degrees granted in the U.S. today are in engineering, compared to one out of 10 back in 1960. Everyone has heard that Japan and the Soviet Union produce more engineers in absolute numbers than we do in this country. What is perhaps more surprising is that, as a percentage of the population, so do countries like Bulgaria, Czechoslovakia, Poland, and Hungary—some of them by a factor of four.

This change in attitude and curriculum spread to our primary and secondary schools. The declining curriculum quality in these schools is reflected in the most common measure of academic aptitude. Scholastic Aptitude Test (SAT) scores have been on the decline for more than a decade. The deterioration has been consistent, regardless of the ever-increasing amounts of money, in constant dollars, that the American public has been willing to spend.

Excuses given for lower scores include the fact that a greater percentage of students are taking the test or that the expectations of today's parents are not high. Others discount the test as not being meaningful. Both of these arguments have their merits, but they do not adequately explain the significant decline of student competency in reading, mathematics, and the sciences.

There is another more realistic premise. Students leaving our high schools are less prepared in the basics than the previous generation of Americans. Today, only one-sixth of all high school students take a junior- and senior-level science course. Today, only one-half of all U.S. high school students take a math course after grade 10, creating a need for math remediation by one-half of all entering college freshmen. Today, just 15% of all high school students take a course in chemistry, and only seven per cent in physics.

The 1980 presidential report on science and engineering education concluded that "more students than ever are dropping out of science and mathematics courses, and this trend shows no sign of abating." We now rank fourth in scientific literacy behind the Soviet Union, West Germany, and Japan.

Students opt for the easy way. A listing of the popular courses in a typical high school would include such offerings as "Teenagers and the Law," "Consumer Math," "Personal Consumer Education," and "Child Behavior." This country simply must challenge its students more.

Our industrial and economic competitors do not make this mistake. Consider these examples:

• In Russia, algebra and geometry begin in grades seven and trigonometry is added in grades eight through 10. All Russian students complete five years of physics, four years of chemistry, and one to four years of high school biology.

• In West Germany, biology is introduced in grade three, physics and chemistry in grade five, and increasingly advanced math and science courses are added each year of high school.

• In Japan, 25% of all class time in grades seven to nine is spent on math and science, with trigonometry added in grade nine.

Unlike in the U.S., there apparently is very little dispute in these countries over the quality of their educational programs.

Another thing happens in our elementary grades, where the teaching process plays a role. Until grade six, both male and female students score about equally on standardized math tests. From that time on, females take fewer science and math courses than their male counterparts. By the 12th grade, according to a recent California study, female competency in math has declined to 51% of that of their male counterparts.

Whereas a substantially higher ratio of high school graduates in many other countries go on to become engineers, our children, because of a dearth in math and science courses, do not have the choice to major in these fields. Most students do not take the prerequisite courses which would allow them to enter engineering colleges, and many of those that do take the prerequisites need remedial work.

It has been estimated that half of the students that are qualified to enter our engineering colleges need remedial work at a cost of hundreds of millions of dollars each year. Even the students who take the necessary math courses are not being taught what they need to know. Between 30,000 and 40,000 students enter these schools unprepared for calculus—usually the first year of math in an engineering college.

Upgrading the Curriculum

To improve the standards of our basic educational system, both the quality of curriculum and of the people delivering that curriculum must be raised. Perhaps it is too easy to say that students opt for taking the easy way. Students should not be allowed the option to choose math or science courses against easier electives at the expense of their basic education. Further, in required courses, students can not be totally at fault for not achieving a minimum of competency. For example, most secondary school systems require four years of English, but the achievement levels are equally as dismal in this subject area. A University of California study, run between 1977 and 1980, found that only half of 50,000 students could demonstrate the reading and writing skills necessary for college-level courses.

It will not be an easy task to change curriculum. It will be especially difficult in math and science, since a serious shortage of teachers qualified in those disciplines exists in our nation's public schools. A 1981 national study of estimated supply and demand of secondary science and mathematics teachers found that 16 of the 46, or 35%, of state science supervisors responding characterized the mathematics teacher supply situation in their state as a "critical shortage"; 16 others said they had some shortage.

This shortage is caused by an inadequate number of teachers trained in these subjects. The production of newly qualified mathematics and science teachers has slowed to a trickle. In 1980, for example, Ohio State University, the University of Nebraska, and the University of Minnesota each graduated only one newly qualified mathematics teacher. In science, Connecticut did not produce a single qualified teacher in 1981, while the state of Minnesota produced one.

This is not surprising. Consider a high school student preparing to enter a teaching college. He or she will not be required, in most cases, to take substantial math or science courses in order to qualify for admission. In a teacher's college, without this preparation, a major or minor in these subjects would require extensive additional courses.

As a result, teachers teach subjects that they are unqualified to teach. In some states, the requirements to obtain math or science certification are absurdly minimal, requiring only 18 semester hours of instruction in the area of certification. For complex, technical subjects, this is less than minimal, especially since the courses given students, because of the lack of this preparation in high school, are often elementary.

A recent study in North Carolina showed that fully 70% of their teachers who hold the science certification are certified only in biology. Only 52% of the teachers who taught science in grades seven to nine were appropriately certified, and almost 29% of the teachers who taught science in grades seven through 12 had no science certification at all.

The situation in math is equally as bad; some 22% of the mathematics teaching posts in this country are vacant, and another 26% are filled by teachers not certified or qualified to teach math. In our primary grades, this situation is even worse. A recent national survey indicated that less than 10% of elementary school teachers felt qualified to teach math or science even at this low level.

Presently, there is little indication that this will improve. From 1972 to 1980, the nationwide decline in SAT scores for education majors was over twice that of all undergraduates. Schools of education are now getting the lowest 10 to 20% of entering students, as measured by these scores. These are the very students that have not taken substantial math or science in high school.

The declining SAT scores of education majors and the change in curriculum from basic to social science and "soft" subjects reflect the change in the perception of public schools that has occurred over the past two decades. Many school systems believe that their function is to care for the social welfare of their students. They have assumed a wide variety of non-essential tasks, from nutrition to driver education. Various school systems have mandated courses in such areas as death education, parenting, television education, morals, and, of course, bilingual education—all consuming class time at the expense of essential subjects.

There is no evidence that bilingual education improves the learning ability of students or that courses in morals have lessened the abortion rate of teenagers. Schools can not cure the social ills of the nation and, in trying to do so, they are failing in their primary function to educate. The very students they try to help with a plethora of social programs—the poor, the disadvantaged—suffer the most since, after graduation, they are unprepared for economic reality. Rather than giving these students the foundation to raise their sights, we have doomed them to a life of mediocrity.

A Program for Change

Changes can be made. Almost all children can be taught. Some of this country's best schools are in the ghettos of our urban cities. Few, if any, children are inherently disadvantaged. This country's youth, be they minorities or not, from low-income families or not, can be taught the essential, basic subjects in public schools which would allow them to become engineers if they chose or math teachers if that is what they want to be. Even if they chose not to enter college, they would have the necessary math and English background for training to become a skilled craftsperson or technician, and not be forced to accept menial labor at minimum wage.

Changes will take time. They will have to be phased in gradually after adequate preparations are made, and they will have to be made not only in the curriculum, but with the very people who teach that curriculum.

Our public schools have to emphasize the essentials. In the past, we have erected magnificent edifices with elaborate sports facilities and barely equipped the science labs. School boards have opened campuses and stressed the social aspects of adolescence. They have required only one year of math and science as prerequisites for a diploma, while insisting on four years of physical education. Somehow, the priorities are wrong.

Graduation requirements have to be raised. Four years of English, two years of history, three years each of science and math, two years of a foreign language, plus geography, government, and art should be mandated basic curriculum for high school.

No child has the basic right to a diploma and no one should be promoted for the sake of promotion. Standardized competency tests should be administered periodically to prove proficiency or the subject should be repeated.

Every child, however, does have a right of access to quality education. If that right is seriously abused by any student, educators should not be forced to keep the offender in the mainstream of the system. Education need not be standardized to the least common denominator at the expense of the rights of others.

Teaching quality must improve. Schools of teaching, in this time of surplus teachers, should upgrade entrance requirements.

These same schools should place less emphasis on methods and more on certification courses. The most dedicated person in the world can not teach, lacking knowledge in the subject.

Teachers have to assume a new degree of professionalism, recognizing that they are primarily educators, not social workers. They have to regain pride in their profession. They need to continuously upgrade their own skills and, above all, those skills should be recognized by increased rewards and community support.

There are signs that progress is being made. California, Ohio, and Texas are upgrading curricula and apparently establishing core subject areas. Texas is planning to give competency tests to both teachers and students. Colleges in several states are upgrading entrance requirements. It is a hopeful trend.

We live in the age of high technology. It is a world of digital watches, electronic communications, computerized games, and home computers. Our work is becoming automated and our cars are acquiring computer controls. We are expected to analyze political and social debates and make informed decisions on nuclear energy, hazardous waste, and national defense. Our home, our workplace, and our world have become increasingly complex, while our children are being graduated with fewer and fewer skills. A return to excellence is essential for their well-being and for that of our nation.

IN MATH & SCIENCE, AN 'F'[3]

In his State of the Union address, President Reagan affirmed that, "We Americans are still the technological leaders in most fields. We must keep that edge, and to do so we need to begin renewing the basics—starting with our education system. While we grew complacent, others have acted." After noting that Japan, with less than half our population, graduates appreciably more

[3]Excerpted from an article by Jeremiah Baruch, pseudonym of a Washington writer with a government position. *Commonweal.* 110:204–07. Ap. 8, '83. Copyright © 1983 by Commonweal. Reprinted by permission.

engineers, the president called for a "quality education initiative" as one of his four major education "goals" (the others being tax-exempt college savings accounts, tuition tax credits, and the school prayer amendment). Aiming to encourage "a substantial upgrading of math and science instruction," Mr. Reagan proposed a block grant to the states: funds to the states for this general purpose and used largely at their discretion.

The president steadfastly maintains that elementary and secondary education is a state and local responsibility, a concern he claims is not being adequately addressed. On March 8, before five hundred prize-winning science and math students in Florida, Mr. Reagan said that the United States is in danger of falling behind West Germany, Japan, and the Soviet Union in scientific advancement unless the nation's educational quality improves.

Unlike the U.S., the central government of these industrialized nations significantly determines the curriculum, sets national examinations, and inspects the quality of instruction. As a matter of national policy, they promote comprehensive science and math for everyone, not only those planning to specialize. Statistics indicate the end result; Japanese and Soviet students get at least two more years of science and math than do American students. Since 1970 there has been a trend in the U.S. toward a reduction in high school graduation requirements—only one-third of America's sixteen thousand school districts require more than one year of math and science for graduation. The growing needs of high-technology and energy-related industry run afoul of declining math and science skills. A.T. & T. alone spends $6 million a year to train 14,000 employees in basic arithmetic and writing skills during office hours. Hundreds of other U.S. corporations also report deficient math skills across a wide range of job classifications. According to a 1980 presidential report on science and engineering, the United States now ranks fourth—behind the Soviet Union, West Germany, and Japan—in overall scientific literacy.

The average SAT math score in the United States continues to decline, from 502 in 1963 (the post-Sputnik high) to 466 in 1981. Between 1975 and 1980 remedial math enrollment in public colleges has increased ten times faster than enrollment. One reason for this decline in student performance has been the loss of qualified math and science teachers. The graduation of secondary school teachers has declined during the last decade by 64 percent in science and 78 percent in mathematics. The schools in 1980 lost five times as many science and math teachers to industry as to retirement. By December 1981, half of the math and science teachers were deemed unqualified by the National Science Teachers Association.

The president has focused his attention on the math and science teacher shortage as the major problem of the educational system. His budget submission to Congress allocates $50 million for each of four years to the Department of Education for block grants to the states for scholarships to college graduates who can become qualified to teach secondary math or science in one year. The funds are to be distributed on the basis of the number of high-school age children residing in each state. Those states wishing to receive a grant would be required to submit an annual report describing how the state or local education agency—whichever operates the program—would distribute the funds. Scholarships would be for $5,000 for twelve months, and recipients would have to agree to teach for a reasonable period of time—to be worked out between the individual and the local or state education agency. Also proposed in the president's budget is an increase of $5 million over last fiscal year for the National Science Foundation's (NSF) secondary school science and mathematics improvement program.

Is there an irony to the president's proposal? Perhaps. The president's consternation at American complacency may reflect, to a degree, a situation of his own making. His fiscal 1982 budget sought virtual elimination of the NSF math and science education program (almost half of NSF's entire budget was once consumed by science education). In the last two years the administration has chipped away at the remaining funds to the point that only $15 million would be left in 1983 for graduate fellowships for secondary math and science teachers, as compared to $81 million in 1981. (President Carter had asked for a FY 1982 funding level of $111.9 million.) Now the president has decided that this NSF program should again be built up—albeit by a relatively small amount. Why the change of heart?

One factor may be the politics of the 1984 presidential election. Over the last two years, the list of senators introducing or co-sponsoring math and science education bills has looked like an Iowa Democratic caucus checklist—Senators Cranston, Glenn, Hart, and Hollings. Obviously the president also sees advantages in positioning himself as an advocate of a high-tech economic renaissance rather than as a protector/protectionist of industry.

Another impetus for the change of heart may be that the president's leadership image has not been served well when the bandwagon on the Hill doesn't play to his tune. The momentum for math and science education assistance has been gathering throughout last year—notwithstanding President Reagan. He won few friends with his written message to a May 1982 conclave of scientists, educators, and business leaders called by the National Academy of Sciences to examine weaknesses in the way math and science are taught in elementary and secondary schools. While deploring the fact that science and math education had reached such an unhappy state that it threatened the nation's military and economic security, the president offered no major administration role.

Congress, meanwhile, has seen fit to ride the defense preparedness and economic development issues for all their worth. Eleven bills have been introduced in the Senate alone so far this year. Senator Gary Hart (joined by Senator Hollings, among others) has introduced his math and science education bill as the "American Defense Education Act," an apparent offspring of the Daddy of federal aid to education—the National Defense Education Act of 1959 which was America's answer to Sputnik. Legislation offered by Senator Claiborne Pell (joined by Senator Cranston, among others) has been entitled the "Education for Economic Security Act," and Senator Paul Tsongas has introduced the "High Technology Morrill Act"—harking back to the Morrill Act of 1862 which created the land grant college system.

Chiefly, the Hart bill calls for participating local school districts to be entitled to a basic payment of two percent of the average per pupil expenditure in the state, with an incentive of an additional two percent payment for those districts which demonstrate that their programs met the proposed goals for the year to improve instruction and student achievement in math, science, communication skills, foreign languages, and technology. (You may well ask what's left out.) Mr. Pell's measure provides, on a matching funds basis, grants to the states to upgrade instruction in math, science, computer learning and instruction, foreign language, and vocational education. Tsongas's High Technology Morrill Act establishes matching federal assistance for joint initiatives of private industry, educational institutions, and state governments to strengthen science, engineering, and technical education. Under the bill's guidelines, a project would be eligible for the 50 percent matching federal grant, if private industry contributes 20 percent, and states 30 percent, of the total cost. The bill would receive its funding from 3 percent of the revenues from the sale of energy and minerals resources on federal lands—hence the historical allusion to the Morrill Act.

Other Senate bills focus primarily on the math and science teacher shortage. [Editor's Note: None of the proposals for alleviating the shortage of mathematics and science teachers has been passed into law at this date. Senate Bill #290, addressing this issue, is in the Senate Finance Committee, where action on it is pending.] Senator Pete Domenici has introduced a proposal establishing merit scholarships for college students and an award program for teaching excellence conducted by the National Science Foundation. Senator Christopher Dodd's bill authorizes financial assistance for a continuing education program to increase competency, and Senator Glenn has introduced a measure which provides for low-cost loans to college students. All of these Senate bills have been referred to the Senate Labor and Human Resources Committee, whose Chairman, Senator Orrin Hatch, introduced Mr. Reagan's proposal, the Science and Mathematics Teacher Development Act, on March 8.

There have also been attempts to address the problem through the tax code. Certain Senate measures have been referred to the Senate Finance Committee (the Ways and Means Committee for comparable bills introduced in the House). For instance, another Glenn proposal (which was originally introduced by Representative Dave McCurdy in the House) provides federal income tax credits for industries participating in a joint employment program, or sharing equipment with educational institutions. Senator

Charles Grassley's bill amends the tax code to encourage contributions of equipment to post-secondary vocational education programs and to allow a credit to employers for vocational education courses taught by an employee without compensation and for temporary employment of full-time vocational educational instructors. The principle of tax credits for equipment contribution has perhaps received the most publicity in the "Apple Bill" (named because of the promotion given by the computer firm), introduced in the House and Senate last session and reintroduced this year, which allows income tax deductions for corporations that donate computers to primary and secondary schools.

An alternative approach, directed specifically at national defense needs, was introduced on March 14 by Senator Strom Thurmond. (Its House companion was introduced by Representative Charles Bennett.) Referred to the Armed Services Committee, this proposal established a program to provide high school graduates with technical training in skills needed by the Armed Forces in return for a commitment for enlisted service.

The house is already much further along in addressing the math and science problem since it considered and passed H.R. 1310 on March 2, by a vote of 348–54. H.R. 1310 contains two titles. Title I is the Emergency Science and Mathematics Education Act, contributed mostly by the Education and Labor Committee. The measure authorizes $250 million in FY 1984 for a new state program of grants from the Department of Education to improve math and science education at the elementary and secondary levels. At least 75 percent of each state's funds must be allocated to local education agencies. The primary use of these funds is to improve instructional skills and knowledge of teachers throughout in-service training programs and to recertify teachers of other subjects as math and science teachers. After meeting teacher training needs, local authorities may use funds appropriated under this provision for curriculum development, for the acquisition of instructional materials and equipment such as computers, and for joint programs with other public and private agencies. Twenty percent of the funds granted to state agencies are to be reserved for an incentive grant program in which any public or private local funds would be matched on a fifty-fifty basis by state funds for activities such as private-sector training of teachers or private-sector instruction programs in schools. An additional five programs are authorized to improve post-secondary education in mathematics, science, and foreign languages (the latter a contribution of foreign-language advocate Rep. Paul Simon), including $20 million for five thousand teaching scholarships in the 1984–85 academic year. Recipients will be required to teach two years for each year of scholarship assistance received, or repay the scholarship with interest.

The second title, the National Engineering and Scientific Personnel Act, drawn up by the Science Technology Committee, authorizes $100 million for an Engineering and Science Personnel Fund to be administered by the National Science Foundation. The fund sets as a national policy the maintenance of an adequate supply of technical, engineering, and scientific personnel, and the monies would be used for grants matching private or public funds on a fifty-fifty basis in such activities as research in engineering, science, and technical fields; for two-year and community college faculty development in high technology and scientific fields; for programs to promote the use of industrial personnel and resources in education programs; and for the promotion of public understanding of science and mathematics. H.R. 1310 also includes requirements that state and local authorities ensure the full participation of women, minorities, and private-school children in these programs.

The House bill, incorporating two separate titles, reflects its parentage in two different committees. A math and science education bill almost passed in the lame duck session, but was stymied by a conflict between the House Education and Labor Committee and the House Science and Technology Committee. The Science Committee, chaired by Rep. Don Fuqua, sought exclusive claim over the measure by choosing to distribute funds through NSF—which is under its jurisdiction. The Education Committee, under the leadership of Chairman Carl Perkins, fought for and gained shared consideration, amending the proposal to distribute funds through the Education Department—which happens to be within *its* jurisdiction.

The two committees could not come to an agreement in the last days of the session, and the measure died. Determined not to be embarrassed by having an in-house jurisdictional dispute block a major proposal—particularly one given presidential attention—Speaker O'Neill and Majority Leader Wright reportedly got Chairmen Fuqua and Perkins to work out a compromise package after summarily dismissing the administration proposal.

The jurisdictional dispute reflects an underlying conflict between contesting interests seeking a piece of an ever smaller pie. On one side of the table are the natural allies of the Education Committee—classroom teachers and their professional associations and unions, and local school officials. These groups all support in-service training, curriculum development, fellowships, or loan programs administered by the Department of Education to improve math and science instruction. (The coalition divides over local school officials' support for initiatives such as salary bonuses designed to relieve the math and science teacher shortage—a device not enthusiastically received by the teacher unions.)

On another side of the table are college and university professors and administrators faced with obsolete laboratory and instructional equipment and faculty recruitment and retention problems. These higher education interests tend to line up with the scientific community, with the scientists' professional associations, and with such groups as the American Association for the Advancement of Science, in favoring the Science and Technology Committee and the programs under the administration of the National Science Foundation. The NSF, they feel, is better situated to attend to the needs of the "hard" science. This coalition of university educators and scientists is often aided by the high technology sectors of the private industrial community, who together with the Armed Service are concerned with the immediate need for technical and professional personnel. High technology industries have shown interest in the potential staffing and tax benefits that would arise from proposed cooperative staffing options with educational institutions.

The administration opposed the House-passed measure because it feels that the funding level is too high, that there is insufficient targeting of programs, and that the bill would lead to undue federal intrusion into local responsibilities. The administration continues to cite the lack of qualified math and science teachers as the major identified problem. Yet the problem is not all that clearly drawn.

Data from the National Center for Education Statistics, based on a survey of local school districts and an *Education Week* survey of state educational agencies, reveal shortages in certain parts of the nation and surpluses in other areas. Teacher supply and demand data are almost always aggregated by state and do not indicate the degree to which some school districts within a state have a shortage and others a surplus.

Teachers willing to relocate, however, are discouraged by the lack of reciprocity in retirement systems and variations in teacher certification requirements. Mobility between states, and at times even within states, is encumbered by differences among local school salary schedules and restrictions on the amount of prior service determining a new teacher's salary. Any attempt by Congress to impose federal standards in relieving inter-state problems related to teacher certification and retirement would not be favored by independent-minded state and local education officials and would be actively opposed by the administration as unwarranted federal intrusion.

Yet the nation faces the responses of 45 states to a 1981 NSF survey—43 reported teacher shortages in mathematics, 42 in physics, and 38 in chemistry. According to a survey of the National Science Teachers Association, 640,000 children who wanted to take science and math courses could not do so for lack of teachers.

Perhaps the most difficult aspect of the problem is the loss of qualified teachers to higher paying jobs in business and industry. Beginning math teachers with bachelor degrees now earn only sixty percent of what bachelor degrees candidates in math and science earn in private industry. Twenty-five percent of those currently teaching math and science were found by the National Science Teachers Association to be planning to leave the profession for better paying jobs in industry. Any long-term solution to the math and science teacher shortage must take the salary issue into account.

Higher salaries for teachers in short supply as in math and science have been suggested to the states by Education Secretary T. H. Bell, but this runs counter to the long-held position of the politically formidable National Education Association and the American Federation of Teachers. Furthermore, the great concern over insufficient federal revenues to control future deficits diminishes the prospects of the congressional proposals using the tax code to provide incentives for private industry to allow employees to be used as part-time teachers or for teachers to be jointly employed by both school and private industry. Moreover, the job of a teacher goes beyond lecturing and supervising laboratory work; he or she is also responsible for the maintenance and evaluation of students' progress—important particularly at the elementary and secondary levels. How do these joint-employment proposals affect the profession of teaching?

The administration offers solutions to these larger, long-range problems of getting and keeping high-quality math and science teachers at all levels of education. Its proposal, in the words of Assistant Education Secretary Anne Graham, "would alleviate the immediate high school shortage while giving the nation's educational system time to solve" the underlying problems. And the schools will have to do it without much federal help. The same well-founded worry about huge deficits that makes the administration oppose H.R. 1310 has also led it to call for drastic cuts in federal education programs. More than one-third of the five-year savings the president proposes in federal benefits and services to individuals are to be obtained from education programs—sharply reducing funds for bilingual and vocational education, terminating the Indian education grant program, eliminating certain grants for support services for low-income students, and so on.

In addition to an extensive private education system, there are almost sixteen thousand local school districts (with student populations ranging from ten to a million) within fifty separate state systems with differing certification requirements and varying degrees of control over curricula. The administration takes the leap of faith that a math-and-science policy beneficial to the nation as a whole will somehow arise from myriad state and local decisions.

In fact, this year both Alabama and Kentucky have initiated state-sponsored college loan programs with a "forgiveness provision" for those who enter math and science teaching. (Of course, it doesn't take a math major to figure out that with a 60 percent wage differential, it's still a better deal to enter industry upon graduation and pay back the loan even at a high interest rate.) The Houston school district, where teachers' unions are not particularly strong, supplements math and science teachers' annual pay with an extra $2,000. Yet a few isolated incidents do not promise a national effort.

Congress, on the other hand, does have faith in itself as the representative body of the nation. Accordingly, the House bill and many of the Senate proposals directly address the concerns which the president would leave to localities or the market. A Senate controlled by Republicans but full of Democratic presidential aspirants may have a difficult time hammering out a compromise with the administration, on the one hand, and the House bill, on the other. What form the measure ultimately takes will depend upon the degree to which the diverse interested constituencies—teachers, parents, school administrators, professors, scientists, businessmen—let their representatives know that decline in math and science education is a national problem demanding a national response.

AGAINST BILINGUAL EDUCATION[4]

This year the United States government, which I am beginning to think is afflicted with a death wish, is spending $150 million on "bilingual education" programs in American classrooms. There is nothing "bi" about it, however. The languages in which instruction is conducted now include: Central Yup'ik, Aleut, Yup'ik, Gwich'in, Athabascan (the foregoing in Alaska), Navajo,

[4]Reprint of an article by Tom Bethell, a Washington editor of *Harper's*. *Harper's*. 258:30–33. F. '79. Reprinted by permission. Copyright © 1979 by *Harper's* Magazine. Reprinted by special permission. All rights reserved.

Tagalog, Pima, Plaute (I promise I'm not making this up), Ilocano, Cambodian, Yiddish, Chinese, Vietnamese, Punjabi, Greek, Italian, Korean, Polish, French, Haitian, Haitian-French, Portuguese, Arabic, Crow (yes, Virginia . . .), Cree, Keresian, Tewa, Apache, Mohawk, Japanese, Lakota, Choctaw, Samoan, Chamorro, Carolinian, Creek-Seminole, and Russian.

And there are more, such as Trukese, Palauna, Ulithian, Woleian, Marshallese, Kusaian, Ponapean, and, not least, Yapese. And Spanish—how could I have so nearly forgotten it? The bilingual education program is more or less the Hispanic equivalent of affirmative action, creating jobs for thousands of Spanish teachers; by which I mean teachers who speak Spanish, although not necessarily English, it has turned out. One observer has described the HEW-sponsored program as "affirmative ethnicity." Although Spanish is only one of seventy languages in which instruction is carried on (I seem to have missed a good many of them), it accounts for 80 percent of the program.

Bilingual education is an idea that appeals to teachers of Spanish and other tongues, but also to those who never did think that another idea, the United States of America, was a particularly good one to begin with, and that the sooner it is restored to its component "ethnic" parts the better off we shall all be. Such people have been welcomed with open arms into the upper reaches of the federal government in recent years, giving rise to the suspicion of a death wish.

The bilingual education program began in a small way (the way such programs always begin) in 1968, when the Elementary and Secondary Education Act of 1965 was amended (by what is always referred to as "Title VII") to permit the development of "pilot projects" to help *poor* children who were "educationally disadvantaged because of their inability to speak English," and whose parents were either on welfare or earning less than $3,000 a year. At this germinal stage the program cost a mere $7.5 million, and as its sponsors (among them Sen. Alan Cranston of California) later boasted, it was enacted without any public challenge whatever.

"With practically no one paying heed," Stephen Rosenfeld wrote in the *Washington Post* in 1974 (i.e., six years after the program began), "Congress has radically altered the traditional way by which immigrants become Americanized. No longer will the public schools be expected to serve largely as a 'melting pot,' assimilating foreigners to a common culture. Rather, under a substantial new program for 'bilingual' education, the schools—in addition to teaching English—are to teach the 'home' language and culture to children who speak English poorly."

Rosenfeld raised the important point that "it is not clear how educating children in the language and culture of their ancestral homeland will better equip them for the rigors of contemporary life in the United States." But in response, a withering blast of disapproval was directed at the *Post*'s "Letters" column. Hadn't he heard? The melting pot had been removed from the stove.

Bureaucratic imperative (and, I would argue, a surreptitious death wish) dictated that the $7.5 million "pilot program" of 1968 grow into something more luxuriant and permanent. As it happened, the U.S. Supreme Court decision *Lau* v. *Nichols*, handed down in 1974, provided the stimulus.

In this case, Legal Services attorneys in Chinatown sued a San Francisco school district on behalf of 1,800 Chinese-speaking students, claiming that they had been denied special instruction in English. The contention that these pupils had a *constitutional* right to such instruction (as was implied by filing the suit in federal court) was denied both by the federal district court and the appeals court. The Justice Department entered the case when it was heard before the Supreme Court, arguing that the school district was in violation of a 1970 memorandum issued by HEW's Office for Civil Rights. This memorandum in turn was based on the 1964 Civil Rights Act, which decreed (among other things) that the recipients of federal funds cannot be discriminated against on the basis of national origin. The 1970 memorandum defined language as basic to national origin and required schools to take "affirmative steps" to correct English-language deficiencies.

Evidently intimidated by this rhetorical flourishing of "rights," the Supreme Court unanimously affirmed that federally funded schools must "rectify the language deficiency in order to open instruction to students who had 'linguistic deficiencies.'" In effect, the Office for Civil Rights had taken the position that the immigrant's tongue was to be regarded as a right, not an impediment, and the Supreme Court had meekly gone along with the argument.

Armed now with this judicial mandate, HEW's civil-rights militants went on the offensive, threatening widespread funding cutoffs. No longer would the old method of teaching immigrants be countenanced (throwing them into the English language and allowing them to sink or swim). No longer! Now the righteous activists within government had exactly what they are forever searching for: a huddled mass of yearning . . . victims! Discriminated against the moment they arrive at *these* teeming, wretched, racist, ethnocentric shores!

America the Bad . . . One Nation, Full of Victims . . . Divisible. (I have in my hands an odious document, the "Third Annual Report of the National Council on Bilingual Education," which remarks that "Cubans admitted after Castro; and more recently Vietnamese refugees . . . became citizens unintentionally." No doubt they are yearning to be free to return to Ho Chi Minh City and Havana.) That's about the size of it in the 1970s, and so it came to pass that the Office for Civil Rights "targeted" 334 school districts, which would have to start "bilingual-bicultural" classes promptly or risk having their federal funds cut off.

"The OCR [Office for Civil Rights] policy is difficult to explain," Noel Epstein remarked in a thoughtful survey of bilingual education titled "Language, Ethnicity and the Schools" and published recently by the Institute for Educational Leadership. "There is no federal legal requirement for schools to provide bilingual or bicultural education." The Supreme Court had merely said that *some* remedy was needed—not necessarily bilingual education. For example, the Chinese children in the *Lau* case could have been given extra instruction in English, to bring them up to par. But the Office for Civil Rights took the position that they would have to be taught school subjects—mathematics, geography, history, et cetera—in Chinese. And the Court's ruling had said nothing at all about *bicultural* instruction. (This turns out to mean teaching that in any transaction with the "home" country, America tends to be in the wrong.)

In any event, the bilingual education program was duly expanded by Congress in 1974. It would no longer be just for poor children; all limited-English speakers would qualify; the experimental nature of the program was played down, and there was the important addition of biculturalism, which is summarized in a revealing paragraph in Epstein's booklet:

Bicultural instruction was elevated to a required component of Title VII programs. The definition of "bilingual" education now meant such instruction had to be given "with appreciation for the cultural heritage of such children. . . . " This underlined the fact that language and culture were not merely being used as vehicles for the transmission of information but as the central sources of ethnic identity. The U.S. Civil Rights Commission had in fact urged the name of the law be changed to "The Bilingual Bicultural Education Act," but key Senate staff members blocked this idea. They feared it would "flag a potentially dangerous issue that might defeat the overall measure," Dr. Susan Gilbert Schneider reports in a valuable dissertation on the making of the 1974 act. Some lobby groups had expressed discomfort about federally sponsored biculturalism. The National Association of School Boards suggested that the legislation could be read as promoting a divisive, Canadian-style biculturalism.

It certainly could. Notice, however, the strong suggestion here that the objection was not so much to the possibility of cutting up the country, as to being *seen* to promote this possibility, which of course might defeat it. As I say, these things are best kept surreptitious—at the level of anonymous "Senate staff members."

At this stage the bilingual seed had indeed taken root. Congressional appropriations had increased from the beggarly $7.5 million to $85 million in fiscal year 1975. The Office for Civil Rights was on the alert. A potential 3.6 million "victimized" children of "limited English-speaking ability" had been identified, and they would furnish the raw material for an almost endless number of bureaucratic experiments. Militant Chicanos, suddenly sought out to fill ethnic teaching quotas, stood on the sidelines, ready to pour a bucket of guilt over any old-fashioned, demurring Yankee who might raise a voice in protest.

Even so, there was a cloud on the horizon—perhaps only a conceptual cloud, but nevertheless an important one, as follows: the idea behind bilingual education was that children would begin to learn school subjects in their native tongue while they were learning English elsewhere—in special English classes, on the playground, through exposure to American society generally. But while they were in this "stage of transition"—learning English— instruction in the home tongue would ensure that they were not needlessly held back academically. Then, when they had a sufficient grasp of English, they could be removed from the bilingual classes and instructed in the normal way. That, at least, was the idea behind bilingual education originally.

But you see the problem, no doubt. At bottom, this is the same old imperialism. It is a "melting pot" solution. The children learn English after all—perhaps fairly rapidly. And at that point there is no reason to keep them in bilingual programs. Moreover, from the point of view of HEW's civil-rights militants, there is rapid improvement by the "victims"—another unfortunate outcome.

The riposte has been predictable—namely, to keep the children in programs of bilingual instruction long after they know English. This has been justified by redefining the problem in the schools as one of "maintenance" of the home tongue, rather than "transition" to the English tongue. You will hear a lot of talk in and around HEW's numerous office buildings in Washington about the relative merits of maintenance versus transition. Of course, Congress originally had "transition" in mind, but "maintenance" is slowly but steadily winning the day.

The issue was debated this year in Congress when Title VII came up for renewal. Some Congressmen, alerted to the fact that children were still being instructed in Spanish, Aleut, or Yapese in the twelfth grade, tried to argue that bilingual instruction should not last for more than two years. But this proposal was roundly criticized by Messrs. Edward Roybal of California, Baltasar Corrada of Puerto Rico, Phillip Burton of California, Paul Simon of Illinois, and others. In the end the language was left vague, giving school boards the discretion to continue "bilingual maintenance" as long as they desired. Currently, fewer than one-third of the 290,000 students enrolled in various bilingual programs are significantly limited in their English-speaking ability.

Then a new cloud appeared on the horizon. If you put a group of children, let's say children from China, in a classroom together in order to teach them English, that's segregation, right? Watch out, then. Here come the civil-rights militants on the rampage once again, ready to demolish the very program that they had done so much to encourage. But there was a simple remedy that would send them trotting tamely homeward. As follows: Put the "Anglos" in with the ethnics. In case you hadn't heard, "Anglo" is the name given these days to Americans who haven't got a drop of ethnicity to their names—the ones who have already been melted down, so to speak.

Putting Anglos into the bilingual program killed two birds with one stone. It circumvented the "segregation" difficulty, and—far more to the point—it meant that the Anglos (just the ones who needed it!) would be exposed to the kind of cultural revisionism that is the covert purpose behind so much of the bilingual program. Put more simply, Mary Beth and Sue Anne would at last learn the new truth: the Indians, not the cowboys, were the good guys, Texas was an ill-gotten gain, and so on.

As Congressman Simon of Illinois put it so delicately, so *surreptitiously*: "I hope that in the conference committee we can get this thing modified as we had it in subcommittee, to make clear that we ought to encourage our English-language students to be in those classes so that you can have the interplay."

As things worked out, up to 40 percent of the classes may permissibly be "Anglo," Congress decreed. And this year there has been another important change: an expanded definition of students who will be eligible for bilingual instruction. No longer will it be confined to those with limited English-*speaking* ability. Now the program will be open to those with "limited English proficiency in understanding, speaking, reading, and writing." This, of course, could be construed as applying to almost anyone in elementary or high school these days.

To accommodate this expansion, future Congressional appropriations for bilingual education will increase in leaps and bounds: $200 million next year, $250 million the year after, and so on in $50 million jumps, until $400 million is spent in 1983, when the program will once again be reviewed by Congress.

Meanwhile, HEW's Office of Education (that is, the *E* of HEW) appears to be getting alarmed at this runaway program.

It commissioned a study by the American Institutes for Research in Palo Alto, and this study turned out to be highly critical of bilingual education. The Office of Education then drew attention to this by announcing the findings at a press conference. ("They've got it in for us," someone at the Bilingual Office told me. "Whenever there's an unfavorable study, they call a press conference. Whenever there's a favorable study, they keep quiet about it.")

In any event, the Palo Alto study claimed that children in bilingual classes were doing no better academically, and perhaps were doing slightly worse, than children from similar backgrounds in regular English classes. The study also reported that 85 percent of the students were being kept in bilingual classes after they were capable of learning in English.

There has been very little Congressional opposition to the bilingual programs, thus bearing out what the Washington writer Fred Reed has called the Guppy Law: "When outrageous expenditures are divided finely enough, the public will not have enough stake in any one expenditure to squelch it." (Reed adds, in a brilliant analysis of the problem: "A tactic of the politically crafty is to pose questions in terms of rightful virtue. 'What? You oppose a mere $40 million subsidy of codpiece manufacture by the Nez Perce? So! You are against Indians. . . . ' The thudding opprobrium of anti-Indianism outweighs the $40 million guppy bite in the legislators' eyes.")

Risking that opprobrium, John Ashbrook of Ohio tried to cut out the bilingual program altogether. Referring to the evidence that the program wasn't working, but the budget for it was increasing annually, Ashbrook said that "when one rewards failure, one buys failure." On the House floor he added, "The program is actually preventing children from learning English. Someday somebody is going to have to teach those young people to speak English or else they are going to become public charges. Our educational system is finding it increasingly difficult today to teach English-speaking children to read their own language. When children come out of the Spanish-language schools or Choctaw-language schools which call themselves bilingual, how is our educational system going to make them literate in what will still be a completely alien tongue . . . ?"

The answer, of course, is that there will be demands not for literacy in English but for public signs in Spanish (or Choctaw, et cetera), laws promulgated in Spanish, courtroom proceedings in Spanish, and so on. These demands are already being felt—and met, in part. As so often happens, the ill effects of one government program result in the demand for another government program, rather than the abolition of the original one.

This was borne out by what happened next. When the amendment abolishing bilingual education was proposed by Ashbrook (who is usually regarded in Washington as one of those curmudgeons who can be safely ignored), *not one* Congressman rose to support it, which says something about the efficacy of the Guppy Law. Instead, the House was treated to some pusillanimous remarks by Congressman Claude Pepper of Florida—a state in which it is, of course, politically unwise to resist the expenditure of federal money "targeted" for Hispanics. Pepper said: "Now there is something like parity between the population of the United States and Latin America. My information is that by the year 2000 there probably will be 600 million people living in Latin America, and about 300 million people living in the United States."

Perhaps, then, it would be in order for the "Anglos" to retreat even further, before they are entirely overwhelmed. This brings to mind a most interesting remark made by Dr. Josue Gonzalez, the director-designate of the Office of Bilingual Education (the head of the program, in other words), in the course of an interview that he granted me. Actually, Dr. Gonzales said many interesting things. He suggested a possible cause of the rift with the Office of Education. "Bilingual education was hatched in Congress, not in the bureaucracy," he said. "The constituents [i.e., Hispanics, mostly] talked directly to Congress. Most government programs are generated by so-called administrative proposal—that is, from within the bureaucracies themselves."

He said of regular public education in America: "I've plotted it on a graph: by the year 2010, most college graduates will be mutes!" (No *wonder* the Office of Education isn't too wildly enthusiastic.) And he said that, contrary to what one might imagine, many "Anglo" parents are in fact only too anxious for their chil-

dren to enroll in a bilingual course. (If Johnny doesn't learn anything else, at least he might as well learn Spanish—that at least
is my interpretation.)

The melting-pot idea is dead, Dr. Gonzalez kept reassuring
me. Why? I asked him. What was his proof of this? He then made
what I felt was a revealing observation, and one that is not nor-
mally raised at all, although it exists at the subliminal level. "We
must allow for diversity . . . ," he began, then, suddenly veering
off: "The counterculture of the 1960s showed that. Even the
WASP middle-American showed that the monolithic culture
doesn't exist. Within the group, even, they were rejecting their
own values."

I imagine that Attila or Alaric, in an expansive and explanatory mood, might have said much the same thing to some sodden Ro-
man senators who were trying to figure out how it was that Rome
fell, exactly.

Dr. Gonzalez had me there and he knew it, so he promptly
resumed the offensive. "There are those who say that to speak
whatever language you speak is a human right," he went on. "The
Helsinki Agreements and the President's Commission on Foreign
Language Study commit us to the study of foreign languages. Why
not our own—domestic—languages?"

Later on I decided to repeat this last comment to George Weber, the associate director of the Council for Basic Education, a
somewhat lonely group in Washington. The grandson of German
immigrants, Mr. Weber speaks perfect English. "Only in
America," he said. "Only in America would someone say a stupid
thing like that. Can you imagine a Turk arriving in France and
complaining that he was being denied his human rights because
he was taught at school in French, not Turkish? What do you
think the French would say to that?"

BILINGUAL EDUCATION IN THE EIGHTIES:
ONE HISPANIC'S PERSPECTIVE[5]

There is no doubt in my mind that the problem of finding better educational responses to the needs of ethnolinguistic youngsters in our schools is still very much with us. Despite the flurry
of recent activities and the mounting of significant bilingual education efforts at federal and state levels, most schools and their personnel still do not respond as positively as they should to culturally
different students. Far too many school people, their public rhetoric to the contrary, continue to insist that the best course to follow
in educating "these kids" is to transform them in the image of the
majority.

I know many school people will deny my contention. Some
may argue heatedly that although perhaps true some years ago,
significant changes have occurred, pointing with justifiable pride
to special programs established through federal and state money
which have effected decided improvements in the status quo. I certainly agree that these are important improvements but my point
is that sadly these positive developments do not negate my base
contention. Rather they underscore it and give emphasis to the
magnitude of the problem.

Let me be more specific about why I am so concerned by listing some of the major current realities which establish the param-
eters of the issues involved. In my analysis, I single out Hispanics
(and Mexican-Americans within that group) because they are the
largest of the ethnolinguistic groups. Incidentally the list is illustrative rather than a complete listing of all the problems and issues.

[5]Reprint of an article by Tomás Arciniega, vice president for academic affairs at California State University, Fresno, California. *Educational Research Quarterly*. 6:25–31. Fall '81. Copyright © 1981 by the Educational Research Quarterly, published by USC School of Education. Reprinted by permission.

Current Realities

1) There are 16 million Hispanics in this country; Mexican Americans make up 7% of the population. More than 60% are Mexican Americans putting their number at approximately 7½ million persons (Pifer, 1980).
2) The majority of Mexican Americans came to the United States after the 1920s. They came in waves; the largest wave occurred in the late 1950s. Although most live in the southwest and west, the number of Mexican Americans is increasing rapidly in the midwest and northwest. This makes the issue a national one (Pifer).
3) Hispanic children are having a tremendous impact on the major school systems of this country. Hispanics comprise 30% of the school population in New York City, almost 50% in Los Angeles, just under 60% in San Antonio and El Paso, 32% in Miami, over 30% in Denver, and 35% in Hartford (Pifer).
4) In the face of such figures, school systems must respond to the educational needs of Hispanics. The biggest question is how since a large proportion of these children are not proficient in English. That issue will be of paramount importance to the United States in the years ahead.
5) Unfortunately, Hispanic children have not fared well in the nation's schools. Hispanics continue to progress through the schools two to three levels behind other students. Only 30% complete high school and in some of the large urban districts the drop out rate is as high as 85% (Pifer, 1980).
6) At the higher education levels, less than 7% have completed college. In 1975–76, Hispanics received only 2.8% of the B.A. degrees awarded in the U.S., 2% of the master's degrees, 2.6% of the law degrees, 2.3% of the medical degrees, and 1.2% of the doctorates (Pifer).
7) Two-thirds of all Hispanic children attend highly segregated schools, schools composed of predominantly minority students; 3.6 million of these Hispanic pupils were judged to be in need of special language assistance last year (Brown, Rash, Hill & Olivas, 1980).
8) Four-fifths of all Hispanics live in homes where Spanish is usually spoken (Brown et al).
9) Income figures for Hispanics continue to run significantly below the national average. In 1978 Hispanics had a median annual family income of $12,600 compared to $17,600 for the nation as a whole. Only 8% held professional or technical positions compared to over 16% for non-Hispanics. Ten percent of Hispanics live in poverty; and, more than half of those above the poverty line are found in low paying jobs in agriculture, or in manufacturing or service occupations (Brown et al).
10) Forty-two percent of Hispanics are under age 25.
11) Unemployment is a serious problem for Hispanics. The unemployment rate in 1978 for Hispanics was over double that of whites and in the urban areas it was even worse. At all levels, Hispanics as a whole earn less that whites (Brown et al).

12) In the courts, the Lau vs. Nichols decision affirmed the concept of language rights. This, along with the Voting Rights Act which mandates bilingual election materials and the requirements for interpreters in the courts, has given official recognition to multilingualism in American society. As part of the Lau mandate, schools are required to offer the curriculum in a manner understandable to the linguistically different child.

13) Finally, recent research on bilingual education is reporting consistently that children who achieve bilingualism through formal schooling are testing higher on IQ and achievement measures. Most importantly such is holding true regardless of ethnic background or language and cultural group affiliations (Lambertis, 1977).

The persistence of the chronic problems and the projected impact of new developments are what concern me most when I look to the eighties. Together these realities underscore the fact that, even with all the efforts and the struggles of the past two decades, the gap continues. From the Hispanic perspective, there is a long way yet to go and the struggle for equality and social justice, as these facts make clear, is still very much with us.

Although school administrators and community influentials don't like to hear about such things, the fact of discrimination is a major reason why Hispanic students continue to have problems in schools and universities. Pifer, the President of the Carnegie Corporation Foundation, in his 1979 President's report stated it even more bluntly:

Schools, as transmitters of society's values, in a variety of ways have made a signal contribution to the school performance rate of Hispanics—by shunting Spanish-speaking children from poor families into educational tracks designed for low achievers, by classifying them as mentally retarded or emotionally disturbed, by denigrating their Hispanic heritage, by giving them the message that they cannot, or are not expected to succeed. In short, the public education system as a whole has neither welcomed Hispanic children nor been willing to deal with their learning problems in any effective way (p.10)

Action for the Eighties

If I were asked to develop a national Hispanic agenda or blueprint for action in the 80s, I would put the reform of public schools at the top of the list. There is nothing more important to the improvement of conditions for ethnic minorities in this next decade than the improvement of the educational level and quality of that human resource pool. I further believe that the principal educational reform issues involved can be specified rather easily. Hispanics face five major problem areas in the public educational systems of this nation (Arciniega, 1977):

1) The inadequate treatment and presentation of the historical, cultural, and economic contributions made by Hispanics in the curricular programs of the schools.
2) The ongoing pejorative and pathological perspective in the schools regarding the appropriateness, worth, and status of the Spanish language as a bona fide medium of instruction in the classroom.
3)The under-representation of Hispanics on school district staffing patterns—teachers, administrators, counselors, etc.
4) The lack of authentic involvement of the Hispanic community in the decision-making structure of the school system.
5) The testing, counseling, and guidance programs and processes in the schools which too often are based on a cultural deficit perspective of Hispanic student needs.

Changing these problem facts of life in schools is what educators must be pushed to address. School people must be motivated to take responsibility for the creation of schools which accept and capitalize on the strengths of cultural and linguistic differences in ways which lead to successful performance in school by ethnolinguistic children. The promotion of cultural difference has to be recognized as a valid and legitimate educational goal.

In a national and statewide strategy sense, the two most important public school programs are Compensatory Education and Bilingual Education, Compensatory Education because of the magnitude of the program dollars involved and Bilingual Education because it represents the most viable programmatic alternative to the status quo and a tremendous victory won over a stormy 12-year period.

Regarding Compensatory Education, public schools need to insist on the flexibility to allow the use of bilingual approaches in such programs. Compensatory programs have not been more successful with Hispanic children primarily because of the propensity to diagnose the educational problems of these youngsters too narrowly. Most programs have assumed incorrectly that the primary and in some cases the only responsibility of these programs was to teach English. Such programs do this rather than teach what these children are supposed to know at the proper age levels by using their home language in ways that can best achieve that end.

Bilingual Education is the most important educational innovation ever launched in this country on behalf of Hispanics. Hispanics are quick to point out that there can be no qualifying or compromising on this. As a concept as well as a program, Bilingual Education has served ethnolinguistic people well.

Crucial Vehicles

Across the nation, bilingual programs have proved to be crucial vehicles whereby Hispanics may press for language rights and these programs have spurred the parents of Hispanic students to action. It is heartwarming to see Hispanic parents fight for the right to have a say-so about the education their children receive. At all levels of the educational system, Bilingual Education has provided needed leverage in moving districts away from those cultural deficit approaches in which minorities have labored and suffered for so long.

In California for example, the issue of language rights has tremendous symbolic value for Mexican Americans. It wasn't very long ago that Mexican Americans were openly barred from white schools (Carter & Segura, 1979). In the southwest prior to 1940, less than 5% of Mexican American children of school age were allowed to go to school. Even as late as the 1950s, this country still had school systems with the good "American" and the inferior "Mexican" schools. And we all know too well the cases of Mexican kids being spanked for speaking Spanish and about the forced anglicizing of Hispanic surnames. That history is deeply etched in the minds and souls of Chicanos. This is too often overlooked and seldom fully appreciated by those who persist in the use of the catch phrase: I just can't understand why Chicanos get so worked up about Bilingual Education.

It is not appropriate to delve any deeper into the specifics of how to change the public schools. But obviously meaningful reform has to begin with the need to effect changes which bring about equitable representation of Hispanics, yield necessary curricular adaptations and insure a meaningful involvement of the Hispanic community.

How best to push for these needed reforms in the face of decreased special program funding is the central issue for the eighties. The nature of that problem for U.S. society is a bit more complex than might appear at first blush. Although many of the implementers of national and state policies have tended to justify projected cutbacks by pointing to perceived problems with existing special programs, the issue is a much broader one. What is really at stake is this country's expressed commitment to act on the needs of the neediest first.

During the last two decades, this country made clear to the world and to future generations its intent to equalize educational opportunities for all Americans. It explicitly recognized the black, brown, red, and yellow peoples of this nation as the most disadvantaged of its citizens. The nation recognized also that only through federal intervention could meaningful redress of past injustices be brought about. Although often overlooked today, it is important to recall that the decision to embark on that national strategy was made only after long and serious deliberations regarding the difficulties involved.

A Nation's Commitment

What remains to be seen in the eighties is how true the new administration holds to that national commitment. If all that is ahead is a change in tactics—in how best to achieve educational equity for ethnic minorities—rather than a pullback from that national commitment, then I foresee only minor adjustment problems. But if what lies ahead is really a decision to abandon that ideal, then this country may well be headed toward the biggest internal civil rights upheaval yet. The social dynamite in the ghettos and barrios of this land, which we heard so much about after the Watts riots, is certainly still there. It would be a serious mistake to think that it is not—an even more serious mistake to underestimate the explosive potential of that social fact. If anything, what should be apparent is that the rise in expectations coupled with the worsening of economic conditions will intensify that explosive potential in the barrios and ghettos of this land.

The Federal Bilingual Education Program, although in dollar terms not the largest of the special federal programs, should prove a very accurate and clear barometer in determining early on what is in store for minorities in the eighties. Hispanics and other ethnolinguistic minorities across the country are watching with intense interest how bilingual education fares under the new administration. Having only recently won the right to construct a national delivery system for bilingual education, Hispanics will not be easily convinced by those rhetorical arguments that maintain the English Only approaches represent a *better solution*.

On the contrary, from the Hispanics' perspective, the involvement of their children in Title VII programs during the past decade has convinced these parents and supporters of the educational worth of bilingual education. They know bilingual programs work for these children and understand also the key role played by the federal government in the establishment of such programs. Thus, it should surprise no one that Hispanics tend to view any and all attempts to cut back or to discontinue bilingual education as anti-Hispanic actions. Early actions by the current administration would seem to indicate a very serious lack of appreciation of that fact.

REFERENCES

Arciniega, T.A. *Preparing teachers of Mexican Americans: A sociocultural and political issue.* Austin, Texas: National Educational Laboratory Publishers, Inc., Educational Resources Information Center (ERIC), 1977.

Brown, G.H., Rash, N.L., Hill, S.T., & Olivas, M.A. *The condition of education for Hispanic Americans.* Washington, D.C.: U.S. Government Printing Office, 1980.

Carter, T.D., & Segura, R.D. *Mexican-Americans in school: A decade of change.* New York: College Entrance Examinations Board, 1979.

Lambertis, W. The effects of bilingualism on the individual: Cognitive and sociocultural consequences. In P.A. Hornby (Ed.), *Bilingualism: Psychological, social and educational implications,* New York: Academic Press, 1977.

Lau et al. vs. Nichols et al., 483 F. 2d 791 (9th Cir. 1973).

Pifer, A. *Bilingual education and the Hispanic challenge.* President's annual report, New York: Carnegie Corporation of New York, 1980.

BILINGUAL MIS-EDUCATION[6]

Bilingual education was one of the first victims of the Reagan administration, and when education secretary Terrel Bell delivered the *coup de grace* to the previous administration's plans for the program, it might have seemed another victory for conservatives and another blow to liberals. The Carter administration's regulations, in Bell's view, were "a symbol of federal meddling," an "intrusion on state and local responsibility," and "incredibly costly." But from the very start bilingual education was a bad cause for liberals. The package looks right, but the contents are wrong. For rather than enlarging the educational and economic opportunities of disadvantaged, mostly Hispanic, children, it diminishes them. And it does so in programs that segregate the children from their black and white peers.

The 1968 Bilingual Education Act made federal funds available for instruction of non-English speaking students in their native tongue, but the initiative had to come from local schools. Bilingual education then was an option, not yet a right or a requirement. However, in the 1974 decision of *Lau v. Nichols,* a unanimous Supreme Court read the 1964 Civil Rights Act to require "affirmative steps to rectify the language deficiency" of children with limited English. While the Supreme Court specified no particular steps, HEW soon did. Departmental regulations known as the "Lau remedies" mandated bilingual education indirectly. It was a revision of these regulations by Carter's education secretary, Shirley Hufstedler, that Bell immediately scrapped.

There is no doubt that some southwestern schools were somewhat brutal in demanding that Spanish-speaking children learn English. As recently as the early 1960s pupils who spoke Spanish

[6]Reprint of an article by Abigail M. Thernstrom, author and specialist on educational issues. *New Republic.* 184:15–17. Ap. 18, '81. Copyright © 1981 by the New Republic. Reprinted by permission.

on the playground at some schools were punished. Nor is there doubt that the school drop-out rate for Hispanic children is high. About 70 percent never finish high school; only about seven percent finish college.

But from the recognition of these problems, the solution of bilingual education does not necessarily follow. Brutality is a problem that can be dealt with directly. A receptive educational environment does not require a Hispanic teacher who conducts classes in Spanish. In a recent report the president of the Carnegie Corporation concluded that "the public education system as a whole has neither welcomed Hispanic children nor been willing to deal with their learning problems in any effective way." American education, he said, has shunted these children into educational tracks designed for low achievers, classified them as mentally retarded or emotionally disturbed, and treated their cultural heritage with contempt. But neither contempt nor erroneous and invidious classification is inherent in all ethnically integrated education. And while some bright children with limited English undoubtedly have been labeled mentally incompetent, the unhappy fact is that many Hispanic pupils—like others from poor families—are indeed poor achievers, with high rates of emotional disturbance. Every child with limited English and low achievement needs help. The question is how best to provide it.

Proponents of bilingual education argue that classes taught in a child's native tongue enable that child to acquire fundamental skills while learning English. English in fact is easier to learn by a Spanish route, it is said. Becoming literate in a simpler language—one which is written as it sounds—eases the task of mastering one that is more complex. But there is no evidence that children in bilingual classes progress faster than peers with comparable language difficulties who are placed in regular classrooms or receive remedial help in English. The most important evidence that we have suggests otherwise. A four-year study of 11,500 Hispanic children conducted by a research institute under contract with the US Office of Education concluded that most children in bilingual programs are not deficient in English. Those who are, it found, are not in fact acquiring it. Moreover, with few exceptions the programs were aimed not at easing the transition to literacy in English (while encouraging competence in other subjects), but at maintaining a separate language and culture. Finally, whatever the language of instruction, children who started out alienated from school tended to remain so. The study found no evidence that children in bilingual programs were more eager to stay in school.

The methods used in that study have been criticized, but the sobering picture that it drew has not been reassuringly revised. Still, support for bilingual instruction, particularly among Hispanic activists, has not lessened. And the reason is clear: the programs provide both employment and political opportunities as schools are forced to hire Hispanics without regular teaching credentials, and as students are molded into an ethnically conscious constituency. Moreover, both Hispanic leaders and their supporters in white civil rights circles are committed to ethnic pluralism. They do not believe in assimilation to a common culture, or in schools as transmitters of that culture. The whole notion of the melting pot, in their view, must be condemned.

The consequence of this commitment to the maintenance of ethnic diversity—to protecting people's differences, as one supportive legislator put it—was the proliferation of bilingual classrooms in which English-proficient students with Spanish surnames were isolated from their non-Hispanic peers and taught not only their "native" language (at the expense of instruction in English), but their "native" culture as well. Bilingual programs have become schools-within-schools, permanently protective ethnic enclaves. Of course not all students in such programs arrive speaking English. But many others have no recognized language at all; they speak a street Spanglish. And for them, becoming literate in English may be as easy as learning true Spanish.

This is not to say that all programs conform to this model. But too many do—or seem to. Hard data are hard to come by, but these programs appear to provide not more equal but more unequal education. By and large, bilingual education is a disservice to Hispanic and other children of limited English proficiency. For in failing to provide these children with a solid grounding in English and failing to integrate them with the culture of their peers, it condemns them to the economically marginal existence that too many of their parents have endured. It closes the door, in other words, to educational and economic opportunity.

BILINGUAL EDUCATION IMPROVEMENT ACT: A COMMON BASIS FOR COMMUNICATION[7]

Thank you, Mr. Chairman. I am honored to follow the testimony of my good friend Secretary Terrel Bell of the Department of Education. He has described in detail the Bilingual Education Improvement Act, S. 2412, which I introduced in the Senate this past Wednesday. [Editor's Note: No action was taken on Senator Hayakawa's Bilingual Education Improvement Act in the 97th Congress, nor on his proposal for a constitutional amendment. None is foreseen in the next congressional session.] I am pleased to work with Secretary Bell on this issue, as we are both committed to giving school districts more flexibility in their teaching methods while targeting the immigrant population in greatest need of English instruction.

Today I would like to address bilingual education as it relates to a much broader issue: the question of what language will be used in the United States. As most of you know I have proposed a constitutional amendment, Senate Joint Resolution 72, which declares as the law of the land what is already a social and political reality: that English is the official language of the United States. This amendment is needed to clarify the confusing signals we have given in recent years to immigrant groups. For example the requirements for naturalization as a U.S. citizen say you must be able to "read, write and speak words in ordinary usage in the English language." And though you must be a citizen to vote, some recent legislation has required bilingual ballots in certain locations. This amendment would end that contradictory, logically conflicting situation.

[7]Reprint of an address by S. I. Hayakawa, U.S. Senator from California. Delivered to the Subcommittee on Education, Arts and Humanities, Senate Commitee on Labor and Human Resources, Washington, D.C., April 23, 1982. *Vital Speeches of the Day.* 48:521–3. Je. 15, '82.

Our immigration laws already require English for citizenship. The role of bilingual education is then to equip immigrants with the necessary English language skills to qualify them for this requirement. The problem is that all too often, bilingual education programs have strayed from their original intent of teaching English. A related issue is the full scale of interpretations for the term "bilingual education." Chances are that when one asks five people for a definition, five very different answers will be given. According to one interpretation, it simply means the teaching of English to non-English-speakers. This is the method I prefer and is usually called English-as-a-Second-Language or ESL. On the opposite side of the scale bilingual education is a more or less permanent two track education system involving the maintenance of a second culture and an emphasis on ethnic heritage. This method is called transitional bilingual education and involves teaching academic subjects to immigrants in their own language coupled with English language instruction. This is the definition used to determine eligibility for Title VII funding.

We all grew up with the concept of the American melting pot, that is the merging of a multitude of foreign cultures into one. This melting pot has succeeded in creating a vibrant new culture among peoples of many different cultural backgrounds largely because of the widespread use of a common language, English. In this world of national strife, it is a unique concept. I believe every member of this committee will agree that it had a fundamental impact on our nation's greatness. In light of the growing emphasis on maintaining a second culture and instruction in the native languages, I ask myself what are we trying to do? Where do we want to go? Demographic research tells us that in some of our states, 10 or 20 years from now there will be a majority of individuals with Spanish background. It seems to me that we are preparing the ground for permanently and officially bilingual states. From here to separatist movements a la Quebec would be the final step. Is this the development which we want to promote?

I believe that my constitutional amendment as well as my Title VII amendments will prevent a crisis similar to the separatist movement of French Canadians. That confused state of affairs is a result of controversy about which language shall be the official one used in Canada. I want to avoid a similar situation here in America where use of another language is encouraged to the point that it could become an official language alongside English. This would perpetuate differences between English-speaking and non-English-speaking citizens and isolate one group from the other. There can be no doubt that recent immigrants love this country and want to fully participate in its society. But well-intentioned transitional bilingual education programs have often inhibited their command of English and retarded their full citizenship.

Congress recognized the importance of teaching English to immigrants in 1968 when it passed Title VII of the Elementary and Secondary Education Act. This Act permitted the development of pilot projects to teach English to underprivileged immigrant children. In 1978 Congress expanded the bilingual education program, dropped the poverty qualification and required appreciation for the cultural heritage of the students served by federal funds. These amendments also introduced the option of providing academic instruction in the native languages of the students, coupled with English classes. This method of instruction, transitional bilingual education, has been interpreted by Title VII regulations as the only acceptable method of instruction for bilingual education. The unfortunate result of Congress' 1978 action was to deprive local schools of their flexibility to determine the best method of instruction for their particular non-English-speaking students.

I agree wholeheartedly that we need to do all we can to teach the English language to non-English-speaking students. However, I cannot support a rigid mandate prescribing a single method of instruction. I believe that given the flexibility to choose their own program, local schools will emphasize English instruction. Without the expensive requirement of a full academic curriculum in foreign languages, schools will be able to teach more non-English-speaking students for the same cost. I have met with many school boards who are struggling to maintain high quality education in the midst of reduced budgets. Through my personal communications studies, I have observed that the more academic instruction children get in their immigrant parents' language, the less quickly they learn English. I personally believe that ESL and immersion techniques allow non-English-speaking students to master our language so they can join the mainstream of society more quickly than through transitional bilingual education. My legislation broadens the range of instructional approaches for serving children of limited English proficiency. I expect school boards to welcome this opportunity to provide more efficient and cost effective instruction to their immigrant students while maintaining their eligibility for Title VII funds.

What the learning of a new language requires, as is well known in U.S. military language schools, is total immersion in the new language, or as close to total immersion as possible. Though I personally support intensive methods of English instruction, I must point out that even my proposed constitutional amendment does not prohibit the use of minority languages to assist non-English-speaking students. On the contrary, it specifically states that it "shall not prohibit educational instruction in a language other than English as required as a transitional method of making students who use a language other than English proficient in English." My bilingual education proposal follows the same line of reasoning by allowing local schools the freedom to choose the teaching method that will best serve their immigrant population and maintain their eligibility for federal bilingual education funds.

Some immigrant groups argue that transitional bilingual education is necessary to preserve equal educational rights for non-English-speaking students while they are learning English. I believe that this requirement can actually result in discrimination in the administration of Title VII programs. The cost of providing academic subjects in a language other than English can exclude many of our recent immigrant groups such as the Indochinese who speak a variety of languages. Many local districts educating these students simply cannot afford to provide academic instruction in the many Indochinese languages which are often represented in one school. Imagine the cost of providing academic instruction in Cambodian, Hmong, Laotian, and Vietnamese in several grades. There students are no more fluent in English than the traditional immigrant groups funded under Title VII. However, because local schools often use intensive English instruction for Indochinese students, they will not qualify for Title VII money. Section 2, subsection 2 of the Bilingual Education Improvement Act would correct this by allowing funding for projects which use a variety of methods for teaching children with limited English proficiency including but not limited to transitional bilingual education, ESL, or immersion. Section 2, subsection B insures educational quality for students served by requiring applicant schools to show that they have selected instruction methods that will complement the special needs and characteristics of the Title VII students.

The acquisition of a new language is far easier for children than for adults. Children at the ages of four to six are at the height of their language-learning powers. In families where the father speaks to the children in one language, the mother in another, and the maid in a third, the children grow up trilingual with no difficulty. From the age of six onward, there is a gradual decline in a child's language-learning powers, so that learning a new language as an adolescent is a more difficult and self-conscious process than it is for a child. For anyone over twenty, it is a much more difficult process, involving conceptualization, like learning rules of grammar. A child picks up unfamiliar grammar without conscious effort. Because of these differences in the rates and methods of language learning among different age groups, school children, especially under the age of ten, should be exposed to English constantly through contact with English-speaking classmates and playmates. They will learn English effortlessly, without the sense of undergoing a difficult experience.

The second provision of the Bilingual Education Improvement Act would give priority funding to Title VII projects which serve children who are both of limited English proficiency and whose usual language is not English. In our current period of limited Federal resources in education, both Secretary Bell and I agree that it is imperative to target Title VII funds to this particular group of immigrant children. It is clear that the proposed Fiscal Year 1983 budget of $94.5 million cannot serve the approximately 3.6 million students who are technically eligible for Title VII aid. This provision of my legislation will target those who are most limited in their ability to speak English without tampering with the current definition of eligibility for Title VII funding. During our discussions, Secretary Bell and I have agreed that this effort to channel Title VII funds to the students who are least proficient in English is not to be interpreted as a Federal mandate which will intrude in the local schools' determinations about their immigrant students. It *is* an incentive to local school officials to set priorities for using limited federal bilingual education funds. We agree that this new provision will be immensely helpful in clarifying a target population of students who are the *most* limited in their ability to speak English.

The third provision in this legislation would authorize several programs under Title VII which were previously under the Vocational Education Act. Vocational training for immigrant adults and out-of-school youth, training funds for teachers of immigrant students, and bilingual materials development have all proved to be small but effective programs. This provision would remove the set-aside for each program required under the Vocational Education Act and would allow the Department of Education to set priorities for the use of these funds. The focus of this funding will be for demonstration projects which will identify successful teaching methods rather than service projects which merely maintain the status quo. I am very encouraged by Secretary Bell's interest in using these programs as catalysts of research and development which will encourage state and local education agencies to share in the formulation of new training methods.

Another small, but extremely important provision of my legislation would require English proficiency for instructors in bilingual education programs. I was shocked to learn that Title VII currently places greater importance on its teachers knowing the native language of their students than on knowing English. My legislation will amend Section 721 (B) of the 1978 Act to fund programs "including only those teachers who are proficient in English, and, to the extent possible, in any other language used to provide instruction." The emphasis is reversed from knowledge of the immigrant language to English, which Secretary Bell and I agree reflects the true intent of federally funded bilingual education.

The issue of English as our official language and bilingual education for immigrants is especially timely in light of the Census

Bureau figures released this past Tuesday. The 1980 census found that 23 million people in the United States aged 5 or older speak a language other than English at home. We as Americans must reassess our commitment to the preservation of English as our common language. Learning English has been the primary task of every immigrant group for two centuries. Participation in the common language has rapidly made the political and economic benefits of American society available to each new group. Those who have mastered English have overcome the major hurdle to participation in our democracy. Passage of my English language amendment, as well as my bilingual education proposal, will insure that we maintain a common basis for communicating and sharing ideas.

MERIT PAY WON'T WORK[8]

"I saw something interesting in *The Washington Post* several weeks ago," President Reagan told a group of elementary and secondary school principals when he welcomed them to the White House last July. "It was a story on how the Soviet leadership is considering ways to get the Soviet economy moving again. Well, one proposal is to depart from the practice of paying Soviet citizens relatively equal wages irrespective of job performance. Now if even Yuri Andropov and the Soviet bureaucracy are beginning to realize the need for merit pay, why can't certain segments of our own educational establishment?" It was a rare moment: Ronald Reagan citing Yuri Andropov as an authority on the capitalist work ethic. It was also a characteristic one: the beguiling anecdote that is as misleading as it is instinctively appealing. Of course good teachers should be paid more than bad ones. Even the National Education Association—at which the President's barb was clearly directed—now concedes as much. But merit pay will not get the system moving again. (Mr. Andropov, take note.) It will not im-

[8]Reprint of an article by Dorothy Wickenden, staff writer. *New Republic.* 189:12-15. N. 7, '83. Copyright © 1983 by the New Republic. Reprinted by permission.

prove the morale of teachers. It will not entice talented new teachers into the schools or prevent talented veterans from leaving. It will not help weed out the tenured incompetents. The clamorous public response to Reagan's call to punish the shirkers and reward the toilers shows that merit pay is a terrific political slogan. But experience has shown that in the school it is a blunt instrument at best.

Like so many education reforms, merit pay means something altogether different to people who know about it in practice, on the one hand, and reflexive critics of "the education establishment," on the other. In essence, merit pay is nothing more than a money reward for exceptional teaching, usually made on the basis of a written evaluation by a principal. It has been widely touted as a daring departure from the standard single salary schedule, which determines teacher salaries strictly according to seniority and academic credentials. But in fact merit pay schemes of various kinds have been tried in hundreds of school districts around the country since the beginning of the century, and they have been abandoned again and again for just the reasons cited by the N.E.A., the American Federation of Teachers, and countless school administrators. Teacher performance, unlike the work of, say, an insurance salesman, is not easily gauged by objective standards of productivity. More often than providing an incentive for teachers to excel, merit pay has played a subtly invidious role in breaking down already tenuous relations between school administrators and staff. It has been an excuse for school boards to perpetuate low salaries; for principals to play favorites and discriminate against women, minorities, and union activists; and for teachers to suspect their colleagues and superiors of nefarious doings.

Around the same time Reagan was urging principals around the country to adopt merit pay in their schools, the San Marino, California, school district dropped its plan which had been in effect for twenty-five years—far longer than the average lifespan. The problems San Marino eventually encountered were typical. The plan worked like this: the school board determined the amount of money to be allocated every year for merit pay (although, since no extra funds were provided, it meant more for the favored few and less for the overworked, underpaid majority). Each year up to 30 percent of the teachers would receive a bonus of between $200 (for a tenured teacher with three years' experience) and $2,000 (for one with twenty years' experience). It was left to the school principals to parcel out the bonuses, purportedly after reviewing a teacher at work a minimum of three times and filling out an exhaustive evaluation form regarding his or her "instructional skills, pupil relationships, parent and community relationships, professional relationships, classroom (or assignment) responsibilities, professional growth, and personal factors." The plan's strength lay in the strict confidentiality of the evaluations. But in 1979, a history teacher filed a grievance stating that he had not been evaluated at all one year, and was turned down for a merit bonus the next because, he was told, he had failed one of the 101 criteria. A three-year investigation was launched, and it developed that teachers throughout the district had similar complaints. There was no appeal for teachers who felt they had been unfairly evaluated, and no reliable standard from which they could judge their weaknesses and strengths.

President Reagan's infatuation with the idea of merit pay derives in large part from the dubious assumption that it will help improve the quality of teaching. His rationale: reward the best teachers and they will be given an incentive to stay on in the field, and perhaps the drones will work a little harder if they know that bonuses are contingent upon their strengths in the classroom. But teachers don't choose to be ineffective out of spite or laziness; for the most part they are doing the best job they know how to do. Furthermore, merit pay does nothing to solve the problem of truly incompetent teachers, who are there because of slack certification standards and rigid tenure laws. Finally, in the real world of classrooms as opposed to the never-never land of Op-Ed pages, teacher "performance" is judged as often on the neatness and thoroughness of one's lesson plans and on one's success in currying favor with the principal as on one's skills in imparting knowledge. One seasoned teacher who has worked in two New York state school systems with merit pay plans says: "I'm pretty sure that I could go into any school and tell impressionistically who the good teachers are. But I'd have less faith in the instincts of a lot of the school administrators I've known, and I don't know of any objective way of making these judgments. Too many things are out of the teacher's control. If I get a class of bright, enthusiastic kids who earn national merit scholarships, I'm going to look great—but what if I'm teaching slow kids?"

Some merit pay plans attempt to get around the troublesome issue of subjective evaluations by devising standards which measure teachers' results, not their methods. They presume that the quality of teachers' work in the classroom is quantifiable in "objective" end-of-the-year measures such as test scores. Take the Dallas public schools, where the superintendent, Linus Wright, has been talking with great enthusiasm about the merit pay plan that just squeaked through the board of education, over the strong objections of the teachers. It's a fancy computer-based program (the first of its kind) that will award merit pay to all teachers in the top 25 percent of those schools where student test scores exceed the computer's projections. Robby Collins, director of employee relations, told Paul Taylor of *The Washington Post* that the plan was designed to eliminate the fractiousness that has so often led to the downfall of merit pay: "Once you have human beings evaluating other human beings, the systems produce jealousies, morale problems. The beauty of our system is that it's done totally by computer." But even high-tech merit pay can't transform lousy teachers into good ones, and this plan may actually perpetuate incompetence. How will Dallas's teachers respond to the new incentive to improve their kids' test scores? Maureen Peters, the president of the Dallas Federation of Teachers, predicts that teacher-assisted cheating, already a widespread problem, will rise. "Everyone in every school knows someone who's cheating— usually inadvertently," she told me. "Teachers get pressure from the principal. They perceive test scores to be the goal of education and a way to maintain their jobs, let alone to get a pay increase. Elementary school teachers leave the multiplication charts on the walls. High school teachers walk around the classroom during tests and nod or shake their heads."

High test scores, although they may please parents and principals, are not the goal of education—or even necessarily the mark of a good teacher, as Maureen Peters points out. All this is not to say, as the N.E.A. has over the years, that it is impossible to judge a teacher's effectiveness fairly. (Only in the past few months has the N.E.A. modified its rigid opposition to any reform of teacher compensation.) But if schools expect high standards from their staff, they must also expect to pay for them—in significantly higher salaries, in the time and planning it takes to hammer out a thorough evaluation system, and in finding ways of encouraging strong teaching techniques. The single salary schedule, which rewards ambitious teachers by relieving them of their teaching duties and "promoting" them into administrative jobs, has clearly failed to do this.

Straightforward merit pay schemes for the most part have fared no better. Those that have succeeded have been in congenial school districts characterized by what Education Research Service describes as "strong, dynamic leadership," where teachers and administrators cooperate on working out the plan, where all salaries are moderately respectable, and where the bonuses are significant. One need hardly point out how few schools have this felicitous mixture. And as the San Diego City school district bluntly put it way back in 1953, "Merit programs too frequently presuppose that all improvement comes through changing the teachers."

The most promising alternatives to merit pay now under consideration in a number of school districts and state legislatures recognize that the only way to get better teachers is to improve the conditions under which they teach, and to upgrade the status of the profession itself. This was one of the rudimentary truths discovered by all of the recently released education reports. One teacher interviewed by the Carnegie Foundation for the Advancement of Teaching said, "I work as a meat cutter in the summer at one of the nearby butcher shops, and I don't usually tell them I'm a teacher. One butcher finally found out that I was a full-time teacher and his comment to me was, 'Man, that's a dead-end job. You must be a real dummy.'" The negligible salary increases over the years, combined with the lack of opportunity for promotion and professional training and the low public repute of teaching, make one wonder that there are any dedicated, competent teachers left in the schools. According to *Action for Excellence,* published by North Carolina Governor James Hunt's task force, a teacher in Montgomery County, Maryland (a wealthy suburb of Washington with excellent schools), who has a college degree, special training, and two years of experience, earns $12,323—less than a liquor store clerk with a high school diploma and comparable time on the job.

The secret of the best new systems—most notably Tennessee's Master Teacher Program and the career teacher plan being devised for Charlotte-Mecklenburg, North Carolina—is their radical transformation of the teacher's role. John Goodlad's book, *A Place Called School,* and the Carnegie Commission's *High School* found that teachers currently spend as much time being wardens—taking attendance, keeping an orderly classroom, fulfilling lunchroom duty—as they do being instructors. Teacher authority is subverted as a matter of course. In the old days principals made announcements in a civil manner, during school assembly or by having a note quietly delivered to the teacher. Now they bark orders and news about school sporting events over the public address system, often in the middle of class. There is little or no time during the day for collegial discussions about ideas and teaching methods. "Frankly, the question of merit as such is a trivial issue," Goodlad told me. "You can raise salaries $5,000 a year, and still have the same old problems on Monday morning. It's a matter of more training and responsibility. The real key is to make teachers feel they have a stake in what they're doing."

Tennessee and Charlotte-Mecklenburg have studied at length—and emphatically discarded—the fundamental premises of merit pay. They take it for granted that teachers teach out of a commitment to the profession, and not out of an expectation of financial rewards; that they burn out and leave not only because of inadequate pay, but because of unrealistic and demeaning demands on their time, a feeling of isolation in the classroom, and a sense of professional frustration.

Under these proposed plans, substantial rewards—in the form of training, regular promotions, and higher salaries for all teachers—are built into the pay scale, not thrown in at the whim of a school board. Evaluations are designed to be both more rigorous and more constructive. For a start, Governor Lamar Alexander has recommended that within the next three-and-a-half years every tenured teacher in Tennessee receive a 20 percent across-the-board raise. And, as in Charlotte-Mecklenburg, teachers will climb "career ladders" over the years as they receive ongoing professional training and take on work during the summer months—in curriculum development, for instance, or in teaching the slow and the gifted. Both programs have requested teachers to help develop and approve the criteria required for advancement, and to be part of the evaluating teams that will periodically review each teacher's progress. Thus they provide a real incentive for all teachers not only to improve their own (and others') teaching methods, but to work with, rather than against, the school administration. A typical teacher today in Tennessee with a master's degree and fifteen years of experience works ten months and moonlights during the summer. Her salary is $18,000. As a "master teacher" (the top rung of Tennessee's career ladder), she would have the option of working ten, eleven, or twelve months, and the opportunity of increasing her earnings by as much as $7,000.

No one who has worked through the laborious process of drawing up these plans underestimates the procedural difficulties in putting them into effect, or overestimates how much they can accomplish. The Tennessee Master Teacher Program was blocked in the Education Committee of the state senate last January because of strenuous objections voiced by the Tennessee Teachers Association. It will have taken a year to work out a compromise acceptable to all, and if the plan passes this time around, it will be an estimated five years before the program is fully under way. The cost will be about $3 million in new state taxes each year—and it is only one part of Governor Alexander's $210 million Better Schools Program, which covers everything from basic skills to university centers of excellence. The Charlotte-Mecklenburg career teacher plan won't be complete for ten years, and will add 10 percent to the district's annual budget. Both plans have the active support of universities (Vanderbilt and the University of Tennessee, and the University of North Carolina), and Tennessee's has gotten as far as it has because of the Governor's role in originating and tirelessly pursuing the idea. Steve Cobb, a Democratic representative who serves on the Education Committee in the Tennessee legislature, who has helped revise the

Master Teacher Program, says: "It will not improve the teaching of the best teachers, but it will reward them more fairly. After a few years it will give teachers an incentive to do better. It will encourage teachers doing well to stay in the profession. It will match the career patterns of other professions. It is not the cure-all, and we don't advertise it as such—don't expect it to repair highways. But it is an important part of a comprehensive education program. It will restore public confidence that we're attempting to motivate teachers and promote change."

In the end, schools will certainly need more than merit pay, and probably more than "career ladders," if they mean to increase the attractiveness of the teaching profession and raise the caliber of its members. Ernest Boyer of the Carnegie Commission has proposed a National Teacher Service which "would enable young people to enlist in the cause of education as they might enlist in the military or join the Peace Corps." Congress's National Task Force on Merit Pay recently suggested that the federal government offer ten thousand scholarships (twenty-three in each congressional district) of $5,000 per year to top-ranking students who pledge to teach for two years for each year of scholarship help, or to repay the scholarships, with interest, if another field is chosen. Last summer the National Endowment for the Humanities sponsored fifteen highly successful seminars in which high school teachers studied lyric poetry, American history, religion, and other subjects with professors at universities around the country; next summer the program will expand to include fifty seminars, involving fifty universities.

But if nothing else, the Tennessee and Charlotte-Mecklenburg plans, with all their inherent limitations, should serve as a model and a challenge: to the school boards and principals who feel that only a dozen or two of their teachers are worthy of recognition; to the legislatures that profess their commitment to excellent schools, but refuse to raise taxes enough to fund them; to the unions that say they seek higher standards, but resist stiffer certification standards and tenure laws; to the President, who simultaneously rails about lousy teachers and cuts aid for the public schools; and finally, to the talented teachers who are leaving the profession in disgust.

EDUCATION REFORMS:
MERIT PAY AND MASTER TEACHER PLANS[9]

. . . The second major event for the year is the appearance of reports that have placed education at the top of the national agenda. For a long period of time we thought this condition could never exist again. After all, the birth rate went down. And the percent of the voting public who are parents dropped from 50 or 60 to somewhere around 20 percent. The issues of public concern focused on senior citizens, or Social Security, and education somehow moved to the background.

But today education is one of the top two issues, second only to the economic and unemployment question on the national agenda. All national polls show that your next president of the United States and next Congress may well be elected on the basis of educational issues.

And we have a series of reports: the National Commission on Excellence, Twentieth Century Fund, the Education Commission of the States and some others about to come out on high schools. By the time the year is over we may very well have 15 or 20 national reports all saying much the same thing. They point in the same direction. They move the emphasis to excellence and to quality. They talk about things that we have been talking about for a long, long time. And they discuss a few things that we haven't been talking about, at least we haven't favored.

They talk about tests—testing teachers, testing students. They talk about a tough curriculum instead of soft courses and electives which don't have very substantial content. They talk about doing something about discipline problems in school. They talk about major investments of money. They talk about policies involving promotion of students and the graduation of students from schools. They talk about changing the nature of rewards for teachers. They all talk about finding some method to deal with the problem of dismissing incompetent teachers.

[9]Excerpted from an address by Albert Shanker, president of the American Federation of Teachers. Delivered at the American Federation of Teachers Convention, Los Angeles, California, July 4, 1983. *Vital Speeches of the Day.* 49:706–12. S. 15, '83.

Many people think this is just one of those fads. Every once in a while the country gets interested in something and you hear people saying: "Well, the country cannot focus its attention for more than a week or a month, or two months or five months. This will all go away."

I don't believe that it will. There are, of course, political, social or economic and religious fads. They do come and they do go. But a fad is generally based on something which is not rooted in a real problem. But what we face in education is certainly very real. Our problem is similar to the fact that several years ago we all of a sudden discovered that we had not been rebuilding our auto plants, our steel plants and our prior industrial capacity. Reindustrialization was a problem. We had to reinvest, reindustrialize, because otherwise we weren't going to compete with the rest of the world and our own standard of living would decline.

Then, after reindustrialization we discovered something else. Not only did our private industry have to be rebuilt, but our public infrastructure was falling apart—roads, bridges, water and sewer systems; in fact, our railroad system, harbors, docks, and so forth.

Again, these are things that don't go away. If you don't rebuild plants, just thinking about it doesn't make the problem go away. It gets worse and worse. If you don't rebuild the bridges, that problem doesn't go away.

Now we have found that neglect in education and neglect of human resources is having and will have exactly the same disastrous effect neglect did in the area of private industry and the area of public infrastructure.

So this is not something that will go away. If we don't do something about educational improvement, we won't have mathematicians, scientists, engineers and computer specialists. Indeed, we won't have enough people who can read and write and think and do the work that the nation needs to do. So, it is not going to go away.

I like the phrase, "a nation at risk" because by using those words the National Commission on Excellence in Education effectively put education on a par with national defense.

A nation at risk means that a country can go down. It can fall apart. We can lose. It can disappear. Those are strong words, and they are good words.

There is a third aspect, a major development this year, and that is a focus on the teacher as essential to education. That wasn't always so.

There was a particular period in the 1950s and 1960s, after Sputnik, when people became very much interested in education. They weren't interested in teachers. Those were the days when various companies were trying to put out what they called teacher-proof materials. That is the equivalent of foolproof.

They had given up during that period of time on teachers. They had instruction books, TV sets and all sorts of things; anything that a teacher can't manipulate, change or break would .work. They would work, but the teachers somehow gummed them up.

Well, not so. And now we have a new and different climate. Now we have governors and businessmen saying that without good teachers we are not going to have a good educational system. That has not been said by us but by those people.

However, these governors and businessmen now realize that teaching in our schools at the present time is a group that is substantially more talented than the group which is about to come in and replace us.

They realize that we had certain unique opportunities in the past to recruit outstanding teachers. Such as during the Depression of the 1930s when it was a decent job in a period when there weren't any others.

Then there were those who came in during and in the aftermath of World War II, with the belief that there was about to be another depression.

I know my mother told me if I wanted to get into a field where I will always have a job—

Then, of course, we had the draft between World War II and the Vietnam war when exemptions were granted to those who preferred to fight in our schools.

We also had a very large number of minority teachers for whom other jobs in the private sector were closed. The public sector, even with some continuing discrimination, was a much more open field. With the success of the civil rights movement, many more talented minority group members began seeking jobs in the open market rather than feeling that they had to come into teaching because that was the place where they would have a better chance.

And, of course, the largest single group of talented people who made sure that education worked over the years was women.

Well, the women's movement has worked to such an extent that we now have an educational disaster. Women no longer feel that teaching and nursing are the two top fields. Women are now going in a big way into medicine, dentistry, architecture, engineering, business administration—

—and into every field where there is money and prestige on the job.

These conditions have brought us a new kind of prospective teacher. We know who they are, because the colleges have test scores, and it is disastrous. The people who are willing to come into teaching—by the way, they don't stay very long, either—are the bottom of all people who are entering and graduating from college.

I am speaking, of course, as a group. There are always a few exceptions, but on a national scale, that is an accurate picture.

A recent report in the current issue of the *Teachers College Record* puts it succinctly. Of those who take a teaching job, 15 percent drop out the first year, and by and large they are the ones who had the best grades. Eight percent drop out the next year, 6 percent the next, and before the end of five or six years half of the most talented drop out.

Another interesting piece of information is that a sample reflecting 36 percent of the nation's prospective teachers flunked tests in reading, writing and mathematics proficiency.

That is pretty shocking, but what was more shocking was that a few months later they went back to find out which of these teachers were hired. They found that while 36 percent of all the prospective teachers sampled were incompetent, 55 percent of all those actually hired by superintendents or principals were among those who had flunked the exam.

In other words, principals or superintendents tend to feel more comfortable with teachers who are less competent.

That should raise some questions about the merit pay issue.

Well, those are the issues before us, and they are also the issues before the nation. It is a period of great danger, and it is a period of unprecedented opportunity.

Now, the reports which have been published bring us very powerful and needed allies who can make a real difference. With fewer and fewer parents out there, we have to help the general community understand that education is not just good for children and parents, but good for our entire society.

Our allies are businessmen, governors and others who realize that there is a powerful and yet simple idea which is sweeping the country. This idea will take two realizations to turn education around and make it work.

First if you need a program which focuses on quality, you can't just keep doing the same things that have proven unsuccessful.

We must keep in mind that for many years we have been negotiating for teachers. We have been winning benefits. We have been advancing collective bargaining, and now we have a nation that believes the reports (I believe them) that the nation is at risk. As we move in the months ahead, we must be sure that the public doesn't see teachers' unions and collective bargaining as an obstacle to the improvement of education.

There is at least one teacher organization that has put itself in that position [Editor's Note: Shanker refers to the NEA, National Education Association, the rival teachers' union whose opposition to merit pay has been more adamant than that of the American Federation of Teachers.] despite the fact that the general public now seems willing to pay higher taxes for the much needed changes in education.

Second, these reports reject tuition tax credits or vouchers either implicitly or explicitly. They recognize that we can't have both tuition tax credits and necessary, massive overhaul of our public education system.

We must show a willingness to move far in the direction of these reports, cooperatively and eagerly, because we stand a great chance that these powerful report sponsors will say yes, the nation is at risk, we were willing to spend a lot of money and we wanted to make a lot of changes, but you know, it is hopeless because we came up against inflexible unions, school boards and administrators. If these leaders of government and industry after having invested time, effort and prestige on a program to rebuild American education find their efforts frustrated, there is no question as to where the tilt of public policy will go. We will lose the support that we now have. There will be a massive move to try something else, and it will all be over.

The American Federation of Teachers is in a very fortunate position. We don't have to sit here and rethink our position on whether our students will be tested. We don't have to rethink whether a teacher coming in who is going to be a math teacher should be able to pass a math test or a language teacher a language test. We don't have to rethink whether we want a tough program geared toward doing something about disciplinary problems.

On almost every program put on the agenda, the American Federation of Teachers was there 20 or 30 years ago working on the problem. I am sorry to say that the other organization hasn't gotten there yet. In normal times, I wouldn't regret that too much because we are winning collective bargaining campaigns by appealing to teachers on these very issues. Let us keep those positions.

We will go out and talk to American teachers and each year we will bring in tens of thousands of more teachers because the other organization doesn't represent the American public on education or the views of teachers either. They have lost credibility with the general public because they are against everything that stands for quality. They are unable to carry a fight on this issue. That is too bad, because it is not just a question of their taking an incorrect position on these issues. They are a larger organization and if we are to maintain public respect and support for public education, it will be important that we be together on these questions.

And so I am here to say that even on issues that we feel uncomfortable with, that we disagree with rather strongly, we have to ask ourselves what are the consequences if we win the fight. What is the price? Is it worthwhile?

In a period of great turmoil and sweeping changes, those individuals and organizations that are mired in what seems to the public to be petty interests are going to be swept away in the larger movements. Those organizations and individuals who are willing and able to participate, to compromise and to talk will not be swept away. On the contrary they will shape the directions of all the reforms and changes that are about to be made. That is what we in the AFT intend to do. We intend to be on board shaping the direction of every change in education.

Now let me turn to the teacher shortage crisis or teacher replacement crisis. What should be done about it? I think the answers are pretty clear, and I think that the changes will be exciting. We need to test teachers.

I must tell you that I felt rather ashamed of something that happened a few weeks ago. The state of Florida has instituted tests for teachers, and some organizations are opposing them. The terrible thing that happened a few weeks ago is that the same test that was given to teachers was given to a normal sixth grade class. The students in the sixth grade class did as well or better than the average of all the teachers who are coming in to teach in the state.

I do not believe that the test of teacher competence is a sixth grade test.

For a teacher who tries to reach the student when a student doesn't understand, it is not enough to do a problem in one particular way or to be able to explain something in a particular way. When a student doesn't understand, you may have to approach it in a second way, third way, fourth way or fifth way and you can't do that as a teacher unless you know a lot more than the student whom you are about to teach.

We ought to support the idea that future teachers should be tested. I would say an absolute bare minimum score on the test ought not to be at the level of what their students are going to be learning, but the teachers ought to be in the top half of all college students in the country, so we are not getting the bottom half.

That is not going to be an easy thing to do. You know why. Every teacher and every superintendent knows why: If you pick from the top half of college graduates, you will not be able to pay 10, 11, or 12 thousand dollars.

You will have to go up to 17, 18, and 19 thousand dollars right now.

There is a second thing we ought to do. A lot of talented people will become teachers because they are interested in mathematics, foreign languages, English or social studies. They are not interested in 36 credits of boring education courses.

We are not against professional education. We are not against professional training. But at the very least professional training should do no harm.

And if it drives talented people away, it is doing harm. That hasn't changed.

We need salary schedules that are not 15 steps long or 20 steps long or with longevity 25 or 30 steps long. There are no such situations anywhere else. Everywhere else you reach maximum in three years, four years or five years. These pay scales were developed when teaching was women's work. They were designed to discriminate. Women would come in at first, second, third step or fourth and leave at the early steps, so only a few survivors who stayed for a long period of time would get a salary that approximated a living wage.

Well, life isn't like that anymore. Nobody is going to start at a horribly subminimum salary and wait for 10, 15 and 20 years to get maximum pay.

The fourth point is we are not going to get people interested in English or mathematics or social studies and languages unless we solve discipline problems and take out of our schools those students who prevent teachers from teaching.

Teachers are not interested in disciplining children. They did not decide to become policemen, or psychiatrists or jailers. They want to be teachers.

Next, I believe that the movement to strengthen the curriculum is something that will be a great help in attracting talented people into teaching. A person interested in English wants to teach that and not remedial reading. Those interested in calculus and geometry and algebra don't want to correct third and fourth grade arithmetic errors if they teach in high schools. As teachers, if we can come in and teach children a subject that we love, it will attract better teachers.

Now I come to something to which I will return in a few minutes: the whole relationship between teachers and supervisors.

Maybe once upon a time school was an educational factory in which teachers were graduates of one- or two-year normal school or training school programs. They were viewed as being just a little ahead of their students. The principal and superintendent were considered the only professionals and college graduates in the school and were made the foreman and boss, while the teachers were the educational workers on the assembly line. That isn't true today. Our teachers are frequently more educated in their own field than the supervisors who supervise them.

We are not going to get people who really know Shakespeare and Dickens and mathematics, who have self-respect and high regard for their work, when someone who knows less than they do comes in and tells them what to do. We have to rethink the authoritarian nature of the schools.

Then finally, there needs to be some public recognition of the importance of the job that teachers do. That includes the President of the United States who I hope will start saying good things about teachers instead of some of the bad things.

Don't do that tomorrow unless we want to re-elect him.

If we do that tomorrow, it will go out through the whole country! "Look how the President was treated! These people are not fit to teach our kids." Not a winner. Not a winner.

There is a reason for this fear of tests. The fear is that if the public finds out that some students are flunking or test scores are dropping, teachers might be blamed. But just as with health care, there are more factors than just the doctor's role that affect my health or your health. The same with education: there are more factors than just the teacher's role that affect educational health and success.

Just yesterday in the *Los Angeles Times* when parents were interviewed and asked what they thought to be the single, most important factor for the decline in the schools, they answered, "Parents, 42 percent." All the other items followed that.

Before concluding, I would like to say one other thing. The new agenda is quality and excellence, and we welcome this. We ought to keep on the national agenda something else, and that is still some unfinished business.

We should stand before the American public when we are talking about standards and continue to advocate a program of quality and excellence. But we should not abandon the poor and needy and the handicapped. We ought to reinvigorate the programs that we have succeeded in all these years.

What about the tough issues? We believe we have the same interest as the general public does in seeing to it that teachers who are incompetent do not remain as teachers. They don't do anybody any good and they don't do us any good. We believe we will develop a new system which will enable us to be rid of incompetents without sacrificing basic process, but it will result in changes.

I want to get to the question of merit pay and the master teachers. I wish we could find some different language because these words cover a fairly wide variety of different programs. I want to say that we were traditionally and still are against schemes of a certain type and we have reasons for being against those proposals.

The first hallmark of the traditional scheme was that it was not an instrument for providing decent and adequate salaries for everyone. In essence it was a way to tell the public that most of the people who were teaching were not good and only a few were worth it.

A second hallmark of traditional merit pay plans was that an immediate supervisor, either a principal or superintendent or somebody like that, would decide who got the money. We all know that principals have their own jobs to do and everybody believes his or her own job is the most important in the world. The principal does not teach children, a principal has to get reports in, and any teacher who gets reports in on time is obviously an outstanding teacher in the eyes of the principal.

Superintendents have to have their contracts renewed. There is nothing more important than that. We understand that the whole future of any given school system depends on whether a superintendent gets his contract renewed; and any teacher who helps by not criticizing or rocking the boat is certainly a fine teacher.

It is very clear that putting the decision process in the hands of supervisors who have different interests could result in either favoritism or irrelevant criteria of selection.

I guess the third major item is that many of these proposals, while rewarding even a few extremely meritorious teachers, are usually put together in such a way that they demean everyone else.

Years ago we started on a program called a "More Effective Schools Plan." No one remembers why it was called the "More Effective Schools Plan." But if we called these few schools the effective schools, that would make all the others ineffective. By calling them "more effective" schools, it made all the others effective.

No school system gains if it recognizes and rewards a certain number of very outstanding people, if it shatters and destroys the will and spirit and morale of all those others who stay on the team.

Well, we have to recognize that on the national scene there are some new proposals. I did not react to Lamar Alexander's proposal the same way I reacted to the kinds of schemes I just talked about because his proposal isn't like any of those three. It doesn't do any of those terrible things that I just talked about. It may create other problems. It doesn't mean it is a good idea, but it is not a merit pay or master teacher scheme in the same sense as those that we have been criticizing.

I am not going to talk about his plan. He will be here Wednesday. He is an eloquent spokesman for that plan. I urge you to give not only the governor but the plan a good deal of consideration.

Remember, if the country is moving in a certain direction, in some situations it may not be whether we have a plan or no plan, it may be whether we have a better plan or a worse plan. We ought to look at the Alexander plan in that light.

I do wish to say that none of these master teacher proposals will accomplish the top priority or solve the top problem that we have in education. We talked about it a minute ago. We are not getting the same talent or quality in teaching as a result of the past history affecting education.

Does anybody really think that a bright, young man or woman graduating from college is going to go to Tennessee and start working at a beginning salary of roughly $10,000 a year? Is this person going to be a talented, wonderful person who will accept the low pay because he feels 8 or 15 years later he will be recognized as a master teacher and get a big salary increase? That is known in psychological terms as delaying gratification. We don't make them that way anymore.

A few minutes ago I said that we will not attract good teachers if we have the same boss/teacher relationship as we have today. If you will listen carefully to Governor Alexander's proposal, you will find that he addressed the problem effectively. It could very well turn out that under the plan half of the people in the state of Tennessee become senior teachers or master teachers. They would remain in the classroom, working longer hours or longer months in order to train teachers, develop curriculum and other things. If half the teachers in the state were doing that, what would the principal do?

It may be that this program will eliminate traditional types of authority and supervision, moving us closer to a college model where the college president doesn't walk into the classroom and ask you for a lesson plan, but treats you as a respected professor.

I am sticking my neck out on this. I hope by the time this week is over that we are all willing to stick our necks out. Twenty years ago when collective bargaining first came in, we were the organization that brought it about and we brought it about by sticking our necks out.

We had only 50,000 members in the entire United States and we were asking that teachers in every district have an election where the majority organization would prevail. Wasn't that an idiotic thing for a small minority to do . . . demand elections?

We did demand elections. We went through a wrenching experience at conventions that if collective bargaining came about because of our efforts against rival organizations, we might be cutting our own throats. Teachers recognized our leadership. We grew as a result of it. This is the time when we need to demonstrate a similar type of courage on the question of educational issues.

One of the key things that is happening—because of a position that another organization has taken—is unfortunate. Merit pay, instead of being one of 15 issues on the national scene today, one of 15 or 20 items mentioned in every one of these reports, has become a life or death issue. The entire national consciousness has been diverted from all the other important issues and recommendations. Everyone is concentrating on this one item.

The American Federation of Teachers will not allow merit pay or the master teacher to become the one single dominant, exclusive issue in this national discussion. . . .

ARE STANDARDS IN U.S. SCHOOLS REALLY LAGGING BEHIND THOSE IN OTHER COUNTRIES?[10]

The question I raise in this article—how standards in U.S. schools compare with those of other countries—is both controversial and provocative. Indeed, it has been a source of concern since 1957, when Sputnik went into orbit—an event that was interpreted as reflecting American inferiority in science and technology. This inferiority in turn was interpreted to reflect badly on the teaching of science and mathematics in U.S. schools. This interpretation seemed to be confirmed by the first international mathematics survey in 1964, which revealed that the U.S. tended to be at the bottom of the international mathematics league, at least as far as 18-year-olds were concerned.

Events in the U.S. today give me a feeling of déjà vu. But this time the concern is somewhat different: the declining competitiveness of American high-technology products. And this time it is not the Soviets but the Japanese who cause concern. One need only mention the lack of competent teachers in key subjects and the decline in the number of students taking these subjects. But how serious is the situation? And what evidence do we have to justify our answer, particularly with regard to the achievement levels that students attain by the end of high school?

As chairman of the International Association for the Evaluation of Educational Achievement (known as the IEA), I have for some 20 years been intimately involved in cross-national comparative studies of the standards achieved by students at various age

[10]Reprint of an article by Torsten Husén, professor in the Institute of International Education, University of Stockholm, Sweden. *Phi Delta Kappan*. 64:455–61. Mr. '83. Copyright © 1983 by Phi Delta Kappan. Reprinted by permission.

levels in a wide range of industrial countries, most of them European but also including Japan and the U.S. In this article I will discuss the limitations and possibilities of cross-national comparisons of academic standards, and I will present some evidence from the IEA surveys about the achievements of comparable groups of students in the U.S. and in some other countries.

Comparing the Incomparable

Comparing the outcomes of learning in different countries is in several respects an exercise in comparing the incomparable. School systems with differing objectives and curricula reflect differing national goals.

In comparing the outcomes of learning in the U.S. with those of "comparable" (i.e., highly industrialized) countries in western Europe—as was done, for example, in the first IEA mathematics survey of 12 countries—one can easily overlook certain basic differences between the school systems. Let me discuss some of the difficulties in conducting meaningful comparisons between countries in terms of what students achieve when tested, for instance, by standardized achievement tests.

The U.S. differs from Europe in terms of the structure of its formal system of education. Historically, European schools have been characterized by a cleavage—both intellectual and social—between primary and secondary education. Secondary (i.e., grammar) schools existed for a small elite that attended private preparatory schools rather than public primary schools. A classical curriculum in the grammar schools prepared students for the university. Secondary schools (*gymnasia*, lycées, or grammar schools) were usually under the control of the central government, whereas primary schools, first mandated in the mid-19th century, were established with strong local influence (though often with considerable central financing). Until the 1960s, children who attended secondary schools with academic programs transferred from grade 4 or 5 of the primary school and completed an additional six to nine years in secondary school. U.S. secondary schools, on the other hand, have for many years been under the control of local school boards and have been far less selective than corresponding European schools.

There are also basic differences between the U.S. and most European countries in the governance and financing of public education. European systems are rather centralized, with both primary and secondary education under the supervision of state inspectors who report to a central agency (as a rule, a ministry of education). Germany, France, and England are, despite many other differences, rather similar with respect to centralization. Appropriations by the national parliament finance secondary schools almost entirely and primary schools in part. Both kinds of schools are under the authority of the national ministry of education. In the U.S., the predominance of local financing and, to a considerable extent, of local initiative means that local school boards are extremely influential.

In attempting to compare academic standards in American and European schools, it is crucial to consider the role of central government in determining curriculum, setting examinations, and inspecting the quality of instruction. Since in Europe a major portion of school expenditures is defrayed by appropriations included in the national budget, it is incumbent upon the central government (and the parliament) to make decisions about the curriculum: what subjects at what stages should be taught for how many periods per week. The recurrent costs of schooling will depend on such decisions.

In addition, the main content of the curriculum in a given subject area is also dictated by the government. This curricular control is the foundation for setting national standards of performance, which are controlled by examination papers in key subject areas set by, for instance, the ministry of education. In some cases, a general agency—such as the National Board of Education in Sweden—is responsible for preparing standardized achievement tests that are given to *all* students in the country at a certain grade level, in order to assure that teachers adhere to a uniform nationwide standard in grading their students.

Such a system contributes to rather concrete, clear-cut performance expectations—to the extent of defining these expectations operationally in terms of examination exercises, be they certain paragraphs that must be translated into another language or mathematical problems that must be solved. In Europe, collections of examination papers have traditionally been issued in book form; these tests, which have been given over the past two or three decades, serve as study guides. They convey rather precisely to the students what topics the final examination will cover. Practice materials of this type are very influential.

As I mentioned above, European secondary schools have historically prepared a small elite for the university. As late as the mid-1960s, when the IEA conducted its first comparative survey of mathematics, only 9% of the relevant age group in Germany graduated from upper secondary school, compared with some 75% in the U.S. The German students were almost all university bound, however, whereas the American group was "comprehensive" in two major respects: namely, 1) size of enrollment in percentage of the relevant age group and 2) range of programs, from highly academic to highly "practical" or vocational ones. It is pointless to compare the quality of learning in a system with a high participation rate with that of countries with very low rates. The former will obviously show a lower average performance than the latter. Thus the IEA mathematics study compared the average performance of the top 9% of students in the 12 participating countries. The science survey made similar comparisons in 19 countries.

One could assume that a comprehensive system of schooling achieves equality at the cost of quality, in terms of *average* performance. As I will show later, however, the international surveys of both mathematics and science demonstrated that the top 5% to 10% at the end of secondary education (i.e., the elite) tended to perform at nearly the same level in both comprehensive and selective systems of secondary education. Thus the elite among U.S. high school seniors did not differ considerably in their performance from their age-mates in France, England, or Germany. The comprehensive systems, where the net is cast more widely, result in a bigger "talent catch." In addition, those who are less able get a better opportunity to develop their potential than in the selective systems of the traditional European type.

The variance between the national educational systems of highly industrialized nations in terms of average performance in key subjects (e.g., mother tongue, mathematics, and science) is rather narrow in comparison with the enormous variance in educational quality between industrialized and nonindustrialized or developing countries. In reading and arithmetic, for example, students from nonindustrialized nations tend to achieve at the third-grade level after about seven years of schooling and at the eighth- to ninth-grade level by the end of upper secondary school. This performance gap is only partly attributable to school resources. On the whole, school resources in affluent countries, expressed in unit expenditures (per student and per year), tend to be rather unrelated to educational achievement. Thus the unit cost in the Swedish comprehensive school almost doubled in constant dollars from 1962 (when the reform was legislated) to 1977, but learning in terms of average student performance has not changed a great deal. No significant increase has been found in average mathematics performance from 1964 to 1980.

The IEA Six-Subject Survey pointed to opportunity to learn as the single factor with the greatest explanatory power in accounting for differences among students, schools, and countries. In school subjects, where learning starts from scratch, this is very striking. John Carroll, who directed the IEA study of French as a foreign language, compared eight countries in terms of time factors, e.g., number of years of studying French, at what grade level French was introduced in school, and number of periods of instruction per week. The U.S., where only two years of high school French are required, recorded a dismal outcome, whereas Rumania, which requires about six years of French, was at the top.

The Role of National Examinations

Most European countries require no national or regional examinations at the end of primary school (which, until recently, often marked the end of mandatory schooling as well). Some countries deem it inappropriate to conduct examinations that aim at assessing *individual* levels of performance in a system where school attendance is mandatory. Failures depend not only on limitations in individual ability and motivation but on the competence of the system to cater to the needs of all students and to enable them to do their best.

However, nationally standardized surveys of student achievement in key subjects (primarily mother tongue and mathematics) have been conducted in some countries. Since the 1940s, for example, all Swedish students at certain grade levels have been required to take standardized tests. These tests are not used to assess individual students but to calibrate the grading scale in order to achieve national comparability.

In most European nations, the upper secondary school examination was—and in many nations still is—a uniform entrance ticket to the university. Such examinations have traditionally been established by central agencies—usually by the ministries of education. This means that such examinations as the *baccalauréat* in France or the *Abitur* in Germany have mainly been external to the school that a student attends. Usually these examinations consist of a written section set by the central agency and an oral part conducted either by outside examiners or by teachers from the student's own school.

Until recently, universities in most European countries strongly influenced the amount of emphasis that secondary schools placed on the various subject areas and the topics that they emphasized within these areas. (Most students who graduated from upper secondary schools went on to universities. In fact, the upper secondary school examination in some countries was often called the "matriculation examination.")

Changes in Sweden are typical of those that have recently occurred throughout Europe. Until 1868 the universities themselves conducted a comprehensive matriculation examination for university entrance. For the next century, until 1968, the upper secondary schools (*gymnasia*) conducted the matriculation examination, but the universities still maintained considerable control. The written examination papers were set by the Ministry of Education and later by the National Board of Education, which also assigned a large number of university professors as "censors" in the oral exam. The content of the papers was determined after consultation with the universities.

This type of system could work as long as only a small elite took the upper secondary school-leaving examination. In western and northern Europe, as late as 1950, this group was no larger than 5% to 10% of the total age group. But when—from the mid-Fifties through the early Seventies—the secondary school enrollment soared to more than 20% of the age group, and when the upper secondary programs became more diversified and less focused on preparation for the university, a uniform school-leaving examination ran the risk of becoming meaningless. When a high percentage of students took vocationally oriented programs, the main purpose of guaranteeing that the graduates had the appropriate academic competence for university study was no longer so central. Sweden's system of centrally established written and oral examinations, administered under the supervision of university professors, was thus replaced by a system of standardized achievement tests that could be used to calibrate grading scales. The resultant comparability in grades was important, since graduates from different schools were competing with one another for entry to selective universities.

Thus European upper secondary education has in certain respects—although with a considerable time-lag—had to face problems similar to those encountered earlier in the U.S. With the growth and diversification of upper secondary education and with the decreasing academic emphasis, the universities have tended to lose both interest in and influence on secondary education—apart from complaining about the poor preparation of many of the students they receive.

For many years most nationally standardized examinations in Europe assessed student performance against an *absolute* standard. From the student's point of view, the key element was the minimum requirement for passing the exam, which in turn was seen as the minimum requirement for being able to profit from university teaching. The important thing was judging the student's potential for university studies.

The nature and the consequences of the final secondary examinations in Europe have changed during the last 20 years, as enrollment in upper secondary education has soared from about 5% to 20% or more of the relevant age group. At the same time, education has begun to be regarded as a decisive factor in employment opportunities and in social mobility. Until the late 1950s, a very low percentage of young people from working-class homes (1% to

3%) went to upper secondary school and from there to the university. The enrollment explosion in secondary school was accompanied by a "revolution of rising expectations." University enrollments began to soar as well, and within the period from 1955 to 1975 enrollments quadrupled. Students were flocking to an increasingly diversified offering of programs, many with a vocational orientation.

Despite the enormous increase in openings at European institutions of higher learning, competition became considerably tougher. Universities that had previously been quite socially selective now tended to become intellectually selective as well. The employment system began increasingly to use the amount of formal education as the first criterion of selection among job seekers. Examination scores began to determine selection for further education. These changes in turn—and in a short time—changed the concept of assessing the quality of learning. Students selected today for upper secondary school and then for the university no longer tend to be assessed against an absolute standard (i.e., whether they have reached the pass mark) but are ranked according to instruments that scale their performance both upward and downward. The main feature of the examination system has tended to be the *relative,* not the absolute, standard. This relative standard can be assessed by means of standardized achievement tests that can also serve the purpose of validating grades given by the teachers.

International Assessments

The idea of conducting a study of cognitive competence among children enrolled in different national systems of education was first raised at a meeting of educational researchers from a dozen countries at the UNESCO Institute for Education in Hamburg in 1958. The year before, that institute had hosted an international meeting of educational psychologists on problems of evaluation. At the time, Europeans had given little thought to this topic. But through Ralph Tyler's pioneering research, evaluation had become an area that provoked great interest among educators.

By 1958, however, educators realized how little empirical evidence was available to substantiate the sweeping judgments that were commonplace about the relative merits and failings of various national systems of education. Concerns about the quality of secondary education in general—and about science education in particular—had begun to surface in the U.S., and American schools were accused of lack of intellectual rigor. Research meetings during the late 1950s pointed out the lack of internationally valid standards for student competence in key subject areas.

Given the lack of hard evidence, the question arose, why not use the experiences gained in some countries (particularly in the Anglo-Saxon countries) from large-scale testing programs and surveys? These techniques had already made their way into authoritative handbooks of social science research. Given the state of the art of comparative social science research, the development of instruments was an impressive achievement. A proposal was advanced for a cross-national study of how schools contribute to shaping the cognitive development of children in different countries. Then a feasibility study was launched to discover whether, methodologically and administratively, instruments could be developed that were cross-nationally valid and could be administered uniformly over a range of countries with different school systems. The feasibility study also aimed to find out whether data could be made accessible, in order to make the processing of data and statistical analyses possible at one central location.

Eventually data were collected in a dozen countries, and the outcomes of the analyses were reported in 1961. Since there was no time for the laborious, time-consuming exercise of test development, those in the group who were experts in test development drew upon items already available, most of them from England and the U.S. A 120-item test was constructed to measure competence in reading comprehension, arithmetic, science, and geography. Some nonverbal, "culture-free" items measuring abstract reasoning were included in order to assess nonverbal intelligence. The participating national centers made the data available to Teachers College, Columbia University, where processing and most of the statistical analyses took place.

The results of the feasibility study were encouraging, and the decision was made to proceed with a 12-country study in mathematics. Mathematics possesses a universal language and a high degree of cross-national overlap in school curricula; it appeared to be an ideal subject for the development of standardized tests. The next step was the establishment of the organizational "machinery" for the research effort, which would span the next decade and cost at least one million (preinflation) U.S. dollars. The resulting organization was called the International Association for the Evaluation of Educational Achievement (IEA).

The Elitist Standard

A comprehensive system provides a publicly supported education for all children of mandatory school age in a given area. All programs or curricular offerings are provided in the same school unit. Another essential feature of comprehensiveness is that no differentiation or grouping practices that definitively determine ensuing educational and occupational careers are employed. Children from all walks of life are served.

The American model centers on a comprehensive high school that accommodates all or most of the students from a given area under the same roof but differentiates by means of programs and ability grouping or by homogeneous grouping within programs. Between-school and between-region diversification is built into the system by means of provisions for local autonomy and by the existence of parochial schools.

In a selective system, by contrast, children are—by means of organizational differentiation at an early age—allocated to different types of schools. Moreover, also at an early age, grouping practices attempt to spot those who are supposed to be particularly academically oriented. Apart from selective admission and grouping, the system is also characterized by a high attrition rate in terms of grade-repeating and dropping out.

The western European model is characterized by the transfer of a selective elite from primary to secondary academic school before the end of mandatory schooling. Until recently, such a transfer typically took place after four or five years of primary school, but the transfer has gradually been postponed by the introduction of "orientation cycles" (e.g., in France and Germany) and other practices. In some countries, provisions for the entire period of mandatory school attendance are under one roof, at least in one type of school.

Critics of the comprehensive system have insisted that the top students in such a system will suffer by being taught together with their slower-learning peers. This is thought to impair their standard of achievement in comparison with students of equal intellectual standing who attend systems where selection for separate, academically oriented schools takes place at an early age or where strict homogeneous grouping within a school is employed. The adherents of comprehensive education, on the other hand, maintain that the top students will not suffer as much in such a system as the great mass of the less academically oriented students will suffer in a selective system—particularly those who are left rather early in the elementary school, after the "book-oriented" have been selected for university preparation in the secondary schools.

The elitists maintain that a system of selection based on fair and equally employed criteria of excellence will open the doors of high-status occupations to those from all walks of life who possess the necessary (mainly inherited) talent. Advocates of comprehensive systems counter by claiming that a selective system is beset with greater social bias than a comprehensive one. As one moves up the ladder of the formal educational system, the proportion of lower-class students is much lower in a selective system than in a comprehensive one, which these advocates interpret as evidence of bias.

The two propositions—both the one on the standard of the elite and the one on social bias—were tested on national systems of education in the first two large-scale surveys that the IEA conducted. The national systems of education differ tremendously with regard to the size of their pre-university groups (as percentages of the relevant age groups). In the mathematics study this group varied from less than 10% in some European countries to more than 70% in the U.S. The science study recorded a variation of the same order of magnitude. The variability in Europe had decreased somewhat, however. Obviously, there is no point in making comparisons between mean performances of school populations representing highly different proportions of the relevant age groups. In the IEA survey we decided to compare students who were in the terminal grade of the pre-university school. Typical illustrations in Europe of this population are, for instance, the *Oberprimaner* in Germany and those students who are about to sit for the GCE A-level in England or for the *baccalauréat* in France.

The problem of "comparing" terminal students is not as simple as it might appear from the popular debate on the relative "standard" of secondary systems that exercise rather strict selection versus the "standard" of those with an open-door policy. Adherents of an elitist system tend to evaluate the schools in terms of the quality of their end-products, leaving out those who are lost in the selection and/or attrition process and attaching a lower priority to their educational fate. Advocates of a comprehensive system prefer to look at what happens to the great mass of students. Their overriding question is, How many are brought how far?

I will look at the standard of the elite in the industrialized IEA countries, using as my criteria achievements in mathematics and science at the pre-university level. The national systems that have been studied vary considerably with regard to retention rate or "holding power" at the upper secondary level. For example, high school seniors account for about 75% to 85% of the relevant age group in the U.S.; those youths who finish *gymnasium* (grades 10 to 12) in Sweden make up about 50% of the age group; and students in the *Oberprimaner* (grade 13) in the Federal Republic of Germany, only about 15%. It is rather pointless to limit a comparison of student achievements in these and other countries to mean performances, simply because the proportion of the relevant age group involved varies greatly from nation to nation. It is more fair to compare *equal portions* of the relevant age groups. (Our governing assumption, of course, is that those who are *not* in school at that age level have not—either by previous schooling or other learning opportunities—reached the level of competence achieved by the elite still in school.)

Critics of our cross-national comparisons have objected that the method of comparing equal portions of the age group is unfair to national systems with a low retention rate (or with high selectivity). Such an objection is simply not consistent with the elitist philosophy. In systems that until recently retained only about 5% to 15% of the entire age group up to the pre-university grade, the prevailing educational philosophy has been that this system rather efficiently takes care of most of the able students and does not bias against any category of them. Thus those who favor an elitist system cannot reasonably object to a comparison between equal proportions of the age group by maintaining that the comparison is unfair to the selective system because it does not retain the able students.

When the IEA mathematics study compared the average performance in different countries of students in the terminal grade who were taking mathematics, we found that American high school graduates were far below those of other countries. In the U.S., however, 18% of the age group of 17- to 18-year-olds took mathematics, compared to 4% to 5% in some European countries. In order to gauge the feasibility of producing an elite in a comprehensive system of schooling, one must compare *equal proportions of the relevant age group in the respective countries.* . . . The range between countries is more narrow for the elite than for the entire group of terminal mathematics students. The top 4% of U.S. students score at about the same level as the corresponding group in other countries.

Similar comparisons were conducted with terminal students in science, but that study compared the top 9% of the age group in the industrialized countries. This percentage was chosen because it represented the lowest proportion of pre-university students in the relevant age group in any of the countries. In order to arrive at measures of the two more limited elites, the top 5% and 1% were also examined. . . . The mean score for the entire graduate population ranges from 30.8 for New Zealand to only 14.2 for the U.S. The pre-university students represent 13% of the entire age group in the former country and 75% in the latter. When we compared the mean scores for the top 9%, we found that countries with a high retention rate experienced sharply increased means. The U.S. doubled its means and scored higher than Germany and France, for instance. By and large, the same picture emerged when countries were compared with regard to the top 5% and 1% of their students.

The assessment of the standard of elite students at the pre-university level does not support the contention that systems with broader access and with relatively high retention rates through upper secondary school do not succeed in producing elite students. An elite *can* be cultivated within a comprehensive educational system. Whether or not the elite produced in such a system is worth its price is another question. One should, however, recognize that, in selective systems, the high standard of the elite is bought at the price of more limited opportunities for the majority of the students.

Conclusion

Finally, I dare to submit that low standards are not the most serious problem with public schooling—neither in the U.S. nor in other nations with comprehensive structures and high retention rates. Standards in terms of average performance can easily be raised by making a system more selective. The real, and most serious, problem concerns the way formal education relates to a highly technical society—and the institutional contradictions and goal conflicts that beset the school operating in a highly competitive society where formal schooling increasingly influences social status and life chances. In my book, *The School in Question: A Comparative Study of the School and Its Functions in Western Societies,* I have tried to "diagnose" the malaise that besets formal education in highly industrialized societies and to discuss problems that emerge, particularly in large-city school systems. I have found that the problems stem from goal conflicts that tend to be ignored or obfuscated by rhetoric.

First, there is the contradiction of equality versus meritocracy that looms large in highly complex, technological societies. It cuts across highly different types of social orders, be they based on capitalist, mixed, or state socialist economic systems. Educated intelligence tends to become more influential, more prestigious, and better paid. The more society depends on advanced and sophisticated technology, the more acute the dilemma becomes. The school provides competences that, in modern societies, increasingly constitute an individual power base.

On the other hand, a marked streak of egalitarianism has affected the polity of most advanced societies in recent decades, leading to a considerable increase in formal equality of opportunity. But it has not led to any increase in equality of results—that is to say, to equality of life chances. On the contrary, differences have become more marked. As a result of policies of widening access to higher education on both sides of the Atlantic, we have experienced a "revolution of rising expectations" and soaring enrollments. There has been an "enrollment explosion," first at the upper secondary and then at the tertiary level. The imbalance between the number of graduates and the number of jobs has reinforced tendencies toward an overreliance on credentials, which in turn has reinforced competition for entry to the next level of formal education. In the IEA Six-Subject Survey, we noticed the paradox that, despite having expressed very negative attitudes toward schooling, a majority of the students in several countries voluntarily continued beyond the mandatory years. They were keenly aware of the fact that they had to "stick it out" in order to be competitive in the labor market. Formal qualifications increasingly tend to determine the place a young person occupies in the line of job-seekers.

After a couple of decades of rhetoric about and efforts to implement increased equality in education, we have by now learned that education cannot serve as an equalizer, as such liberal educators as Horace Mann once proclaimed. At least, education cannot do it alone. Formal education in our technological society exists to impart competences and is, therefore, *creating* differences. The school—particularly in a technologically sophisticated society— cannot at once serve as an equalizer and as an instrument that establishes, reinforces, and legitimizes differences. Such goal conflicts make it extremely difficult for the school to pursue genuine educational goals conducive to self-fulfillment and social education, goals that traditionally play a prominent role in curricular rhetoric. On the one hand, the school is expected to pursue intrinsic goals, to foster "inquiring minds" that enjoy learning for its own sake. On the other hand, the rewards for pursuing learning are extrinsic to the learning process: grades, degrees, jobs. Again, on the one hand, the school is expected to foster a cooperative spirit, primarily through group work. On the other hand, the rewards always go to individual accomplishments.

Let me suggest that the most serious problem faced by schools on both sides of the Atlantic is the rise of a new educational underclass. The "old" underclass was, in the pre-meritocratic society in many countries, virtually excluded from the advanced education that was available to a small social and intellectual elite. (A supposed characteristic of the meritocratic society is that all are thought to have equal access to education.) What characterizes the "new" underclass is that it consists of those who from the very beginning tend to be school failures. They also tend (rephrasing Orwell) to be less equal than others, by coming from unprivileged homes, though not necessarily unprivileged in material terms. Their parents often have lower levels of education and are suspicious of the school as an institution. Very early during their school careers these children give up competing for success; they are highly overrepresented among truants, nonreaders, vandals, and, in the long run, among the jobless. Those who are from the beginning (to quote Orwell correctly) "more equal than others," by virtue of coming from proper backgrounds with better-educated and more school-conscious parents, tend—irrespective of the school system—to have an advantage. A formally equal treatment in a competitive milieu does not lead to greater equality of outcomes.

THE TUITION TAX DODGE[11]

The man from New Hampshire had never heard of a "tuition tax credit" but he thought it sounded like a good idea. He and his wife were both working, he said, and because their state doesn't provide kindergarten, they had to send their daughter to a private

[11]Reprint of an article by John Merrow, producer and co-host of "Options in Education" on National Public Radio. *New Republic*. 236:594–5. My. 14, '83. Copyright © 1983 by the New Republic. Reprinted by permission.

school. He wouldn't mind, he said, "getting some of that tuition money back at tax time."

This may be his year. A tuition tax credit bill came close in the last Congress (passed the House, lost narrowly in the Senate). This Congress is more conservative, and President Reagan, unlike his predecessor, supports the idea, as does the secretary of education. The idea is simple: if you send your child to a private school or college, you may subtract from your tax bill a specified amount (but not more than half) of the tuition. How much credit parents get depends on the bill, but the most publicized, the Moynihan-Packwood-Roth bill, provides $250 in the first year, $500 thereafter. Anyone who owed the IRS less than the credit would get the money in cash. [Editor's Note: The Moynihan-Packwood-Roth bill has not yet come up for a vote. At present ten different bills regarding tuition tax credits are up for consideration. All are in the House Ways and Means Committee or the Senate Finance Committee.]

Tuition tax credits may have friends in high places in Washington, but most liberal and public education groups oppose them. The *New York Times* and the *Washington Post* are condemning the idea with even more vigor than they did last time around. Other opponents are calling tuition tax credits a "pernicious danger" to the public schools, a "blatant raid on the Treasury," and—at least by implication—a threat to the stability of the Republic. Thirty organizations, including the PTA and associations of school principals, superintendents, school boards, and teachers have formed the National Coalition for Public Education to fight against tuition tax credits.

The opponents have a lot of ammunition available to fire at tuition tax credits, though some shells are more explosive than others. First is the constitutional or "church-state" argument: because about 85 percent of nonpublic school students are in parochial schools, giving tax credits amounts to state establishment of religion, which is expressly forbidden by the Constitution. Earlier attempts to aid nonpublic schools have been overturned on this ground, notably in the Supreme Court's rejection of New York State's plan, in the 1973 *Nyquist* decision. Supporters of tax credits argue that their legislation is different because the credits will go to families, not to religious schools or to churches. Senator Moynihan argues that if all religions are eligible (as they are under his bill), then no one religion is "established." If tax credit legislation passes, there is sure to be a church-state court test.

Another argument is that tax credits will go, indirectly, to white-only, segregationist academies (true), and directly to parents who are purposely buying segregated education (also true). Moreover, credits will encourage segregation-minded parents with children still in public school to flee (probably true). On the other side of the case, it's good to remember that private schools are, on the whole, more integrated than public schools. It isn't strictly true—as often claimed—that tuition credits benefit the rich the most. The prime beneficiaries, in fact, would be middle-class families. Most parents paying $4,000 to $5,000 to send a child to Andover or Groton don't need, and probably don't care about, a $500 tax credit. Parochial school tuition, though, is normally in the $400 to $1,200 range. Poor people would not benefit unless they could find a way to come up with half their children's tuition money, and then benefits would be delayed each year until after tax time.

There is a big question whether the US can afford the cost in lost tax revenues, which opponents such as Senator Ernest Hollings of South Carolina estimate will be four billion dollars a year. Because most members of Congress seem to have taken vows at the altar of the balanced budget, passage of tuition tax credit legislation would seem to mean even deeper domestic budget cuts, presumably from programs such as Title I, school breakfast and lunch, CETA, and other programs that help the poor.

It seems clear that tuition credits would be yet another advantage for private over public schools. Already public schools are required to serve everyone, but the private schools are selective, and don't have to enroll—or keep—the handicapped, the unmotivated, the unintelligent, the anti-social, and other hard-to-educate children. It's not fair for government to encourage more "skimming off the cream." Advocates of tuition credits claim that parents of private school students have to pay taxes to support public schools and tuition and that this is not fair. By that faulty logic, though, people who belong to country clubs or drive to work in their own cars should get tax credits for those outlays because, after all, their taxes are already paying for public parks and mass transit and they shouldn't have to "pay twice."

Tuition credits seem to invite the federal intrusion into education that conservatives claim to abhor. Who, for example, will distinguish between real and phony private schools? The logical investigator is the IRS rather than state education authorities. In reality, the IRS might do the job better. Private schools in most states are virtually unregulated, having only to meet fire and health code standards and teach US history. Fear of federal "meddling" does seem to have diminished, perhaps extinguished, the enthusiasm that fundamentalist Christian schools once had for tuition tax credits. Other private schools, like those in the National Association of Independent Schools, are talking bravely about finding "workable solutions."

Despite their dislike for each other, both US teacher unions, the National Education Association and the American Federation of Teachers, vigorously oppose tuition tax credits. Part of their reasoning is that with public enrollment already declining, teachers cannot support anything that might shrink the student population further. Teaching jobs are at stake, in their view. The fact is, though, that nobody knows how many students would leave for private schools if tuition tax credits pass. Some opponents predict a whopping five percent—more than two million students. Other observers predict almost no movement, on the grounds that the tax credit is too small to induce parents to change. If the pessimists are right, though, tuition credits are likely to undermine public education and to spawn creation of thousands of new private schools, some of which will specialize in mischief as much as education.

All this represents a strong case against tuition tax credits, but there is one good argument on the other side: the need to shake up the public schools and the monopolistic-minded people who run them. Public educators as a group have forgotten that they work for the public. They have built up bureaucratic walls to protect themselves and have coated their policies in layers of jargon. It will take a drastic threat to make them responsive. Congressional and presidential moves toward tuition tax credits might do the trick. Clearly there are exceptions to the pattern of inadequacy in the public schools, but too few. Tuition tax credits are probably bad education policy and bad tax policy, but the threat they pose just might force the public schools to improve the quality of the education they offer and scare them into opening their doors to parents. Something has to do this, and soon.

MR. REAGAN AND TUITION TAX CREDITS[12]

In an Easter Week speech at the National Catholic Educational Association's convention in Chicago, President Reagan announced that he intends this spring to introduce legislation giving tuition tax credits to families with children in private elementary and secondary schools. Before that speech was delivered, however, editorial writers for The New York Times, The Washington Post, and The Christian Science Monitor hit the proposal with preemptive strikes. The Times elegantly observed: "The idea is awful and the timing is worse."

Even defenders of tax credits agree that the timing was suspiciously bad. In this season of record-breaking deficits, any tax credits seem inopportune. Moreover, the Administration is acting so late in the session that Congress may not have enough time to deal with the tuition tax credit question. In fact, Senator Robert J. Dole (R., Kan.), chairman of the Senate Finance Committee, has predicted that the measure will never even reach the floor.

Since it must be supposed that the President's advisers, if not Mr. Reagan himself, were quite aware of these unfavorable prospects, the discussion of tax credits has taken off in two directions. The President's motives have become nearly as much of an issue as the plan itself. It has been charged that Mr. Reagan, knowing perfectly well that Congress will not pass tax credits this year, went to Chicago to win the votes of those middle-class and blue-collar families who send their children to parochial schools. Oddly

[12]Reprint of an editorial from America. 146:331. My. 1, '82. Reprinted with permission of America Press, Inc., 106 West 56th Street, New York, NY, 10019. Copyright © 1982. All rights reserved.

enough, this interpretation is advanced along with the claim that tuition tax credits would mostly benefit the well-to-do whose children go to exclusive private schools.

But having dismissed the President as grandstanding and his proposal as certain to fail, critics of tax credits have been carrying on as though Mr. Reagan's rather modest proposal really does have a chance after all. In this plan, tax credits would be introduced in 1983, and it is calculated that they would mean a loss of about $100 million in revenues the first year. Once the plan was fully phased in, this loss would amount to $1 billion annually, which would, of course, be only a fraction of the defense budget. Since public schools are financed almost entirely from state taxes and local property taxes, their funds would not be diminished by a Federal income tax credit. But Mr. Reagan's tax credit plan is admittedly compromised by the cutbacks he advocates in education programs at the national level. However, the President might reasonably argue that just because the Federal Government does less for education in general is no reason why it should do nothing at all for private lower schools in particular.

In any case, the opponents of tuition tax credits concede that they would resist them even in boom times. If it is assumed, in an excess of charity, that all of these critics are free of anti-Catholic bias, their arguments come down to two. Tuition tax credits, they say, would be unconstitutional. But since many members of Congress and the legal profession think otherwise, surely the constitutional question can be left to the U.S. Supreme Court to adjudicate.

It is further said, however, that if tax credits were ruled constitutional, public schools would be harmed because private schools would then lure the best students away. This is a thoroughly unrealistic objection. Tax credits to parents would enable more children from moderate-income families to attend private schools, but they would not make any capital expansion possible. The well-being of public schools must indeed be a concern of all citizens, but it neither requires nor justifies a total monopoly of public support. The writers of the Constitution said nothing about education because they considered it to be the function of the family. They were right. When Government enters the field of education, it finds the family already there, and so its first interest should be to help parents provide for their children the school of their choice. Whatever is to be thought of President Reagan's timing or intentions, he is at least to be credited with having recognized this basic requirement of equity.

TUITION TAX CREDITS:
A SOCIAL REVOLUTION[13]

The Packwood-Moynihan tuition tax rebate legislation is, as Professor E. G. West aptly calls it, "a crucial event in the history of education."[1] Its "revolutionary potential for low-income groups"[2] has been missed by most other commentators and critics and deserves further exploration.

Why is this bill so important—and to whom? It is most important to those who are mentioned least: the poor, the working class, and all whose children are trapped in educationally deteriorating and physically dangerous public schools. Few groups have so much at stake in the fate of this bill as ghetto blacks. To upper-income families with children in college, the maximum $500 tax relief is hardly of decisive importance, when annual college costs range up to ten times that amount. The campaign of misrepresentation by the education establishment has depicted the affluent as the chief (or sole) beneficiaries, when in fact the opposite is nearer the truth. There are many times more students in elementary and secondary schools than in college, and among those children enrolled in precollege private institutions, there are more whose parents earn from $5,000 to $10,000 a year than those whose parents are in *all* the brackets from $25,000 on up.

Even the current enrollees in private education are not primarily the affluent. The average family income of private elementary and secondary school children is about $15,000. But since the

[13] Reprint of an article by Thomas Sowell, research fellow at the Hoover Institution, Stanford University, Palo Alto, California. *American Education*. 18:18–19. Jl. 1982. Copyright © 1982 by American Education. Reprinted by permission.

whole purpose or effect of the tuition tax rebate is to extend to others the opportunity for private education, the question is not so much who *now* goes to private school but who *could* go after this legislation is in effect. No doubt those who went to college in past generations, before the G.I. Bill and other educational subsidies, were far more affluent than the general population, but to object to the G.I. Bill as aid to the affluent would be to miss the whole point—that it extended a privilege previously enjoyed by a few into an opportunity open to millions more. That is precisely what this bill does. That is precisely why it is being opposed and misrepresented by those whose jobs, pensions, and power derive from the public school bureaucracy.

The Question of Expenses

While $500 does not begin to cover college costs, it does cover all or most of the cost of sending a child to many private day schools. Most of those private schools are not the expensive Andover or Exeter stereotypes but rather schools costing a fraction of the tuition they charge—and having costs per pupil that are a half, a third, or a fifth of the per-pupil cost in the public schools. It is not uncommon for Catholic parochial schools costing a few hundred dollars a year to have test scores higher than public schools in the same neighborhoods with per-pupil costs well over a thousand dollars. One of the misrepresentations by opponents of the tuition tax rebate is that it would cost billions of dollars. They are talking about Treasury disbursements, which may be politically important. What is *economically* important is that a shift of students to lower-cost private schools can save billions of dollars for society as a whole.

Most of the private schools do not have the runaway pay scales or plush pensions that teachers' unions have extracted from politicians handing out the taxpayers' money. Few parochial schools are surrounded with tennis courts or contain many of the other expensive amenities or status symbols that add little to the education of children but which have become part of the fringe benefits of public school administrators. Indeed, most private schools have far fewer administrators per hundred pupils, which is no small part of the reason for their lower costs or for the opposition of public school administrators to allowing parents a choice of where to send their children.

The crux of the controversy over this bill is *choice* and *power*. If parents are given a choice, public school officials will lose the monopoly power they now hold over a captive audience. That monopoly power is greatest over the poor, but it extends to all who cannot afford simultaneously to pay taxes for the public schools and tuition at a private school. Public schools in affluent neighborhoods where parents already have that option must pay some attention to those parents' wishes and be responsive. But parents in poorer neighborhoods and ghettos have no such leverage to use to get attention, response, or even common courtesy. The mere prospect of being able to remove their children to private schools changes all that. In other words, the benefits of the availability of tuition tax credit do not end with those who take advantage of it but extend to those who keep their children in the public schools and never collect a dime from the Treasury—but whose children's needs now have to be taken seriously by public school officials no longer insulated or assured of a captive audience.

Much has been made of the fact that most of the enrollment in private elementary and secondary schools is in Catholic parochial schools. Like many other statements about the situation before this bill is passed, it is far from decisive in determining what the situation will be afterwards. The government is constantly overestimating the revenues to be gained from imposing a given tax by assuming that the pretax situation will continue unchanged except for the collection of the tax. In the same way, some are now assuming that the social, economic, and religious composition of families with children in private schools will remain unchanged after a subsidy that will put such education within reach of tens of millions of other people. Moreover, not all of the children enrolled in Catholic schools are Catholic. In urban ghettoes, especially, it is not uncommon for many Protestant black families to send their children to Catholic schools, as an escape from ineffective and dangerous public schools. About ten percent of the ghetto youngsters in Chicago are in parochial schools. In some places, a majority of the enrollees in a Catholic school are non-Catholic. A

parochial school can be a social-service activity, like a denomina-
tional hospital that does not limit its medical care to co-
religionists.

The Constitutional Issue

The Constitutional ban on government support for religious
establishments raises legalistic issues for legislation whose initial
impact may be more pronounced on Catholics. The First Amendment, as written, would not prohibit tax rebates for individuals
to do with as they please and the G.I. Bill is used at Catholic colleges and universities, but the Supreme Court has sometimes
drawn an arbitrary line between higher and precollege education
and made the constitution more restrictive on the latter. However,
the uncertain course of the Supreme Court in this area in recent
years and some evidence of at least a pause in the trend toward
judicial policymaking under the guise of interpretation leaves reason to hope that extremist extensions of the "separation of church
and state" doctrine will not nullify a bill that offers major benefits
to all segments of the population. As things stand now, there is
no Constitutional limitation on an individual's choice to donate
money received from the government—whether as salary, tax re-
fund, or Social Security benefits—to a religious organization. To
say that the individual cannot choose to *buy* an educational service
from the same religious organizations with money originating
from the government seems inconsistent at best.

Another red flag to many is the possible effect of parental
choice on racial integration. Visions of "segregation academies"
are sometimes invoked (even though the tuition tax rebates cannot
be used for any institution practicing racial discrimination). Quite
the contrary is the case. In most of the nation's largest urban public school systems, there are not enough whites left to integrate,
so any further racial integration in such places may be achievable
only by the voluntary movement of black children into private
schools. But even this is objected to by some "liberals" because
blacks who take this opportunity to get ahead and leave the ghetto
public schools would leave behind only the children of "the least
educated, least ambitious, and least aware."[3] In other words, black

parents who want to make a better future for their children must be stopped and their children held hostage in the public schools until such indefinite time as all other people in the ghetto share their outlook. Ethnic minorities in the past rose out of the slums layer by layer, but for blacks it must be all or none! This arrogant treatment of millions of other human beings as pawns or guinea pigs would be impossible when parents have individual choice. That is precisely why both the education establishment and the social tinkerers are opposed to it.

NOTES

1. E.G. West, "Tuition Tax Credit Proposals: An Economic Analysis of the 1978 Packwood/Moynihan Bill," *Policy Review,* (winter 1978) p. 62.

2. *Ibid.,* p. 64.

3. "Kissing Off the Public Schools," *The New Republic,* March 25, 1978, p. 6.

BIBLIOGRAPHY

An asterisk (*) preceding a reference indicates that the article or part of it has been reprinted in this book.

BOOKS AND PAMPHLETS

Adler, Mortimer J. The paideia proposal: an educational manifesto. Macmillan. '82.

*Boyer, Ernest. High school: an agenda for action. Carnegie Foundation for the Advancement of Teaching. '83.

Coleman, James S. and others. High school achievement: public, Catholic, and private schools compared. Basic Books. '82.

Cusick, Philip. The American high school and the egalitarian ideal. Longman. '83.

Feistritzer, Emily C. The condition of teaching: a state by state analysis. Carnegie Foundation for the Advancement of Teaching. '83.

Goodlad, John I. A place called school: prospects for the future. McGraw-Hill. '83.

Lightfoot, Sara Lawrence. The good high school: portraits of culture and character. Basic Books. '83.

*The National Commission on Excellence in Education. A nation at risk: the imperative for educational reform. U.S. Department of Education. '83.

National Science Board Commission on Precollege Education in Mathematics, Science and Technology. Educating Americans for the 21st century. National Science Foundation. '83.

Ravitch, Diane. The troubled crusade: American education, 1945–1980. Basic Books. '83.

Sizer, Theodore R. Horace's compromise: the dilemma of the American high school. Houghton Mifflin. '84.

Task Force of the Business-Higher Education Forum. America's competitive challenge: the need for a national response. Business-Higher Education Forum. '83.

Task Force on Education for Economic Growth. Action for excellence: a comprehensive plan to improve our nation's schools. Education Commission of the States. '83.

*The Twentieth Century Fund Task Force on Federal Elementary and Secondary Education Policy. Making the grade. Twentieth Century Fund. '83.

PERIODICALS

*America. 146:331. My 1. '82. Mr. Reagan and tuition tax credits.

America. 147:86. Ag. 21, '82. Public school teachers; targets. J. W. Donohue.

America. 150:89-92. F. 11, '84. Consumer report on schools. J. W. Donohue.

American Education. 18:4-9. My. '82.; 18:7-13. Je. '82. Public support for private education. C. E. Finn, Jr.

American Education. 18:16-19. My. '82. Tuition tax credits: the president's proposal. Ronald Reagan.

*American Education. 18:18-19. Jl. '82. Tuition tax credits: a social revolution. Thomas Sowell.

American Education. 18:30-40. O. '82. Federal policy in bilingual education. I. C. Rotberg.

American Education. 18:18-19. N. '82. Tuition tax credits—a dialogue. Edwin Meese.

American Education. 19:9-12. Ja./F. '83. Some observations on the reported gap between American and Soviet educational standards. I. C. Rotberg.

American Education. 19:8+. Mr. '83. The administration's commitment to federalism. R. S. Williamson.

Change. 15:15-17. O. '83. Preparing for the millennium: finding an identity and a future. Theodore M. Hesburgh.

Change. 16:8-11. Mr. '84. Graduate education: signs of trouble and erosion. John Brademas.

Change. 16:9-13. Ap. '84. Opportunities for optimism. Howard R. Bowen.

Christian Science Monitor. p 2. My. 6, '83. Panel criticizes teachers' unions.

Christian Science Monitor. p 22. Ag. 3, '83. No merit in merit pay.

*Chronicle of Higher Education. 27:80. F. 15, '84. The Ph. D. outside academe: some appalling facts. Edward Tenner.

Commentary. 75:45-54. Jl. '83. How the schools were ruined. J. Adelson.

*Commonweal. 110:204-7. Ap. 8, '83. In math & science, an "f." Jeremiah Baruch.

Current. 246:45–49. O. '82. Toward bilingual education. Erik Larson.

Current. 257:15–24. N. '83. College graduates and the market. S. M. Ehrenhalt.

Education Digest. 46:32–35. Ja. '81. "Static maintenance" in bilingual education. Ricardo Otheguy and Ruth Otto.

Education Digest. 47:2–5. Ja. '82. The debate about standards: where do we go from here? Diane Ravitch.

Education Digest. 47:2–6. Ap. '82. The Reagan administration and federal education policy. D. L. Clark and M. A. Amiot.

Education Digest. 48:21–23. O. '82. The case against tuition tax credits. T. A. Shannon.

Education Digest. 48:66–68. O. '82. Japan: a learning society. D. P. Schiller and H. J. Walberg.

Education Digest. 48:27–29. N. '82. Characteristics of effective schools and programs for realizing them. L. W. Lezotte.

Education Digest. 48:2. F. '83. The challenges facing American education. Walter F. Mondale.

Education Digest. 48:2–5. Mr. '83. The Reagan administration: its record on education. E. B. Fiske.

*Educational Research Quarterly. 6:25–31. Fall '81. Bilingual education in the eighties: one Hispanic's perspective. Tomás A. Arciniega.

Fortune. 108:60–64. S. 19, '83. What to do about the nation's schools. Peter Brimelow.

Futurist. 17:55–60. Ag. '83. The changing university. S. L. Dunn.

*Harper's 258:30–33. F. '79. Against bilingual education. Tom Bethell.

*Harper's. 258:35–40. F. '79. The unlettered university. John C. Sawhill.

Humanist. 44:9–12, 32. Ja./F. '84. Making schools work again. Robert A. Blume.

*Nation. 236:594–95. My. 14, '83. Arming education.

National Review. 34:1537–38. D. 10, '82. Our listless universities. Allan Bloom.

National Review. 36:42–44+. Je. 15, '84. Ethnic studies, campus ghettos. Jacob Neusner.

Nation's Business. 71:5. Jl. '83. The crisis in our schools. J. J. Kirkpatrick.

*New Republic. 184:15–17. Ap. 18, '81. Bilingual mis-education. Abigail Thernstrom.

*New Republic. 184:23–27. Ap. 18, '81. The schools we deserve. Diane Ravitch.

New Republic. 186:7-9. My. 5, '82. Savaging the schools.

*New Republic 189:12-15. N. 7, '83. Merit pay won't work. Dorothy Wickenden.

New Republic. 189:2-22. N. 7, '83. Why Jonathan can't read. Leon Botstein.

New Republic. 189:27-29. N. 7, '83. Scapegoating the teachers. Diane Ravitch.

*New Republic. 239:594-95. Ap. 18, '81. The tuition tax dodge. John Merrow.

New York Review of Books. 28:34-36. N. 5, '81. Wasteland of American education. Jacques Barzun.

*New York Review of Books. 31:35-40. Ap. 12, '84. The schools flunk out. Andrew Hacker.

New York Times. p A 24. Je. 16, '83. President presses school merit pay. Francis X. Clines.

New York Times. p 20. O. 4, '83. But will anything come of all those reports? Fred Hechinger.

New York Times. p 1+. Je. 17, '84. U. S. pupils lag from grade 1, study finds. Edward B. Fiske.

New York Times. p A 11. Jl. 3, '84. Teachers' group resists change in evaluations and rewards. Gene Maeroff.

New York Times. p C 8. J. 3, '84. Step to upgrade teachers is taken at a critical time. Fred Hechinger.

*New York Times Magazine. p 46-58. My. 1, '83. Higher education's new economics. Edward B. Fiske.

Newsweek. 99:56+. Ap. 12, '82. Does college cost too much? Dennis Williams.

Newsweek. 99:86. Je. 14, '82. The college brain drain. Dennis Williams.

Newsweek. 100:68. Jl. 19, '82. Is SAT a dirty word? Dennis Williams.

Newsweek. 100:81. S. 20, '82. The trickle-down effect. Dennis Williams.

Newsweek. 100:64-65. O. 4, '82. Go to the head of the class. Dennis Williams.

Newsweek. 101:54. My. 9, '83. How the Japanese do it. Charles Leerhsen.

Newsweek. 101:100. My. 16, '83. Creating a learning society. Meg Greenfield.

Newsweek. 101:26. Jl. 11, '83. A new turn on tuition credits. Aric Press.

Newsweek. 102:75. Ag. 1, '83. How to reform the schools. Dennis Williams.

Newsweek. 102:83–84. S. 19, '83. Longer, harder school days. Dennis Williams.

Newsweek. 103:47. Ja. 16, '84. A report card for the states. Dennis Williams.

*Phi Delta Kappan. 62:707–8. Je. '81. Japanese education: its implications for economic competition in the 1980s. M. W. Kirst.

Phi Delta Kappan. 63:33–47. S. '81. 13th annual Gallup Poll of the public's attitudes toward the public schools. G. H. Gallup.

Phi Delta Kappan. 63:73. S. '81. NEA-White House rift widens as teachers union declares political war. Stanley M. Elam.

Phi Delta Kappan. 63:653. Je. '82. Tuition tax credits proposal generates hot debates in U.S. capital and elsewhere. F. S. Rosenau.

Phi Delta Kappan. 64:5. S. '82. States move to reestablish academic standards in public schools and colleges. Cris Pipho.

*Phi Delta Kappan. 64:455–61. Mr. '83. Are standards in U. S. schools really lagging behind those in other countries? Torstein Husén.

Phi Delta Kappan. 64:525. Ap. '83. Tennessee governor proposes sweeping statewide school reform. Cris Pipho.

Phi Delta Kappan. 64:564–68. Ap. '83. Bilingual/bicultural education: its legacy and its future. C. J. Ovando.

Phi Delta Kappan. 64:722–24. Je. '83. Excellence in education: Tennessee's master plan. John Parish.

Phi Delta Kappan. 65:165. N. '83. Merit pay-master teacher plans attract attention in the states. Cris Pipho.

*Phi Delta Kappan. 65:167–72. N. '83. Education moves to center stage; an overview of recent studies. Harold Howe.

*Phi Delta Kappan. 65:181–82. N. '83. Just among us teachers. Harry N. Chandler.

Phi Delta Kappan. 65:463–68. Mr. '84. Should the U. S. mimic Japanese education? Let's look before we leap. John J. Coogan.

*Phi Delta Kappan. 65:684–85. Je. '84. A nation at risk: another view. James Albrecht.

*Science. 215:1077–78. F. '82. Budget tailors education to Reagan pattern. John Walsh.

Society. 19:4–9. Ja./F. '82. Public and private schools. J. S. Coleman and others.

Society. 19:11–14. Ja./F. '82. Neither direction nor alternatives. G. S. Thomas.

Time. 119:15. F. 1, '82. The White House sensitivity gap. L. I. Garrett.

Time. 119:21. Ap. 26, '82. A boost for private schools.

Time. 120:59. S. 6, '82. Quality not quantity. Richard Stengel.

Time. 120:69. N. 15, '82. Peering into the poverty gap. Philip Faflick.

Time. 121:64. Ja. 24, '83. Bleak view from the ivory tower. Ellie Mc-Grath.

Time. 121:62–63. My. 9, 83. A rising tide of mediocrity. Ellie McGrath.

Time. 121:53. My. 30, '83. Dear dad: send lots of money.

Time. 121:56. Je. 6, '83. Have degree, will travel. Ellie McGrath.

Time. 121:21. Je. 27, '83. School is in.

Time. 122:66. Ag. 1, '83. Japan—schooling for the common good. Ellie McGrath.

Time. 122:58. O. 10, '83. The bold quest for quality: the nation's schools are shaping up. Ellie McGrath.

*USA Today. 110:29–31. S. '81. The continuing controversy over bilingual education. Francesco Cordasco.

*USA Today. 111:30–31. S. '82. The money pinch in higher education: the end of the American dream? Don M. Flournoy.

*USA Today. 112:47–49. N. '83. Meeting the needs for a high-technology America. Robert P. Henderson.

U.S. News & World Report. 90:59. Je. 8, '81. Are public schools about to flunk? Stanley Wellborn.

U.S. News & World Report. 91:53. S. 7, '81. Today's high-school is fraudulent. John R. Silber.

U.S. News & World Report. 92:12. Ja. 25, '82. A touchy turn around on private schools.

U.S. News & World Report. 92:46–47. Ja. 25, '82. Hard times come to graduate schools. A. P. Sanoff.

U.S. News & World Report. 92:68. F. 1 '82. Tax exemptions for private schools.

U.S. News & World Report. 92:53. My. 17, '82. Ahead: a nation of illiterates?

U.S. News & World Report. 93:43–45. S. 6, '82. Schools open—with lean year ahead. Lucia Solorzano.

U.S. News & World Report. 93:34+. D. 13, '82. Grim days ahead for class of '83. J. L. Sheler.

U.S. News & World Report. 94:81–82. Ja. 24, '83. Degrees gathering dust for frustrated grads. D. A. Wiesler.

U.S. News & World Report. 94:33–34. Mr. 28, '83. Are Soviet schools as good as they look? Nicholas Daniloff.

U.S. News & World Report. 95:60. Ag. 29, '83. Bilingual classes? In U.S. but few other nations.

*Vital Speeches of the Day. 48:521–23. Je. 15, '82. Bilingual education improvement act. S. I. Hayakawa.

*Vital Speeches of the Day. 49:706–12. S. 15, '83. Education reforms. Albert Shanker.

Wall Street Journal. p 1. D. 14, '82. Requiescat in pace: the death of a college underscores the plight of private institutions. Anne Mackay-Smith.

Wall Street Journal. p 1 E. Jl. 22, '83. Reaganites scent political success in pressing the education issue.

Washington Post. p A 5. D. 19, '82. Ivory towers are bending to hard times; enrollment lower, cost higher. Bill Peterson.

Washington Post. p A 19. My. 3, '83. At bottom, Americans don't give a damn. J. J. Kirkpatrick.

Washington Post. p A 10. My. 9, '83. The state of public education. Susan Coryell.

Washington Post. p A 1. Je. 15, '83. California may pass incentive pay plan for teachers. Jay Mathews.

Washington Post. p A 2. Je. 15, '83. Reagan says schools are too easy: "sorry state" of education is blamed on his generation. David Hoffman.

Washington Post. p A 2. Jl. 1, '83. NEA conventioneers boxed in by Reagan's education issues. Kathy Sawyer.

Washington Post. p A 2. Ap. 9, '84. Parents' disenchantment with bilingual education found rising. Paul Taylor.

World Press Review. 31:27–29. F. '84. Japan's education edge. Gene Gregory.